Angels in My Life
An Inspiring Life's Journey

Mathell Givens

iUniverse, Inc.
New York   Bloomington

Angels in My Life
An Inspiring Life's Journey

Copyright © 2010 Mathell Givens

All rights reserved. No part of this book may be used or reproduced by any means, graphic, electronic, or mechanical, including photocopying, recording, taping or by any information storage retrieval system without the written permission of the publisher except in the case of brief quotations embodied in critical articles and reviews.

The views expressed in this work are solely those of the author and do not necessarily reflect the views of the publisher, and the publisher hereby disclaims any responsibility for them.

iUniverse books may be ordered through booksellers or by contacting:

iUniverse
1663 Liberty Drive
Bloomington, IN 47403
www.iuniverse.com
1-800-Authors (1-800-288-4677)

Because of the dynamic nature of the Internet, any Web addresses or links contained in this book may have changed since publication and may no longer be valid. The views expressed in this work are solely those of the author and do not necessarily reflect the views of the publisher, and the publisher hereby disclaims any responsibility for them.

ISBN: 978-1-4401-6235-0 (pbk)
ISBN: 978-1-4401-6233-6 (cloth)
ISBN: 978-1-4401-6234-3 (ebk)

Library of Congress Control Number: 2009933354

Printed in the United States of America

iUniverse rev. date: 04/8/2010

amiracleonflight1483@yahoo.com

I pray that many blessings be bestowed in your life!

To:_____
From: *Mathew Greene*_____
Date_____

Thank you sincerely!

Contents

Acknowledgments		ix
Introduction		xv
1.	In the Beginning	1
2.	My Roots	4
3.	Growing Up Too Soon	17
4.	Reality Sets In	25
5.	Home Again	35
6.	Family Separation	45
7.	Making a Way Out of No Way	56
8.	When All Else Fails, Pray	80
9.	Grandmother's Journey	88
10.	The Prophecy	108
11.	Multiple Situations	112
12.	Cruising with a Blind Man	124

13. The Storms and the V-Boys   138
14. Conspiracy Hits   152
15. Wanna Be Like Mike   206
16. A Miracle on Flight 1483   213
17. Life Goes On   221
18. Meeting Spike Lee   236
19. Little Girl Next Door   244
20. Divine Inspiration   248
21. The Miracle Ending   256
22. Angels in My Life   258
About the Author   259

Acknowledgments

I give honor to my spiritual father, God Almighty, who is the orchestrator of my life. I believe Him to be the creator of all things. I must express my gratitude to God, for He is the true author of this book. Thank you, merciful and gracious father, son, and precious holy ghost, for my journey.

To Bishop Simon Gordon of Triedstone Church, thank you for all your prayers and kindness.

To Pastor Steve Munsey of Family Christian Center, God has sustained my life and living in a very special way through you and I am grateful.

To all my supporters, thank you! I can't thank God enough for you.

To my dad, I thank God for his timing to restore our love. God's time is the right time, and his love is the greatest love. Love ya, Papa!

To my three sons, I love you all with my heart and soul. I thank God every day of my life for each of you. As I bow each day looking up toward heaven, I give thanks and salute the Lord for his promise of your safe return to me and our entire family. Your repenting souls have blessed you to be an inspiration, and you have become very positive men of God. Your trials and tribulations have turned into miracles. I pray your stories will give someone hope and a lifeline to hold on to and believe that they, too, can experience a miracle. I pray as I give my testimony of some of our trials that someone can see their way out of theirs. I am grateful to God that he looked beyond your faults and even mine. It is evident that you V-boys have a purpose and were predestined to survive the odds of life. I bless the Lord God Almighty for your valley moments. Now lift up each of your heads and allow the Lord to continue to be your shepherd. Love, Mama!

I am forever indebted to God for my grandchildren's and great-grandchildren's safety while in such a horrific storm. Babies, I have been praying and believing that God would not allow your minds or your destinies to be destroyed. Each of you has suffered greatly, and I believe that opportunities for your futures are bright. Your pain and struggles have encouraged my fight for your rights! Sincerely, Mama May loves each of you to "life"!

To my sisters, Deloris Allende and Paulette Duke, and to my stepsister, Patricia Thompson, I love each of you with all my heart.

To my brother in Christ, William Dixon, thank you for all your time and love dedicated to your nephews.

To the original IMAGE (Intelligent Men Are Going Everywhere) Brothers—Vincent, Joe, Khalid, Daniel, Duran, Demetrius, Craig, and in loving memory of Brother Brian Edwards—you are the greatest.

To my son in Christ, Walt Whitman, I bless God for the anointment on your life and the ability you have to soothe and hear a mother's cry. God bless your heart. Love Mama May!

To all of you that call me Godmama or Mama May, I love you dearly!

To all of my loved ones I did not mention, it was not intentional. So charge it to my head and not my heart. Love you!

The Lord has graced me with many to love and see me through my life's journey, and I feel that I am one of God's special children, chosen to be loved by God through his grace and mercy over and over again. He has designated me to be surrounded by mother figures who are the most precious jewels in my life. How blessed I am to have arms to still embrace me, shoulders to lie on, and most importantly, ears to hear me. Their words of encouragement and guidance nurture my heart and soul. They each are very unique and have beautiful smiles that charm me. They are placed in my life as angels, and I am grateful that as God took the mothers that have gone on before, he gave me these other mothers to love: Mama Rosia Slaughter, Mama Lola Cooper, Mama Mary Elizabeth Elmore, Mama Marion Rogers, Mama Alice Davis, Mama Artis Bryant, Mama Doristein Tijerina, Mama Levietta Smith, Mama Doris Hurd, and Mama Gurtrude Valentine. I am grateful, also, for my one and only Godfather, Artis Elmore.

Special thanks to DePaul Law School Professor Barbara Bressler, the Student Law Team and all attorneys assigned. Professor Jay Williams, Roosevelt College, thank you for all your counseling. Chicago Heights Library, thank you for your computer assistance. Mark Whitman of Eagle's Nest Production, I could not have captured a vision of what God did for my sons without you. Adam Bruce, camera technician and videographer at WUPC TV Channel 4, thank you for continuing the vision of my journey and sticking close to me. Christel Allen, station manager of WUPC TV cable University Park, Illinois, thank you for the use of the cameras and studio, and for your kindness toward me.

Mark Timejardine,Gm. Of Red Lobster, Matteson IL you always made time to hear my troubles and encourage me. Thank you and your team for all you did for me. Janet, Ed and the entire team at Cracker Barrel in Matteson IL thank you for your love and support. Dr. Shanda Evans, Women of War ministry at WSRB 106.3 fm radio Chicago, thank you for your prayers, love and all of the interviews. Sabrina Peden, steno typist, thank you for your willingness to help and your long hours.

Aileen Johnson, thank you for lending your helping hands to get me started writing my life's journey. You are the best. Also Pastor John Rice Jr. and Cherry Lynn Rice, thank you for your thoughtfulness. Alex Cox-Fuller, thank you for your compassion and all the advice. Veda Vanarsdale, executive editor and reviser, thank you sincerely for all your time and expertise. I truly could not have done this without you. Veda, your hospitality was great. Geraldine Goodlow, you are fantastic thank you for your spontaneous efforts. Martha Faye Ikner, thank you for proofreading and editing. Shelia Bruce and Ladrena BoBo, thank you for all of your suggestions and assistance with proofreading. Joanne Brodanex, thank you for being there for me every step of the way. You are a jack of all trades, and the best little angel that anyone could have.

Christine Robinson, thank you for your daily prayers along with the late great Mr. Bill Robinson. Stephanie Stephen, principal of Cottage Grove Upper Grade Center, thank you for all your loving greetings and your great staff. Dr. Yolanda Wallace, thank you for opening the door to your heart and being compassionate to help me in any way you could. Rose McGill, thank you for encouragement to write this book. Also, thank you for all the toys at Christmas time to make my grandchildren happy from the Toys for Kids organization. Rose, you are the greatest. Kevin Turnbo, Chief/Owner of Southland Caterers, Park Forest IL. You, my friend have the spirit and compassion of a righteous man. I thank God for your heart and your empathy. Prem Kanoth, you are my encourager and my spiritual friend. While in this storm, these sisters were always near. Vickie Shy, my dear sister in Christ, thank you for your ways of keeping me uplifted through inviting me out to eat with you and your mother. You shared me with your family and made me feel love in some of my lonely hours. You gave me hope for restoration between me and my family. To Rose Rogers, at Sutton Ford, my friend, thank you for all those hugs and gifts of angels. To Nancy McDaniels, girlfriend, your kind words of encouragement will be remembered forever. Linda Washington, thank you for all you did for me. To Lesley Jackson, thank you for all the beautiful birthday and Christmas gifts. To all my friends, I could write page after page of thanks to each of you that I couldn't mention. You hold a special spot in my heart and I love you just as much.

Last, but not least, to my dearest friend, you have been supportive and caring through all my storms. To you I am eternally grateful!

I pray a special prayer for my brothers and sisters in Haiti. I pray that continued help ripples your way. Keep the faith that "Angels" are being dispatched on your behalf. Don't give up and keep believing that God is working things out.

Finally, to all the men and women serving our country thank you, I want you to know that I pray for you and honor you everyday.

Introduction

I wrote this story to provide encouragement to other women or men in this human race who may be fighting for their lives. Reader, I speak directly to you when I say I am writing this book for both of us. The war you find yourself in is not with another two-legged being, man or woman. Nor is it with the government. Your fight is not with your family or even a friend. The fight is with a subtle, clever enemy—the spirit of the devil. This enemy has been around for generations and has studied you as his opponent. He is the unseen adversary who knows what makes you tick and what buttons to push to make you afraid. The fight is with a spiritual foe who fights dirty, plays by no rules, and makes up stuff as he goes along. The fight is with a wicked general who has a great military arsenal at his disposal and weapons of mass destruction. The fight is with a wise old dog that has an unquenchable thirst for blood and sees nothing but your death and the death of your children. If you are reading this and still breathing, you still have time to fight and make a difference.

This book is dedicated to all the mothers in my life who have been called by "our father who art in heaven" to rest in peace. They are Mama Mildred Johnson, Big Mama Lucille Jones, Mama Virgie Adger, Mama Verona Brown, Mama Jimmie Lanfair, Mama Clara Ikner, Mama Cornelia Elders, and my precious grandmother, Rosie

Lee Ikner. As the good Lord called each of these mothers, he still continues to show his favor.

All Bible verses can be found in the King James Version of the Holy Bible.

Some of the names have been changed to protect the innocent.

Based on a true story.

In the Beginning

It was a hot day in July when I came into this world. The two people responsible were a woman who was not ready or equipped to be a mother and a man who did not want to claim fatherhood. My name is Mathell Givens. I was born on July 6, 1952. My birth parents are Mildred Johnson and Nathell Ikner. When I was conceived, God assigned several mothers to care for me. My birth mother became restless when I was three weeks old and decided she wanted to go out and party. Mildred lived in the basement of Mama Rosia Lee Slaughter's house, and she would take me upstairs and ask Mama Slaughter to watch me while she went out clubbing. This went on for a few weeks, until Mildred finally asked Mama Slaughter to raise and care for me. Mama Slaughter and her husband, James, took care of a lot of the neighborhood kids. Several other mothers had turned children over to the Slaughters to raise, then returned unexpectedly to take their children back. When Mildred asked Mama Slaughter to take me, Mama Slaughter said it had to be done legally—Mildred would have to sign adoption papers. But she could not sign me over, so I never lived with Mama Slaughter permanently.

Though she didn't want me to be adopted, my mother still had no desire to assume the responsibility and challenges of motherhood. Her best friend Verona, whom I affectionately called Godmama, was asked to take care of me, and she did just that. Across the street from Godmama Verona lived her good friend Mama Lola, who would lend her a helping hand with me. Mama Lola was well known for her fashion shows and social events. When I was old enough, I became one of her models and began to travel with her. She sparked my interest in the fashion world.

I lived with Godmama and her father, Deacon Brown, who I called Grandfather. It was an awesome life living with people God picked especially for me. They introduced me to the finest things they could, and I grew up appreciating my life and my guardian-angel family. Godmama's mother had died when she was twelve, leaving her motherless and Grandfather a widower. He remained a single parent raising his daughter very well and never remarried. Godmama didn't have any children, and we never really talked about it. God gave Godmama and Grandfather enough love to nurture and teach me to see that I was chosen to be with them. They never wanted me to feel that I was merely filling a void in their lives, so they never mentioned that Godmama could not have children of her own.

By the time I was nine years old, Godmama had me participating in our household chores. On Saturday mornings, Godmama would play jazz, blues, and doo-wop, and we would sing and dance and have great times as we cleaned. It's partially due to those good times that my boys and I are singers and entertainers. I would watch Godmama bob her head and wiggle her hips to the musical beats. She had a special kind of love for all types of music. When I was ill or wasn't able to attend church services with Grandfather, I would be at home with Godmama, praising the Lord and listening to all of her special gospel music. She would hold me close to her bosom and sing "Baby, You Are the Best Thing Jesus Did for Me." We would have some great times bonding, fellowshipping, and growing with the Lord. I now realize that I am very much like Godmama. I have raised my children to love God, music, the entertainment business, and Godmama's great cooking. I truly cherished and enjoyed her when I was growing up.

The Illinois town I grew up in was called Summit and was also known as Argo. I lived in a three-flat building on Sixty-second Place on the side of town called "Down in the Valley." It was called that because it was the only street in the town that was at the bottom of a hill. At the top of the hill, there was a dairy. On the right side, in the middle of the block, there was a trucking company. At the dead end of the street was a fenced-in lumber company. Our building was red and gray, fenced in, and well-manicured. It was a busy neighborhood. When the sun would go down and all the businesses closed, the action would begin "Down in the Valley." We would play baseball and other games and have summer parties. There was a concrete gangway that led to our backyard patio where the adults would play music while my friends and I would dance in the gangway and have so much fun. We would take the party to the garage when it started to rain. Those were the good old days! Biblically, when you refer to being in the valley, you are at a low point in your life's journey. But this did not seem to be my plight. I was very happy and content in my world with my God-sent parents in this valley.

I was born to a mother who gave me up and a father who wouldn't claim me as his daughter, but God sent me the parents I needed, and I am truly grateful for each of them. This was the beginning of my journey and part of God's magnificent plan for me.

My Roots

My natural father and mother were raised in much different circumstances than I was. Nathell, my father, was born November 18, 1921, to Rosie Lee and Garci Ikner in Shreveport, Louisiana. Garci was a dice maker, gambler, and hustler type of man, so it's clear where Nathell got his talent. Garci whittled dice out of wood and carved the snake eyes in the dice for gambling. There was a farm up the road from Grandmother's house that needed workers every day. Rosie Lee would rush to get in line to work the farm. Her earnings were needed desperately to supplement the family income, and she would have Nathell strapped to her back while she picked cotton and tended to the farm animals. Nathell worked the farm picking cotton as a young man, but his main trade was gambling. This was his hustle until he went to the military.

Garci died when Nathell was nine years old. Rosie and Garci's "little boy" had to become a man well before his time. Nathell became the man of the house and took care of his mother. His father's death affected him greatly, but he learned to depend on his mom. He wasn't strong enough to accept death, and he found himself without a male role model. As Nathell got older, he set up a shoe-shine stand to help make ends meet. Grandmother had a yard that was a mini-farm. It needed tending, and Nathell would help out as much as a young boy could. However, his mother was emotionally hurt by her husband's sudden passing, which made her a single mother. This situation wasn't easy for my father or grandmother because they found themselves struggling to survive. Unfortunately, poor decisions and choices were made during this transition that made their living situation even harder. My dad witnessed men abuse his mother, emotionally and sometimes physically. He wanted to hurt them for hurting her. He was just a young boy and couldn't take all the sudden negative changes in his life. He was very disturbed by his mother's transformation and her poor choices in men. He would strike out at them because of his anger. So it was decided that he would move to Keithville, Louisiana, to live with his mother's sister, Aunt Effie.

The move tamed Nathell's anger and temper, and he became a very well-adjusted young man. When he was old enough, he joined the armed forces and served in WWII. After being released on an honorable discharge, he moved to Chicago, Illinois. Several years later, he moved to Summit, Illinois, and met my birth mother, Mildred Johnson.

Nathell was a tall, thin man. He wore his coal black hair slicked back, and he had long black eyelashes and very thick eyebrows. He made women's hearts skip a beat. He had a shining smile that showed his gleaming gold tooth. Nathell was charming and handled a lot of money; people called him Big Ike. This turned on Mildred and a lot of other women in a mighty way. They loved the sound of his voice. He would serenade Mildred by singing the song "Mona Lisa" to her.

He was a great dresser and loved the fashion industry. He worked at Division Lead Steel Mill, but got into the garment-selling business after losing his position. He sold a variety of different apparel to city employees, politicians, lawyers, and people in the neighborhood. He specialized in men and women's clothing and eventually got me into the clothing business with him. This was his way of providing me with clothes to wear.

However, there is a dark side to all of us, and Nathell was no different. Unfortunately, Nathell's dark side happened to be a violent one. He liked to drink and would get drunk sometimes. I remember, when I would visit Nathell and Mildred, he would smoke Camel cigarettes and gamble all night long. It wouldn't make a difference what gambling game it was, he would play. He especially liked shooting craps and handling dice just like his father. Making his mean streak more dangerous was the fact that he kept a gun—a .45 magnum—with him at all times.

My mother, Mildred Johnson, also had a horrible temper and became belligerent when she drank and smoked. She became a heavy drinker after moving in with Nathell. What came out of Mildred's mouth would cause her and Nathell to get into awful fights. Nathell was very hard on women. After all, he was living a double life. He maintained control by being abusive and calculating with the women in his life. When he and Mildred would get into it, she would run to my Godmama's house for comfort and shelter. I was always sent to my room so I could not hear the grown folks talking. However, I would put the pieces together from what I could hear them saying.

Mildred was born January 27, 1926, in Cairo, Illinois. She never knew her birth mother. Her mother's last name was Johnson. I have always thought of this side of my mother's family when I hear of a Johnson Family Reunion. Could this be my family? She knew her dad, and his name was Ira Jones. Mildred's mother already had children when she met Ira. She took those children with her when their short romance ended, turning the infant Mildred over to Ira to raise. He took Mildred to his sister Lucille's home, and it was determined that Mildred would be raised by Lucille—who we all called Big Mama—with her two sons, Vernell and Claude. Lucille had a sister we called Aunt Pete. Aunt Pete was an adult diabetic and leg amputee who lived with Lucille. Aunt Pete and Lucille nicknamed Mildred "Sister" and the name stuck. She was raised as part of their family. Mildred and the family's adjustment went well until she found out the facts of her birth.

Mildred was unaware of her true family history until she was a young teen. She overheard Ira and Lucille talk of a woman who would come and see Mildred from time to time. They said, "She's beginning to be a big girl and she needs to know her mother." Mildred began to ask Ira questions about these conversations with Big Mama, and Ira told her the truth about her birth mother. All Mildred's life, she had believed that Big Mama was her mother, and Vernell and Claude were her brothers. She was very disturbed to learn that her birth mother had abandoned her. Mildred began to rebel and became a bit of a "swift girl," as the old folks would say. She disobeyed the strict rules that governed the household. This was very stressful for everyone in the family, and it was decided that Mildred would attend an all girls' boarding school. Ira hoped that she would become disciplined and gain control of her actions and behavior. He wanted her to settle down and become a solid citizen, contributing to society. This only made Mildred more bitter and distant, and she drifted off into a world of drinking and partying.

Though she spent several years in boarding school, it didn't get in the way of her good times. Mildred slipped away one Saturday night and hitchhiked a ride to Argo. She found herself floating between two nightclubs there. One club was called The Greeks and the other was called Steps. One night she was in Steps, dancing and wiggling very seductively. Nathell had just gotten off his knees in Steps' bathroom, where he had won at the regular crap game. Suddenly, he laid eyes on Mildred. He liked her moves and began to dance up to her. They had a couple of drinks, and he asked her questions about herself. She shared with him that she had run away from boarding school. Nathell told her that he would fix her situation the next day, and that he would take her back to school and sign her out properly.

Mildred had jet black, naturally curly hair. She was a woman of average height and medium build, with big beautiful legs and an ample behind. She was what one would call a full-figured, sassy woman. While she lived with Nathell, she acquired a taste for Crown Royal and Coca-Cola. She was a born dancer, and I loved watching her dance to the song, "How Low Can You Go." She would bend her body low to the ground and sweep the floor with her rump. I could see the dust from the floor on her rump as she rose and continued to dance. It would always make Daddy smile. She would have a Kool cigarette hanging from her lips and would be woozy from drinking. I was told that you never knew how Mildred would behave. At times she would break down and cry; occasionally, she would curse you and your mother and father. When she became angry—which was often—she would fight, bite, and turn as mean as a junkyard dog.

Mildred had another daughter, Penny, when I was six years old. There was suspicion that Penny was Nathell's, even though Mildred went to New York to have Penny with another male friend. The male friend turned out to be the type of man who mistreated her, and after Penny was born, Mildred returned to Argo to raise her daughter. Later, when Mildred would become intoxicated, she would say Penny was Nathell's daughter. No one really knew for sure. Mildred asked Godmama to take care of Penny, too, but Godmama told her no. Penny stayed with Mildred during her formative years, but she said it was a very dysfunctional situation.

While growing up, Penny and I were not very close, even though we shared the same mother. I lived with Godmama, and I always wondered why my real parents didn't keep me. Penny, on the other hand, was resentful that Godmama wouldn't keep her. We've only acknowledged this situation since we've become adults, and I thank God we eventually discussed the issue and straightened out our relationship. Unfortunately, Penny grew up with much more verbal abuse from Mildred than I did. I was taunted by Mildred's mean words and cursing, but only when she came to visit and had too much to drink. For me, those times were limited—but not for Penny. I felt very bad for my little sister, but there was absolutely nothing I could do for her then but pray.

Penny was not my only sister. When Nathell met Mildred, he mentioned that he was married and had a daughter named Deloris. Years later, I had a conversation with my dad and he shared with me that he had a daughter. I asked if I could meet her. He said he had not kept in touch with Deloris or her mother, but he gave me her mother's name—Cornellia Bell Elders. I called directory assistance. There was a listing under that name, but it was unpublished. I explained my dilemma to the operator and she connected the call, explaining the situation to Mrs. Elders. The woman was very accepting and understanding and was willing to let me meet my big sister. The connection between the two of us has not gone the way I would have hoped. Today, I keep my arms open wide for the day my sisters and I relish one another. I believe God will grace us as a family with abundant love that will bond us forever.

The fact that Nathell already had a wife was one of the reasons he and Mildred never married—the other was Mildred's behavior when she drank. There was another side to her, though, a soft and kind side, very giving and good-hearted. During those times, Mildred would tell me she loved me, and we would talk about her past. She would explain why she and my father were living a common-law existence. This was when I learned why I did not live with Mildred and Nathell. She also told me about how she met her best friend, Verona, while out clubbing at Steps.

Most of what I know about my childhood, I learned from Godmama Verona. Godmama was a jazzy woman who bought herself a brand new car regularly. She was a precious and beautiful lady inside and out. She was five feet seven inches tall and what some would call pleasingly plump. She was beautiful! She always kept her hair pressed, and she would adorn her beautiful face with beautiful big hoop earrings and her body with stylish classy clothes. Even though she had fair, blemish-free skin, she would wear makeup and look just like one of the beautiful movie stars I watched on television. I would be amazed to watch her put red blush on her cheeks, and I couldn't wait to grow up to follow Godmama's womanly style. She would throw kisses at the mirror as she looked at herself and say, "Girl, you are looking good." I would always smile because she was right. She did look good. Godmama had a wonderful way of motivating herself, and it was a blessing to witness her character and adapt it into my own style. Her favorite perfume was Avon's "Here's My Heart."

I loved it when the weekends rolled around. It was inspiring to see Godmama and her girlfriends entertain and have fun with one another. Witnessing their relationships helped me to develop female relationships that have lasted through my lifetime. My childhood friends were like my sisters, just like Godmama's neighborhood buddies. I was truly a witness to their love for each other.

Godmama was quite the hostess, and was very pleasing to all she knew. She would solicit a menu and beverage request from each of the ladies and have it prepared every Friday evening. Godmama loved to cook, and she taught me her skills. I was her little helper, and I learned to become a good cook. The first to arrive would be Aunt Bertha Bridges, Auntie Heloise, and Auntie Alberta Aldridge. Auntie Alberta and Auntie Heloise were married to Mildred's brothers, Uncle Claude and Uncle Vernell. We would hear their knuckles strike our wooden door around 9:00 PM every weekend. They were always willing to help with the final preparation, so Godmama would be completely prepared when the other guests arrived. The early birds would express their concern that the weekend preparation was too much work for one person. Godmama would smile and shake her head and say, "I have help."

I could hear them say in unison, "Who?"

Godmama would call my name, "Mathell!" and say, "Come here, baby." I would walk real fast to respond to her. Back in the day, when I was a youngster, we were taught that when an adult called you, you'd better answer loud and clear. Don't let a grown-up call you twice; if you didn't respond immediately, you could very well get a strap to your tail end. When I entered the room, she would say, "I've got my baby."

Godmama would set out her fine crystal each week for her friends. There were always arrangements of fresh hand-picked flowers from our backyard sitting in the middle of the table and in strategic spots around the apartment. It was very refreshing to see the beautiful colors and arrangements, and exciting to see the yard while it was in full bloom. Godmama and Grandfather kept a very well-manicured front and backyard landscape. The aroma from the beautiful flowers was wonderful.

A few of Godmama's best friends lived in our building. Gloria and Lillian lived on the third floor; they were more like sisters to my Godmama than friends. They were involved in all of the parties and were so much fun to be around. At one time, Lillian had been married to Godmama's Uncle George. After years of marriage, they divorced. I am not sure what really happened, I wanted to ask Godmama, but I was mindful of staying in a child's place.

Aunt Lillian was like a daughter to Grandfather, and she was more like a real sister to Godmama. My godparents showed her much love and helped her reorganize her life after the divorce. She and Godmama sat on the front porch every night. They enjoyed each other's company. I heard Aunt Lillian tell Godmama how she loved both her and Grandfather. Aunt Lillian said she did not believe she could have made it without their support during her separation and divorce. She expressed such gratitude for their assistance, and I felt good that she was comforted by my godparents.

Aunt Lillian was very loving to me and to everyone she met. She was a petite lady with a friendly smile. She wore her hair pressed, short and sassy. I loved the way she would tell me to be a good girl in such a soft voice with a beautiful smile. The way she spoke to me made me want to be the best little girl I could be. I would give my cute little smile, and her eyes would light up the room. She would bake cakes and pies, and the aroma would filter downstairs. I would run upstairs just in time to lick the bowl. I would anxiously wait by the stove and watch the clock until the pastry was completely baked. If Aunt Lillian had pastries in her apartment, she would reward me with her treats for being her sweet, precious little girl. Aunt Lillian never had children, so I felt privileged that she treated me special as a kid. Now that I am an adult, she still calls me her little girl, and her disposition has never changed.

Big Dee and Willie Penn lived in the garden apartment of our building. Weekly gambling games would occur in their apartment. When Grandfather took his winter trips to San Diego, the card games and board games moved to our apartment. Big Dee had two daughters named Anna Laura and Marilyn. They were my childhood playmates.

Godmama had a very good telephone partner who she called her "Ace Boon Coon." I would love for Godmama to refer to her friend, Mrs. Louise Gary, in this manner. Mrs. Louise would not gamble with the partiers, but she would tell the funniest jokes and was always the life of the party, indoors and out. She loved to come to the backyard outings and sip a cold beer while listening to the beautiful music that Godmama would be playing. Mrs. Louise died one year before Godmama. She left a son and a daughter. The daughter, Debra, was one of my childhood friends. It broke Godmama's heart something awful. I watched her become ill from grieving over the passing of her "Ace Boon Coon." I would watch her cry and would bring her tissues and try to console her while she mourned the loss of her telephone buddy. I would give her a big kiss and listen to her tell me how she missed her girlfriend. I would tell her, "You got me, Godmama." She would smile and say she felt better. Those tender moments and musical memories with Godmama still bring bittersweet feelings when I think of them. Godmama would play the music Mrs. Louise would listen to and become rejuvenated. She would croon and drink a beer while she jammed around the house and saluted Mrs. Louise's memory.

Another one of Godmama's good buddies was Bertha Bailey. Bertha lived two houses down from us with her handsome husband, N.C. Bailey, and their nine kids. Everyone in the neighborhood called Bertha "Pig." I never understood why we called her that because she looked nothing like a pig. She was a beautiful woman, approximately five feet two inches tall, with a small frame, medium brown skin, and a beautiful head of hair.

Bertha was a remarkable mother with an awesome personality. She was the mentoring mother on the block and was very instrumental in my development as I was becoming a woman. One of her daughters, Pamela, became my best friend and still is today. I am the godmother of her daughter Brittney. Bertha's second daughter, Gloria, has a daughter named Ashley. She wanted me to be her godmama, too. So, I became the godmother to both sisters' daughters, and I took them both to church with me and had them christened.

Pamela is a mixture of both her mother and father. She is an attractive woman, medium brown like her mother, with beautiful long hair. Pamela and I have been through some terrible storms together, and we supported each other through it all. We have been together since we were very young, and I believe we will be together to the very end.

Nadine was another one of Godmama's party buddies. She would say some of the funniest and coolest things, and I would get so tickled when she was around. She was a lot of fun. We would sit and have long talks about the ups and downs of life. She was the one we would call the "jigger" or dancer. I remember that Nadine was one of the few women who would shoot dice with the men on party night. She would curse and talk about the men as she placed her winnings in her bosom for safekeeping. It was very entertaining to watch her mingle with the men. Godmama was crazy about cool Nadine.

I remember that Godmama smoked Winston cigarettes, and her favorite cocktail was Crown Royal mixed with Pepsi-Cola. She would be the life of the party. The more she drank, the more fun she would be. In the mornings, she would be up cooking a wonderful breakfast of salmon croquettes, bacon, rice, scrambled eggs, and toast or a hot pan of homemade biscuits. As soon as breakfast was over, we would clean the kitchen and begin preparing dinner. When I began assisting her with meal planning and preparation, I learned to cook collard greens, hot-water cornbread, black-eyed peas, great northern beans, baked sweet potatoes, fried chicken, and homemade biscuits with warm syrup. Three days a week, Godmama would bake pound cakes, sweet potato pies, peach cobbler, and bread pudding. Soon, I learned to become a great cook just like Godmama. Godmama would say things to me like: "You little ole sweet girl, my baby." "Godmama don't know anything about having no baby, but I sure know how to raise one." "Godmama has been blessed to be able to love and take care of you. I could not love you more than if I gave birth to you myself." "Baby, I love you so much." Those words will remain with me forever.

When I think about my grandfather, I remember that he was a very cool man. Grandfather was born March 8, 1888, and was a veteran of WWI. He had a medium brown complexion. He was a man about five feet eight inches tall. Grandfather wore thick black glasses that looked very much like the ones Malcolm X wore, and he loved to smoke cigars. His features were large. His nose and ears were pretty big, and I would call him Rudolph the Red-Nosed Reindeer. I would also play with his ears and call him the big bad wolf. We would have so much fun.

He would leave the state of Illinois every winter season. He realized drinking and gambling was going on in our building, but I never remember him and Godmama talking about it. When he was home, the parties would be held in the basement apartment where Big Dee and Willie Penn lived. Grandfather didn't claim to be a perfect man, but he was very gracious, loving, and one of the most nurturing men I've ever met. At one time he had been a drinker and gambler too, but he became a saved Christian man. The world's way was no longer his way. When someone would meet him on the porch or in route to their gambling game of choice, he would say a little prayer and would delay them as they walked passed. He would read a Bible scripture to them before they went to gamble their money. He would share with them that time and living would bring about a change, and that every man must work toward salvation. However, when I was growing up, I never wanted for anything. When I had children, they never wanted for anything, either. I guess one would say I was spoiled, but I called it privileged, blessed, and favored. I remember that if I walked by a store and saw something I wanted, or merely mentioned that I wanted something I saw in the window, it was mine. My grandfather would go into the store and tell the cashier that the item belonged to me.

Another thing about Grandfather was that he loved to play games. He would put me on his back like a horse and make up games to play with me. One game would be what I called the money game. He would hold money in his hands and I would either have to jump for it or catch it with only two fingers when it fell from his grasp. If it fell on the floor, I would not be able to keep the money. Most of the time, I would catch it and hold on to it with all I had. This was Grandfather's way of giving me an allowance.

Grandfather was my knight in shining armor in those days. We lived near railroad tracks that were surrounded by open fields. We would get uninvited guests—mice. I would be petrified when I would see one running around and scream. Grandfather would rush to my rescue pick me up and carry me on his back to make me feel safe. When Godmama would go out, I had to go to bed before she left. I would sit still in my bedroom and hear all types of scary noises. I would knock on the wall, and Grandfather would know I wanted him to come and get me. He would bring me to his bed and we would watch television, talk, and play until I fell asleep. Grandfather was the most instrumental spiritual teacher in my life. He would take me by the hand, lead me to the sanctuary, and instruct me on the teachings of the Lord.

Growing Up Too Soon

When I became old enough to understand the facts of my birth, Godmama would encourage me to visit my birth parents from time to time. During my visits, I would witness a lot of gambling, drinking, and adult socializing. There were a lot of people going in and out of the house, and I saw more than a child my age should. I came to realize that Mildred was an alcoholic with emotional issues, and that my father, Nathell, was denying me as his daughter. However, I learned to love them just the same. It was at this point in my life that I learned Nathell was well known in the neighborhood as a person not to be reckoned with. He was a gambler, womanizer, and hustler. But I didn't care about his reputation; I desperately wanted his genuine fatherly attention—and my mother's attention too, for that matter.

Instead, I attracted the sexual attention of a pedophile. It started when I was seven years old, during one of my visits with Nathell and Mildred while playing outside. I was very traumatized by what was happening to me, but I blocked it out of my mind and could not tell anyone about my predicament. Godmama continued to send me to visit my birth parents. I remained silent, and pretended the violation had not happened until I got a voice in my early teens. One day, during a visit to Mildred and Nathell's house, the man who had been molesting me in my young tender life attempted to grab my breast and pull me to his body. I snapped!

Reality had set in, and I began to scream: "It was you who hurt me, it was you!" I had blocked this situation out of my mind for years. I thought that my little girl thoughts wouldn't be believed. As the Lord would have it, this was the day everything came up and out and I was not going to be violated again.

I believe this was a small turning point in my relationship with Nathell. He felt horrible when he heard about what I had endured. Nathell regretted not having done much for me in my life, but the most disheartening thing was ignoring my existence as his daughter. In my adult years, my father contacted our family attorney and legally signed my birth certificate so the "father" status no longer stated "omitted." He now recognizes me as his blood daughter without taking a DNA test.

My relationship with Nathell became a little bit stronger while I was in my first year in high school. However, at the age of fourteen, I became smitten and sexual with a man ten years older, who was high-ranked in a black political organization. I believe that the longing for my father's affection is what led me to be attracted to him. He was known by the nickname of Denny Doo Whoop. That name really turned me on. I know you're wondering what I could have possibly known about being turned-on at my age. But I used to sneak around with him. I would ditch school and go to motels when I should have been in class. I would stay all day until it was time to get out of school. This was my trick to make Godmama think that I had been in school. It soon caught up with me, though, when the attendance officer called Godmama. I can't begin to tell you the trouble I was in or for how long.

My first sexual encounter was not a memorable experience. But I got pregnant and was totally thrown off course. When I informed Godmama that I was no longer menstruating, she took me to the doctor and we found out I was pregnant. She said, "You must have gotten tired of playing with dolls and forgotten all the things we discussed about sex." Godmama had schooled me on how to protect myself from pregnancy and disease when I began to develop breasts and had my monthly cycle. Once she expressed her disappointment about my situation, Godmama insisted that I continue my high school education and promised she would help me through it all. However, after she spoke with Mildred about my pregnancy, the two of them came up with a plan for me to have an abortion. I was petrified by the notion of abortion. I knew that killing a fetus was an illegal act, and that many times coat hangers were used. I decided to talk to Nathell about my dilemma, and told him my fear of abortion. He went to Godmama and Mildred and stood up for me. He told them I would not have an abortion, so I didn't. Godmama tried to shelter me from the ridicule and the shame teenage pregnancy carries.

At first, my family would not allow him to come around when they found out he had fathered my child. However, once Godmama thought about it, she concluded that the damage was done. Godmama realized that I had suffered sexual abuse at an early age. She also understood my need for a father's love. She thought that I had to have provoked him. She was right. I had told him I was older than I was because I looked very mature for my age.

When I was fifteen my son, Vaughn, was born. He was a sickly baby who had asthma and developed juvenile diabetes at the age of eight years old. He was admitted to several hospitals and was in many diabetic comas. Due to being the only baby in the family and not a well child, he was spoiled by all. Godmama and Grandfather bought him everything a child would want and need. As I look back at the situation, it was much like when I came into their lives. I have to admit motherhood was not easy for me and really affected my social life. Godmama made me raise my son. She would watch him when I went to school and did my homework, but that was just about the extent of her babysitting duties. I really did learn the hard way to be responsible for my actions and my son. I must say the teaching was good for me. Mildred helped me with her new grandson also, and we began to bond a little.

When Vaughn was two months old, Denny Doo Whoop told me about his other children and their mother, Ann, who was a mature woman of his age. He told me he had ended their relationship before I became pregnant, and he wanted to introduce me to his kids and their mother. I thought I knew what I was getting into. I was too young for this introduction, but I had placed myself in a woman's position by having sex, so I had to step up to the plate. I discussed this arrangement with Godmama and she told me this was an act of a gentleman. She stated that I should forgive myself and understand that we can not undo the pregnancy. She emphasized that I was a young woman now and that I should go forward.

Finally, I agreed to meet Denny Doo Whoop's other family. He took Vaughn and me to Ann's home to meet her and her children. Her children were in their rooms playing, and she summoned them to the living room where we were. Ann introduced her daughter Marilyn, who was two years old, and her son Pat, who was one.

Lo and behold, Ann and I had already known each other through our families. Her aunt and grandfather attended the same church I attended. Summit was a small town, and just about everyone knew each other. It was important to us as mothers that the kids get acquainted and establish kinship. This lady was very nice to me, and so was I to her.

As time passed, Ann and I had a very difficult time raising our children. Denny Doo Whoop had to go underground because of illegal activities. She decided to leave Summit and move her family to California.

Vaughn's male role model was Grandfather. He loved Grandfather "Jack," as he called him. As he grew older, he secretly longed for his father. I understood his feelings because that was how it was for me with my father, Nathell. When Vaughn was a small infant, his father was a part of his life. Vaughn was too young to really understand his father's nurturing, and shortly thereafter his father disappeared from Summit. We didn't see him again until Vaughn was nine years old.

When I was sixteen, my Godmama pulled me aside to let me know that she was getting married. She explained that she was going to take a real job, for the first time in a long time. In the past, she had been a party girl. She gave house parties. She charged guests for food, drinks, and admission. Everything had a fee of twenty-five cents. There were rooms to play cards of any sort, shoot dice, and dance all night long. Now that she was getting married, she shared with me that she would be taking a job cleaning houses. Godmama explained she didn't want her new husband to complain about having to take care of me. Godmama married Mr. Buchanan, a wonderful man, who had a daughter named Deloris. She was the big sister and friend I longed for, and I welcomed her as my godsister. Her dad was heavy built, had dark skin, and wore a hat. He was a sharp dresser like Godmama, and she called him a "cool cat."

When Deloris would visit us, she was filled with fun and love. I remember hiding her shoes and playing pranks when it came time for her to leave and return home to Missouri. Once during her weekend visit, Deloris came down with the flu. She was in bad shape. Godmama, Mr. Buchanan, and I nursed her back to health. I hated seeing her sick, and I never wanted her to leave. We were divinely blessed to love one another.

Deloris was tall, with a light brown complexion, and was very prissy. She wore glasses. She was a person who liked to smile, a sharp dresser like her dad, cheerful, and a super mother of one son.

Godmama had been married for one year when Mr. Buchanan died. He was from St. Louis, and his services were held in his hometown. Godmama and I went to St. Louis for the services and prepared to stay at a hotel. Deloris's mother, Virginia Williams, would not hear of it and offered her home to us. She would not take no for an answer. She was a most gracious host and a lovely woman. Miss Virginia has passed now, but her generosity will never be forgotten. Deloris and I grew closer, and as my troubles began, she started ministering to me. She grew up in the church and is a pastor today.

Anxious to leave home and to be grown, I was seventeen when I got married to a man named Harold Givens. Vaughn and I moved in with my new husband and his brother Johnny in south suburban Chicago Heights. Ironically—and fortunately—Harold's sister, Marva, lived next door to us. She and I became friends. I was in my last year in high school and would commute to Argo every day to complete my education.

Argo High School is actually where Harold and I met. He was a security guard there. One day in September, I was walking down the hall and he stopped me. He asked if I was a senior. I told him yes. When I saw him, I thought he was so fine. He was about five feet eleven and twenty-five years old. He had a sparkle in his eyes. His pupils were a light shade of green. They had the glare of cat's eyes in the dark of the night. He was wearing a cap bent down above his eyebrows. The front of the cap had the name of the agency he worked for. This was very impressive to me, a teenager. He had nice white teeth and a beautiful flirty smile. I was attracted to him at first glance. He asked me out for dinner, after school, and I accepted with no hesitation.

After our lovely date, full of laughs and fun, I took him over my birth mother's house so she could meet him. She lived across the street from my school. While we were visiting, she asked him if he could get her on as a security guard. He told her he would talk with his supervisor. I knew he was, of course, trying to get to my heart. Days after they met, Mildred went for an interview and was hired. She became fond of Harold. She began calling him son-in-law. I guess this is when the dream of being his wife entered my mind—and his, also. Godmama Verona had not met him yet. Our relationship was growing strong. It was important that he meet Godmama, who was my guardian. I took him to meet her. She felt we needed more time to get to know one another, and she felt that I should complete the twelfth grade. Even though I had had a baby, I was able to complete my last year of school ahead of my class, in January; I had gone to summer school every year after Vaughn was born. I had the option of going back and walking across the stage on graduation night of the next year. I did not want to wait to marry. Godmama did not approve of our hasty decision. She explained to both of us that she wanted to give me a nice wedding, but only if I waited until after the graduation ceremony.

I went behind her back to my birth mother. That hurt Godmama very much. Mildred was indebted to Harold for getting her the job. I manipulated her. I waited until she was tipsy and asked her to sign for me to get married. Going against Godmama's wishes caused friction between my two mothers. In December of that year, I was married. I realized soon after that Godmama's decision was the best. I was wrong for going over her head. I should have listened to her, because my poor decisions in the past had caused me many setbacks and mental stresses.

On my wedding night, approximately thirty minutes after crossing the threshold into my new abode, the telephone rang. My new husband told me to answer the telephone, since I was the new woman of the house. I answered, and the caller was a woman who seemed surprised to hear a female voice answer the telephone. She stated that she had been with my husband the night before our wedding, and that they had a very serious sexual relationship.

She believed she was pregnant. I had married a man who would cheat, double-cross me, and generally be a disloyal human being. However, I replied by saying, "A one-night stand does not mean you are pregnant."

She replied, "Yeah, I rocked him hard last night to get a baby, and I should have been the one he married, not you."

I later found out that the ring he had placed on my finger the night he proposed (which was a little tight) was initially bought for her. I was excited to be proposed to and never thought about the ring being too small. I would slide it on and off with Vaseline. I was young, silly, and on top of that, I was ecstatic to be getting married and finally grown. When I found out that I wasn't his first choice, I was overwhelmed and felt as though I had been misled and emotionally abandoned.

Reality Sets In

Just when I was feeling all alone, Bea came into my life. Bea was a tall stately woman with a smile that welcomed you into her heart. She possessed an aura of kindness, concern, and great sympathy for those around her. It's amazing to have someone in your life who treats you the way they want to be treated, with no strings attached. I met Bea when I was seventeen and she was twenty-two. I was married and had a two-year-old son to care for. I had just relocated to the town my husband grew up in, Chicago Heights, Illinois. The move and my marriage made me unhappy, but it turned out to be a blessing in disguise. God created a divine connection between Bea and me. It started over thirty years ago and still exists today. Our paths in life have been inseparable, spiritually and mentally. Bea is the best friend a girl could have.

I had decided to look for a job. Not knowing the area, I accidentally came upon the town's Community Economic Development Association, or CEDA. I walked in and approached the reception area, where I was greeted by the receptionist sitting at the front desk. I told her that my name was Mathell Givens, and I was seeking employment. She greeted me with a warm smile and said, "Everybody calls me Ms. Bea." I was given an application for the position of Assistant Youth Coordinator. Ms. Bea and I immediately connected; she felt that I would qualify for the position and scheduled me to be interviewed. The person who interviewed me was the administrative assistant, Ms. Shirley. I watched her as she slowly walked to the reception area, called my name, and introduced herself. I smiled at her, and she asked me to follow her into the interviewing room. Her words were very clear and formal. She had a big smile on her face as she led me to her office and asked me to have a seat. This lady was amazing to look at. She was blonde and adorable, and I told her so. She laughed out loud while stating how beautiful and charming I was, as well. I remember that day vividly. Ms. Shirley was wearing a two-piece purple suit accented with a bold-colored gold blouse that had a single row of buttons down the front.

She was a short lady, approximately five feet three inches tall, but wore a pair of purple high-heel shoes. Her skin was chocolate and her neck was accented with layers of gold chains. She had a ring on every finger. After the interview, I was told that I would receive a call within the next few days. I was a bit surprised when I received a call the next day from Ms. Bea, telling me I had the job, and I was to report to work the next day at 9:00 AM sharp. She excitedly shared that the center provided a new academic program offering college credits at Prairie State College, located in Chicago Heights, Illinois. This program was created to enhance our skills while working with young women ages thirteen through eighteen years of age. Ms. Bea and I took advantage of the program. We both were single parents, and the program would enable us to better ourselves.

Ms. Shirley was a jazzy supervisor, a woman with flare and very down to earth. I was so happy and thankful for meeting such nice people and getting the job, I showed up for work earlier than expected.

Ms. Bea asked me out for lunch on my first day, and I was filled with joy. I not only had a new job but a new friend as well. We chatted at lunch and told each other things about our families and our lives. I told her that I was only seventeen years old, recently married, and had a two-year-old son. I shared with her that I had just moved from Summit, Illinois, where I grew up. During our first lunch conversation, Ms. Bea suggested I call her Bea, and we hugged to solidify our new partnership.

My second day at work, I decided to return the favor, and I treated Bea to lunch. We had a chance to talk about some of our likes and dislikes. We found out that we both were raised in the church, and that we both liked to sing. She told me about two other young ladies she knew who loved to sing, and she wanted us all to get together. One of these ladies was her cousin, Karen Bell, and the other singer's name was Aurelia Kennedy. Bea arranged for us to meet, and it was a match made in heaven. We met and began singing along with the songs on the radio. We discovered that we all had harmonious voices and formed a singing group called the Brown Sugars. We exchanged phone numbers and, from that day forward, our friendship soared. We made a pact to be there for each other as sisters, through the good times as well as the bad times.

At the center where Bea and I worked, fundraisers were held all the time. We went to Ms. Shirley, told her about our singing group, and asked if we could audition to perform at the next community-center fundraiser. She wanted to hear us first and asked if she could bring along her sister, Myra, for a second opinion. We assumed she needed to make sure we could sing. None of us had any problem with her request. Bea planned the audition at her house. Ms. Shirley introduced Myra to the Brown Sugars, and we introduced ourselves. The Brown Sugars had prepared for our tryout, and now we changed into one of our glamorous outfits. We came out singing, with Bea as the lead singer. We sang "Don't Mess with Bill," as our audience watched in amazement and delight. At the conclusion of that song, Myra and Shirley—she had asked us to drop the "Ms." except at work—screamed for one more. Shirley jumped up out of her seat and started dancing and humming. She encouraged us to please sing more. The four of us sang a song by the Emotions, "So I Can Love You." I was the lead singer of that song, and I rocked it. I looked down and my toes were tapping to the beat.

Shirley told us that we would have to audition for the board members. She scheduled the audition, and we sang the same two songs. They were delighted and overwhelmed by the Brown Sugars' audition. The spokesperson for the board assured us that we would be able to perform and claimed we would be a hit. The four of us were excited and encouraged to know that this big organization would showcase us. However, it was explained that, due to the tight budget, the Brown Sugars could not be paid for our performance. We didn't care about the money, we wanted the exposure.

The first thing the Brown Sugars had to do was shop for new outfits to wear for our debut. We had about two weeks until show time, and we put in a lot of hard rehearsal time every day after work for three or four hours. When it was show time, we were the stars of the show. We had great reviews. One would have thought that we had been together for years. We had many people giving us their phone numbers for bookings. We didn't realize a photo had been taken during our performance, and it appeared in the next issue of the local newspaper. Our first time out was quite a success, and the community organization was so proud of and pleased with our performance that they booked the Brown Sugars for their next fundraiser, with pay. Our dreams of becoming a successful singing group were coming true. We suddenly had more bookings than we could handle.

However, the excitement of Brown Sugars was short-lived. We were all faced with common problems. How could we as performers continue to raise our children, please our husbands, and work a full-time job? At that time in our lives, we didn't know how to multi-task all of our family life responsibilities and reach our career goals at the same time. Appearing in show after show became problematical with our husbands. It was especially hard for me, because my marriage started off rocky. My music career eased my troubled home life. When I was on stage and at rehearsals, I was very happy. However, Bea had trouble with her husband, too. Neither of our husbands wanted us to sing and be in the limelight. As young women, we thought our husbands or significant others would be happy for our success and supportive of our dreams. But that was a one-sided belief. We didn't know our ability to achieve our singing dream would soon fade. Many men believe that a wife or their woman should cook, work, or stay home, performing wifely duties and raising the children. Many had the barefoot and pregnant frame of mind, and this made it difficult to have a singing career. With so many issues, we decided to disband the Brown Sugars after a two-year ride. However, Bea and I remained the best of friends.

It seemed that my marriage to Harold was a disaster from day one. Exactly nine months from my wedding day, I received another call from the same woman who said she was pregnant by my husband. She called to announce that she had given birth to a bouncing baby boy. She called me at my job to inform me that she had given birth to my husband's son. I informed her that she should speak to my husband about the situation and asked her, "How did you get my work number?"

She arrogantly replied, "I know everything I need to know about you."

I hung up immediately and called Harold at his job. He explained that he had already received a call from her. I then encouraged him to visit the hospital, along with me, to see this new baby boy. I must tell you it didn't feel good to be hit with such blatant disrespect. I was seventeen years old, caring for an asthmatic two-year-old and facing the end of my ten-month marriage to Harold. I was seriously contemplating hurting the person I had married.

He had conceived a baby boy, and we had been married less than a year. We had made vows to one another. Where was the respect I should have been given? When I was growing up, the male and female relationship was based on love, togetherness, compassion, and consideration. My grandfather loved me and his daughter, my Godmama. When Godmama married Mr. Buchanan, they also had a loving relationship. When he brought his daughter into the picture, more love poured out. I didn't understand how I chose to marry a man who would mistreat me in such a manner. However, love was, still is, and always will be with me. Even old Harold couldn't take that away from me. God gave that gift to me, and no one but God can take it away from me. I believe that was the main reason I was so angry. No one had ever messed with my soul. That is where my love resides, and Harold had severely disrupted the flow of things. It was the first time I'd felt this type of emotion. Normally, when mistakes were made in my life, it was because of my doing, and the brunt of the impact was on me. Not this time. I didn't like it one bit. I wanted revenge, even though I knew that vengeance belongs to God.

When the dust settled and Harold and I were alone, there was absolutely no conversation. I continued to clean house, and finally Harold went to bed. That was his biggest mistake. By now, I figured Harold didn't know anything about nurturing a teenage mother or respecting his young teenage wife. I was angry as hell! No need to guess, it was definitely his child; it was determined that my husband was the father of this male infant. This situation brought major tension into our marriage. However, I purchased clothing, diapers, milk, and toys for the baby. Together, we delivered the items to the mother's home, attempting to do the right thing during this difficult time.

Later that evening, when we returned home, the tension mounted between us. When we went to bed with our backs toward each other, I was very disheartened and saddened by my new husband's behavior. The next morning, I decided to skip school, take Harold to work, and keep the car. When I returned home, I began to clean and wash to take my mind off of the drama I was living. I was really attempting to work out the blues my heart and mind were experiencing. I went into the clothes hamper and took out the dirty clothes and began to sort them. This was when I discovered a set of soiled sheets that I knew for sure I had not used. The week before, I had stayed at Godmama's house and went to school from there. So there should not have been soiled sheets in our hamper. I became enraged, and then there was a knock at the door.

When I asked who was there, a low voice responded. I couldn't hear what was said, but I knew it was a female. I opened the door and there stood a small young woman dressed in a navy overcoat and tennis shoes. Her hair was very short, and she had a worried look on her face. She asked who I was. I quickly replied that I was my brother-in-law Johnny's wife. I now realize the Lord wanted me to see what had been going on in the dark that was now about to come to the light. She asked if Harold was there, because she saw his car outside. I stated that Harold had had car trouble, and that was why his car was in front of the apartment. Internally, I was steaming and was ready to whip some butt. I tried very hard to keep my composure. First, the baby boy, next, the soiled sheets, now, a woman, live and in color, at my door is looking for my cheating husband. I had seen several of Johnny's lady friends, but I had never seen this woman. This was the reason I lied about whose wife I was. My woman's intuition went into overload. She asked if she could come in and wait for Harold to get home from work. I opened the door to let her in. I went immediately to the telephone to call Marva, because I was feeling myself getting out of control. I was thinking I potentially had two women and a baby competing for my husband's affection, and the nice Mathell had had enough. I told my sister-in-law that there was a woman in my apartment waiting for Harold to come home from work. I told her what was happening, and what I had said to the woman. She knew this situation meant trouble, and she came right over—but not before contacting Harold to tell him to come home immediately.

The young woman walked toward my bedroom and was attempting to go lay down in my bed.

I said, "No baby, you can't go in there."

She said, "Why? This is Harold's room."

I replied, "Johnny and Harold changed rooms last night, and this is me and Johnny's room."

She replied, "This is Harold's furniture."

I said, "Yes, but we changed rooms last night."

Marva intervened. She told the woman, "Honey, you come in here with us. Harold will be home soon."

I began to tap my foot to keep from strangling this woman who was claiming my man. The air was thick during the fifteen minutes we waited for Harold to come through the door. It seemed like an hour before he came storming through the front door, but it really was a short time. Harold borrowed someone's car to come home early, and this is when all hell broke loose.

He came in the door and briskly stated, "Dion, you fool, what are you doing here? Do you know who you are sitting with?"

Dion replied, "Yes, this is Johnny's wife and your sister."

Harold said, "Fool, you are sitting next to my wife, not Johnny's." Harold stormed into the bedroom and retrieved our marriage license and threw it in Dion's face.

Then I looked at Dion and said, "It is time for you to get out of my house." I flashed my wedding ring in her face.

Harold said, "You got to get out now."

Dion said, "But she told me she was Johnny's wife."

Harold screamed, "She lied to you, get out!" He forced her to the door.

The woman looked at me and angrily screamed, "He'll never be yours because he belongs to me."

I felt like I had been hit with a brick. I didn't have a clue until Harold told me that he had married me on the rebound. I was devastated!

When Dion left, I began to cry and scream and became violently enraged. How dare he continue to mistreat me in such a fashion? He had previously accused me of sleeping around and being a whore. He made me give up a thriving singing career with the Brown Sugars, and I was very angry about it all. How dare he accuse me of being all the horrible things that he was!

I decided I had had enough. When he went to sleep and I heard him snoring, I took a butcher knife and began to slice the sheets where his legs were located. I began to cut him with the butcher knife until I saw blood. Once I saw the blood, I wanted to kill him. He woke up and screamed, "Are you crazy?" He balled up his fist and punched me in the face so hard that he knocked me down. He left the house and stayed out all night. I was destroyed and didn't know what to do about my dilemma. This was not the type of life I had intended to lead, and I was hurt to the core.

Harold stayed at his son's mother's house that night. The next day, the woman called me to brag about having my husband with her. I called Marva to go over to the woman's home with me. Harold had left by this time, and the woman came out of her house to confront me. She had her girls with her, but Marva wouldn't let them intervene because the problem was between the mistress and me. The woman stepped up to me and all I can remember was banging her head upside the closest garbage can I could find. After a few bangs, two policemen arrived. They put their arms around me and handcuffed my hands together real tight. I was flabbergasted and asked what was going on. The police said, "You are disturbing the peace." I yelled that the lady was the one at fault. Needless to say, I was through. I was taken to jail and the policeman told me that I needed to remove myself from this situation. He said that I seemed to be a very nice young lady, but I was dealing with some rough characters. He also advised me to move on with my life and try to create a great future for myself.

The first time I spoke about my husband's infidelity to my Godmama, she told me, "If you leave, be prepared to leave permanently. You will not move in and out of my house. But if you plan to leave his ass for good, then you can come back home." The next day, I left my husband of one year, never to return to him again. I worked out a plan and went back home to Godmama and Grandfather.

Home Again

Godmama told me she overheard some women talking while she was out finger-popping and partying one Friday night. She heard that a big industrial company in Clearing, Illinois, was taking applications that Tuesday. She explained that they did not quote a month or date, but we both agreed it was an opportunity worth checking out. We found out where the interviews were taking place. The company was Johnson & Johnson.

Godmama was an encourager. This mama was truly a motivator, as long as you were trying to do the right thing. If things did not work out, it was always all right. She would reassure me that at any given time, I was going to get a job. I sought out the opportunity at Johnson & Johnson. This is when I met Faye Carter. We were both hired on the same day.

Faye was a beautiful sister. She looked like she had a tan all year round. She was five feet seven inches tall, slim build, with shiny black hair. Faye's hair was flawless every time you saw her, and the first day we met was no different. At one time, she was contemplating going to beauty school. She would practice her hair-styling techniques on me and a few of her other girlfriends. She had a massive shoe collection, an awesome wardrobe selection, and her style was very classy. Faye spoke with a Southern accent and always kept a friendly smile. She was from Smithville, Mississippi.

Faye and I became godsisters. She was quite friendly and very generous with her love. She and I seemed to have a lot of the same interests, and we both loved to cook. We would often cook while talking on the telephone all night long. Before leaving for work every day, she would clean the house, as well as prepare meals for her husband and their three pretty, precious little girls.

Faye explained that her husband, Louis, worked all of the time. She was trying to help her husband make ends meet. She said that her family had been through some hard times. She wanted to make sure that Louis wouldn't have to work too hard. He was working two jobs, preparing to become an ordained minister and she did not want him to work himself into an early grave.

Faye really wanted to work, but she also wanted to be a great mother and wife. I encouraged her to respect her husband's wishes for her to take her place in the home and just be a wonderful homemaker. I told her that I wished I could have a man thinking of me the way her husband thought of her. I was truthful to Faye and shared my marriage story. I strongly suggested that she should accept the role her husband offered her. I held her by the hand as I cried while telling her about Harold and his awful conduct as a husband. Faye was very saddened by my story, and it encouraged her to consider quitting the job and going home to her family. She needed to allow her husband to be the man of the house and father to their children as well. She should maintain her wifely and motherly responsibilities.

After Faye and I had worked together for about two months, she invited me to her home in Chicago to meet Louis. They had a fabulous brick home. It was fully furnished in a French provincial style. The rooms in their home were very spacious. Every piece of furniture was polished, and you could see your image as you looked upon each piece. The style of her dining room stayed in my mind. There was a big beautiful piano positioned in the center of the room. As I entered their bedroom, I noticed that Faye's dresser looked like a display at Marshall Field's department store. Faye had the best perfumes on her dresser, and it was set up very nicely with glass trays full of good-smelling body lotions and make-up.

Faye's husband had a friendly smile when I met him. He was a very delightful and humble spirit. He knew I was worldly, but he also knew I had a desire to know all about the Lord. He never placed judgment on me. I felt very comfortable meeting him and talking with him. It was like I had known him all my life. He was such a good man to his family and others. Minister Louis Carter was very dark in complexion, and he stood about five feet six inches tall. When he walked, his steps were slow and easy. He'd come into the room and take his hat off leisurely. It was a calming motion to watch. His spoken words, especially to me, were soft and sometimes just a whisper.

Every time I would visit them on a Saturday, Minister Carter would be in his study seeking to know all about God. Minister Carter had told me that he dreamed of retiring and becoming a full-time pastor. He did just that and not only became a pastor, but was elevated to a bishop. He was a very quiet man until he would speak about our Lord and savior. I loved to visit with him and hear him speak about all the beautiful stories and miracles that the Lord performed in the Bible. I would feel the excitement stir in me as Minister Carter read from the scriptures.

I began to feel a spiritual zeal inside me and knew exactly where it was stemming from. I had thoughts of Grandfather Brown, and how he would take me to church. Godmama would play and sing a variety of gospel songs that would intrigue my soul. I realized that I had greatness inside me, and I was born to do great things.

Faye and I were laid off after working at Johnson & Johnson for approximately three months. We both felt the lay-off came right on time. We were line workers, and we were both tired of the fast pace. Faye was already considering quitting, but I was ready to go back to a desk job.

I was determined to get a steady job to support my three year old son and myself. My lay-off lasted only two weeks. Then I got another plant job at a company called Lever Brothers. The company's specialty was Pepsodent toothpaste. The plant's location was right down the street from my last job. On my first day, I met a very distinguished-looking man with salt-and-pepper hair. He had a deep, sexy voice and a sensational smile. I was assigned to work on the toothpaste-tube line. There were many jam-ups, and our line would stop and be backed up and overflowing, with empty tubes falling to the floor. This man was in charge of the sanitation department and had a crew that did all the clean-ups for the entire plant. When this smooth operator of a man saw me bending down to pick up some of the tubes, he whistled as I lifted my head up. I began to rise up in a standing position. He was facing me. He then smiled and introduced himself as Cannon, and in return I told him my name. He started flirting with me by telling me I was pretty. I smiled at him and turned my head and looked in the opposite direction. I did not know how to take this man making a move on me. I had experienced a great deal of disappointment in a marriage that ended with a broken heart just a few months prior. It was too soon for me to let thoughts of another man go to my head.

While I was trying to analyze the meeting between us, the lunch buzzer went off. My first few hours on my new job were interesting. However, learning the skills to work on a steady running conveyor belt was different from my past jobs. I needed a break. Lunch time could not have come soon enough. When I entered the lunch area, it seemed as though all eyes were on me. I began to slowly look around the room as I stood in line to select what I wanted to eat. I had not made acquaintances, and so any table would be okay. I sat down where there were only two ladies, and I introduced myself.

One of them hinted that she saw Cannon wink at me. She thought it looked like I had caught a big fish on my first day. The other lady said that she had heard a rumor that he's a ladies man. Many ladies had an eye for him, but you must be the lucky one, Mathell. I asked them what makes me so fortunate. They said, almost in unison, that a lot of women around there had pursued him. Cannon was cool, and he didn't make a move on any of them. They said that from the looks of it, he's after you. Soon, lunch was over, and we were all back in our designated areas. One lady who worked on my line was Marie. She saw Cannon passing slowly by me, whistling and making comments to me. As he walked away with a smile on his face, she teased me about hearing him say that I was a fine brown lady. Marie gave me a little history of what a nice person he was, and also the length of time he had worked for the company. She said he was very dedicated.

I laughed at her and said, "Are you Cupid?"

She threw her head back and said, "Go for it, girl."

It was not hard for me to reach a decision after that kind of information. I was strongly attracted to this man, as though a spell had instantly been zapped on me. I was a fine young thing with a beautiful smile. I had personality plus. I could sing, as the old folks would say, like a hummingbird. At the end of my first week of work, Cannon was standing at the exit door when I was punching out. He asked me, as I was getting in my car, if I would meet him at the nightclub called Before and After Lounge. This lounge was located at the top of the viaduct. It had a circular shape like a horseshoe. It was at the dead end of town where most of the local bars were located.

I told him I would meet him at the lounge. I stopped by my apartment first to check on things. Everything seemed fine, and Godmama did not mind watching Vaughn. She wanted me to get out and be social again, anyway. When I arrived at the club,

Cannon was already in there. We embraced one another and even gave each other a smooch. We both ordered a cocktail and began to enjoy the music and one another's company. While we were having fun, he suddenly asked me out to a gala affair. His eyes started to gleam as he looked at me and asked me to go to a retirement party in two weeks in honor of a friend of his in Chicago. I was very interested and answered quickly, "Yes, I would be delighted." He was excited to tell me that he lived in Chicago and the party was in the vicinity of where he lived. He was used to the convenience of city cabs or riding the CTA bus line. He smiled and said, "They run all night long." As he was talking, I was wondering why he didn't drive. I knew his position at the plant paid him well enough to buy a car. This man was a supervisor of the sanitation department. As my thoughts were running wild in my head, he began to tell of an accident he caused while under the influence of alcohol a few years earlier. Fortunately, no one was hurt. He came out of it with a few bruises and a skull fracture. Cannon was grateful that there was no one in the car with him when he struck a utility pole. He then explained, with a frown in his face, that after his life was spared, he never attempted to drive again.

But he would be happy to come to my home and we ride in together. I welcomed him to come out and pick me up. This was really thrilling for me, and I looked forward to being with him. We confirmed a pick-up time, and he was at my door promptly. It was important for him to make an entrance with me on his arm. He was an older man escorting a twenty year old pretty young thing. There was nineteen years difference in our ages. I looked at him, and he smiled and winked his left eye. I was a cool young woman. I had been raised by the best and had been around a lot. He gave me a charming line of flattery. I was curious, and my imagination was running wild. After his explanation, I let him know I would be his private driver.

My aim was to blow his mind in my foxy red miniskirt, flaming red halter top, and tall patent leather red boots, with a red leather bag trimmed in gold. I was gorgeous when he arrived. I must say this "cat" was looking fine as a glass of cold mellow wine. He was a chocolate drop styling a pinstriped, chocolate brown leisure suit. He wore a sharp brown shirt with gold thread sparkling through it. He was clean from head to toe. He had on a pair of cold-blooded brown pointed-toe shoes. When we pulled into the parking lot, I turned off the car ignition. Our hearts were thumping, and there were sparkles in each of our eyes. It was "on" in the parking lot. Our lips touched as his arms reached out to hug me. These were exciting and sizzling moments. We were too hot to trot.

We both tried to compose ourselves before entering the club. He was proud to have this pretty young sexy looking lady on his arm. I, as well, was excited to have this fine distinguished-looking man by my side. Because of our age difference, he felt like he was a bad dude. He greeted many people. He was a very popular man. The ladies were coming up to him and the closer they would get to him, the more he would squeeze me. He wanted to make sure that I felt secure. I knew that I was his lady that night. As the evening went on, the disc jockey played this "bad jam" that was a duet. We started singing to Harold Melvin and The Blue Notes' "Hope That We Can Be Together Soon." We discovered that we both could sing and could truly blow that song. We sang it like we owned it. At one point, we were on our feet dancing to the beat. We were touching and blowing kisses at one another as we sang. People began to applaud us and request that we sing it over and over until it was time to say goodnight.

We stayed on the nightclub scene each weekend. We were beginning to be a couple. People on our job started to notice how we played with one another as he would pass my area. The rumor was that I was too young for him. He had an answer back for them. He felt I was more woman than a lady his age could be. He used the old cliché, "Age ain't nothing but a number." Everywhere we went, people loved to hear us sing that song. I must tell you, he thrilled my soul when he would look at me. I do believe I was infatuated.

I knew that this man was living with someone when I met him. I found myself trapped now that we had been intimate. While lying in his arms one night, I suggested we move in together. He then explained that he was married, had four kids, and was separated from his wife for about fifteen years. The woman he was living with was taking care of his two little girls. Cannon explained that he could not jeopardize his girls' home. They were used to her kindness, and he was grateful that this woman was nurturing his girls. I should have turned around then. I sometimes believe that because of my past hurts and disappointment, I found myself stuck on stupid. Godmama tried to tell me about the games men could run, especially on a young girl. She felt he was too old for me, but of course, you couldn't tell old fast me anything.

A few years after meeting Cannon, I became pregnant again with my second child. I was informed by the doctors that my baby had a big body and a small head. They said the child was maybe fifteen pounds, and would probably be born deformed or not survive birth. I consulted Godmama and we decided to let the Lord determine the fate of my unborn infant. What we didn't know is that I was pregnant with twins.

At the same time, my friend Myra was also expecting. However, she knew she was having twins. As her due date approached, Myra's sister Shirley became very concerned about her sister's risky pregnancy. Myra had become huge, and it was very difficult for her to do normal things for herself. I could not imagine the hard time she was having, because my first pregnancy wasn't that rough. I called her one day to check on her, and she explained that she could not walk without assistance. I decided to go visit her and give her a helping hand for a week. The day I arrived, she went into labor and delivered a healthy boy and girl. It was amazing to see her care for two babies. Little did I know, two months later, at the age of twenty-two, I would give birth to twin sons.

I was playing softball at a July 4th outdoor celebration the day my water broke, and I was immediately taken to the hospital. My son Vaughn was seven-and-a-half years old at the time and was anxiously waiting for the baby to arrive. Little did we know our little one was about to arrive early—one month early to be exact. I was in labor for twelve long, hard hours. It wasn't from just the labor pains it was also from not knowing God's plan for my baby's life. I knew I was about to find out something, and I prayed that I could handle the blessing God was about to give me. All I could do was surrender and totally lean upon the arm of God.

While I was in the delivery room, doctors and nurses would come in and check on the baby's heartbeat every fifteen or twenty minutes. Each hospital worker who checked me during labor seemed very pleased with the way things were going with my high-risk pregnancy. I noticed each time the stethoscope was placed on either side of my stomach; the "strong heartbeat" comment was made. It briefly ran across my mind that it was odd for an unhealthy baby to flip so fast, especially since the baby was early. I must admit I felt a small sense of relief and continued to pray for God's mercy and grace, but also added "Thank you Lord" to my prayers.

Finally, the doctor ordered an ultrasound. I was wheeled to the examination room. Once the ultrasound was given, the technician said, "Oh my, call the doctor. I believe she is having triplets." Another technician checked and said, "No, it's twins, and they are ready to come out." I was now overwhelmed with the blessing of two babies. I welcomed the doctor's instruction for an immediate C-section. I was in shock, disbelief, and thankful that I was having two healthy sons.

I called Myra late in the midnight hour to inform her of my multiple births and told her I thought she was contagious. She did not believe me and wanted the hospital phone number to inquire about my delivery. Myra called the hospital and identified herself as my sister and was in shock when the nurse congratulated her for becoming an aunt to healthy twin boys.

I couldn't concentrate on names for five days after their birth. The first two days of my twins' lives, we called them "Me First and My Turn Next." I know this sounds silly, but it is true. The doctors had misdiagnosed my due date by one month. The twins were born on July 5, 1974. They weighed in at approximately six pounds ten ounces and six pounds eleven ounces. I became the proud mother of three sons, instantly. They were the V-Boys—Vaughn and the twins, Victor and Verdell. God's plan was perfect! Awesome! Magnificent!

Five years after Myra and I had twins, my best friend Bea got pregnant and had a set of twins, a boy and a girl. It seemed as though our lives were really becoming interconnected. We were all tight like "white on rice." We still are.

Family Separation

As we well know, time waits for no one. Godmama's health began to fail, and it was very saddening to watch. Her doctor recommended she have someone with her at all times. I needed to take care of my sweet loving Godmama. Bea and I had become very close friends, and she would come over and help me care for her.

Then my grandfather's property, along with the entire community, was sold. These properties were then developed into a new community and our family had to relocate. I found myself having to move from the community I had lived in since I was six weeks old. We did not want to separate. But as we searched for a new home, it became difficult to remain together as a single family unit. I moved to Palos Hills, Illinois, and Godmama and her father moved to Maywood, Illinois. Our close family unit was now spread out.

Vaughn was fourteen and refused to leave his grandparents. So, we collectively decided he would move to Maywood with them. I believe this was poor timing, because Godmama was ill and Grandfather was in his nineties. All of our hearts were broken because we had never been separated before.

This was the first time since Bea and I met that we were logistically separated. The distance did not stop my Sista Bea from coming to visit me. We were like two peas in a pod, and our children were very close also. We often planned sleepovers at Godmama's house so we could all be together. During these visits, Bea would assist me with Godmama's medical needs. When I think of Bea, I am reminded of the song "Ain't No Mountain High Enough." She was always right there with me giving Godmama her loving care. What a beautiful angel!

One night, after Godmama and Grandfather had been in their new apartment about two months, I telephoned Vaughn and was informed that the husband of Godmama's closest girlfriend had died. Godmama had taken some food over to her grieving friend's house to provide support for the family. While Vaughn and I were talking on the phone, he informed me that he saw Godmama approaching the building. We continued to talk as we waited for her to climb the stairs and get into the apartment. As time passed, I realized we had been talking for a long time with no word from Godmama. I interrupted our conversation and asked what was taking Godmama so long to get into the apartment. Vaughn looked out the window and could not see her. He looked at her car and she was not there, either. I became concerned and asked Vaughn to go downstairs and check to see if Godmama was having trouble opening the door with her key.

Vaughn followed my instructions and ran down the stairs. When he reached the landing, he had to jump over Godmama so he wouldn't trip or step on her. Godmama was unconscious on the hallway landing. Vaughn ran back to the phone and yelled with more anguish in his voice than a mother should have to hear, "Mama, Godmama is laid out at the bottom of the stairs." I told him to call 911 immediately, and that he needed to get the paramedics for Godmama quickly. He was very diligent in getting help for Godmama. She was taken to the nearest hospital and diagnosed as having had a massive heart attack. They worked on her for about an hour, but there was nothing the medical unit could do to revive her.

When I arrived at the hospital, the doctors were hesitant to say anything to the family about Godmama's condition. I approached the reception desk and informed the staff that I had Godmama's medicine, so they could be aware of any prior conditions. I had arrived to help Godmama, the one person in the world God picked for me. I was totally unaware that she was gone forever. When the doctor got the courage to mention Godmama's death, I interrupted him by showing him Godmama's medicine bottle and telling him what each prescription was for. The doctor looked at the bottles and became concerned for me. He knew that I was about to have a traumatic experience. When I think about it, his facial expression said, "I wish I could give you hope, but I can't." After wrapping his arms around me and holding my hand, the doctor told me that they were unable to revive Godmama. I cried out, "Lord, what do you mean?" As reality struck me, my heart went out to poor Vaughn.

Godmama's death brought the type of agony that never left Vaughn's soul. He had found her dead. I was terrified for him. He ran out of the room when the doctor broke the news to the family. Vaughn ran out the hospital doors in misery. This was all so unexpected and difficult to accept. As a juvenile diabetic, he found Godmama's death too overwhelming. Vaughn passed out eventually after finding out that his grandmother was gone. We had to admit him into the hospital on the same day. Vaughn was mentally, physically, emotionally, and spiritually traumatized. I truly understood how close Godmama and Grandfather were to him. This loss would be insurmountable. He had a lot of different challenges going on in his young male life, and the scars were piling up pretty darn high. He needed the security and comfort of the two people who were now dead. The first was his father, and now Godmama.

Due to all of the traumatic experiences in Vaughn's fourteen years of life, he began to exhibit suicidal behaviors. He would come home from school after thinking about Godmama being gone and would go into his room and take an overdose of insulin to make himself go into a diabetic coma. I believe Vaughn was reaching out for more of my love and affection. This loss was very difficult for my son. I would rush him to the hospital where they would place him under psychiatric care. I shared with the psychiatrist that Vaughn was having serious emotional issues. He had lost some very close people in his short lifespan. When I became seriously ill with asthma, Vaughn was convinced that I was going to die and leave him also. Fortunately, my health slightly improved, and this helped Vaughn somewhat.

It was unfortunate that I did not know enough about death to comfort my son at this crucial time in his life. I was desperately trying to deal with death myself.

The twins who were seven were hurt by Godmama's death, but Vaughn was the firstborn. He had been with his grandparents all of his life. Godmama never had children, and my children became her children. Vaughn was her first grandchild. Grandfather and Godmama had been Vaughn's God-sent family. He had them all to himself for seven years and had never, ever been without them. He had been blessed, as I had been, with Godmama and Grandfather.

When Vaughn's father resurfaced, he was a professional certified accountant and became active in our son's life. I began to see a remarkable change in Vaughn's behavior and demeanor. The strong bond they developed was just what my son needed. One year later, when Vaughn was ten, tragedy struck his life very hard. His father died in a tragic car accident. He lost control of his vehicle and hit a brick wall. The impact caused the brick wall to collapse on top of the automobile, instantly killing his father. This disaster was very traumatic for Vaughn. I believe to this day that he has never been the same.

I remember Vaughn's grandmother, his father's mother, telling me, "Mathell, the Lord had His arms wide open ready to receive my boy." I clearly understood what she meant by that statement, but Vaughn couldn't handle the finality of his father's death. He had absolutely no understanding of what was happening in his life. On top of everything else, Vaughn's pressures were compounded by the neighborhood gangs. He eventually succumbed to the gangs mainly to fit in, but also he was tired of getting into the many fights that were beginning to arise in the area. So I sent him off to California to be with Ann and his stepsister and stepbrothers. The arrangement did not work. Every time I sent money for him, it would come up missing. Ann was unable to care for a sick, troubled diabetic and asthmatic teenager. However, I truly thank her for all of her efforts and offering her home to him.

The Lord is an awesome God, and I love the way he plans situations. There is a purpose for everything, and this is where Mama Love Joy comes into my life. Mama Love Joy's mother was a spiritual mother or godmother to Mildred, my birth mother. Mama Love Joy's mother taught Mildred a lot about life, and Mama Love Joy had a part in teaching me. She knew about my upbringing and the hard times I had with Mildred and Nathell. Mama Love Joy also knew Mildred was an alcoholic and did not have the moral fiber to raise my sister or me. So, as God would have it, Mama Love Joy intervened and assisted me in becoming the woman I am today. Mama Love Joy was brought into my life to bring me joy when Godmama died. She had always been a part of my world, but she became the nurturer I needed at one of the lowest points in my life.

My mother, Mildred, moved into Mama Love Joy's building when her mother died. Mama Love Joy and I became very close. When I would visit Mildred, Mama Love Joy would always stop me on the way up to Mildred's house and invite me in to chat for a while. If Mildred had been drinking and became mean-spirited,

I wouldn't stay long and Mama Love Joy would feel my pain and always comfort me. She would leave her door open to listen out for me when I'd come down the stairs and would say, "Baby, come on back here and talk to Mama." Mama Love Joy was a great help to me after Godmama died. She decided to take me in as her God-sent daughter, and I can't thank God enough for her. In the less joyous times of my life's journey, Mama Love Joy brought me peace and love. The day after Godmama died, I ran into Mama Love Joy as she was getting out of her vehicle. I ran to her shouting, "Ms. Joy, oh, Ms. Joy. My Godmama has had a heart attack and has suddenly passed."

She replied, "Oh baby, I am so sorry to hear that. Is there anything I can do for you?"

I said, "Yes. I am going to need you to be a mother figure to me." It seems like the sudden death of Godmama, at the age of fifty-four, left me feeling like a motherless child. I felt as though I still needed mothering. I'd grown up around Mama Love Joy, and we had become very close. She had known me since the day I was born, and I had grown up with her in the church where Grandfather was one of the deacons. All my life, I had only seen Mama Love Joy's encouraging character as she related to me, just like a genuine mama. I needed her desperately and was extremely grateful God elected to bless me with the exact person I needed in my life in order to move forward.

Mama Love Joy gladly accepted my request to mother me after Godmama died, and I immediately began to call her Mama Love Joy instead of Ms. Joy. She was another God-sent mother-angel in my life. She was caring for her mother, who was bedridden at that time, and was very encouraging in supporting me in caring for Grandfather after Godmama died. I've always felt a special connection to Mama Love Joy because her mother looked out after my mother when she left the boarding school. Just as Godmama took care of me, Mama Love Joy's mother looked after Mildred. I was raised in church with Mama Love Joy, and she was the church secretary. I would attend all special church events with her and my play aunt, Lorenza Porter. I was a choir member at Antioch Missionary Baptist Church in Summit, Illinois. Mama Love Joy loved our family and she stood with us through many storms.

I sang in the church choir, and Mama Love Joy would love to hear me sing. One of my most special memories of Mama Love Joy was when I would come from the choir stand singing one of her favorite songs, "You Can Depend on Me Lord." She would reach out and embrace me with her beautiful smile and mellow voice. She was such a tender person. She was a very sharp dresser and wore perfume that would fill the air with her beautiful fragrance. It would linger long after she'd left the room. She was a very smart woman and oh, so beautiful. Mama Love Joy was cinnamon colored and roughly five feet six inches tall. She was a thick, very sharp, and attractive woman. She carried her ample size with class and dignity. She had a mellow voice that always spoke tender words. Mama Love Joy was very encouraging. She worked for many years and retired as a secretary for a team of doctors.

My precious angel, Mama Love Joy, was a bundle of joy. Her sense of humor was always positive and comical. She was a lot like Godmama Verona. Mama Love Joy was another mama angel assigned to guide me in my next steps toward my destiny. As I think back, this beautiful woman of God was chosen to be there after the loss of Godmama. How precious it is to be mothered all along your life's journey by women endowed with a great deal of love. I pray to be able to give the same mother's love to a multitude of children or whoever requires it. I have had many experiences of how love can and will rejuvenate you. This awesome woman was a lover of all people. She truly admired her good friend, Frank.

Frank was a cool daddy who I affectionately nicknamed Big Daddy. He always wore leisure suits and color-coordinated all his accessories down to his shoes. He was a great lover of music, and

I loved to hear him call Mama Love Joy "Jazzy Mama." He was originally from Summit, Illinois, but he moved to California for a change of scenery. He kept in close contact with Mama Love Joy and always professed how he cared for her.

Mama Love Joy and I would go to a lot of gospel shows with Aunt Lorenza. Mama Love Joy and Aunt Lorenza had a dear friend, Mrs. Marguerite Gatling, who was the owner of Gatling funeral home in Chicago. Inside the funeral parlor was an annex, a special section built especially for gospel shows. I remember Mama Love Joy telling me she wanted me to work two gospel shows with her. One was in the annex at Gatling and the other one was at The House of Blues. I was thrilled as she described the events as a big-time concert showcasing "The Dixie Humming Birds, The Gatling Singers, and The Argo Singers." Mama explained that Aunt Lorenza needed us to work the display table.

All we had to do was sit, smile, and look pretty. That seemed easy, and I was honored to be included. The sitting part was great because neither of us was able to stand for any length of time. We both loved people and enjoyed greeting them. We agreed that these two events were going to be a lot of fun. Mama Love Joy and I loved to coordinate our colors. Red, purple, orange, and black were our favorites. We chose to wear pretty red dresses for the concert and a purple three-piece skirt set with red threads streaming through for The House of Blues. Mama Love Joy and I went to her furrier, and she had the most beautiful fur coat made and told me to wear it for the next event. We were matched from head to toe.

Mama Love Joy and I decorated our table in silk cloth with a mix of red and black. We then placed each artist's CDs and cassette tapes in sections and were ready to greet the guests. There were many encouraging words from the attendees as they approached our table. Our coordination fascinated them. People said that we were a beautiful mother and daughter team. Their kind words touched both of our hearts to the core. We were encouraged that we were a dream team, and Mama called us showgirls. Our sales for the artists were complete. We sold out of everything and were taking orders. We could hardly wait to work the next gospel show planned at The House of Blues by those same groups. We knew by the love of Jesus Christ that we were His gift to each other. She would say to me that she would pray that one day my dad, Nathell, would come to recognize the precious jewel that I was. We were blessed to know each other.

I had absolutely no doubt that I would be responsible for Grandfather Jack in his golden years, after Godmama Verona died. I could not leave him. I would never have left him or forsaken him. Grandfather and Godmama were the two core people in my life.

Grandfather's behavior began to change as time passed. He reached a stage where he would make a mess of everything to get my attention. When I was not around, he would have a fit and tear up the house. In extreme situations, he would have bowel movements on himself. On these occasions, my sons would jump in quickly and provide assistance. Vaughn would put Grandfather into the bathtub and wash him down. The twins would follow up with drying him off and rubbing him down with body lotion. Finally, they would dress him.

All of Grandfather Jack's immature actions were designed to change my plans and stop me from leaving him alone, in the house with the boys. I was forced to quit a job working for CEDA in Summit, Illinois. Doris Robinson was the executive director; she was a beautiful young woman a very compassionate person and very professional. She had a passion for seniors and had befriended our family. My grandfather became special in her heart. Grandfather made good on a threat that he would set the apartment on fire if I left the house. One day, I proceeded to go to work as part of my daily routine and left the apartment. Once outside, I looked up at our apartment window and saw that Grandfather had set the curtains on fire with his cigar. The curtains were in flames, and I was hysterical. The fire department was promptly notified, and we got Grandfather out of the house safely, without much damage to the apartment. I explained to Grandfather that this kind of behavior would not be tolerated, and I was going to send him to live with his family in California. Deacon Caldwell Sr. and Aunt Lillian were close family friends. They advised me to call his relatives and tell them that he would have to come and live with them.

The day I contacted Grandfather's relatives, he overheard the conversation. He heard one of his family members say, "Oh, no, we can't take him." That really hurt Grandfather's feelings. He really thought his relatives were going to take care of him in his old age. I explained to him that he had it made if he would just stop acting out like a kid. Later, Grandfather sat me down and said, "Listen, Mathell, I am ninety-one years old. But you should treat me like a nine-year-old. You have to do me like you have to do the boys, sometimes. You have to get on me, and I promise you I'm going to do all I can to be good. Remember, the Bible said, 'Once a man and twice a child.' I'm just a child now. You must treat me like I'm a child. I asked God to bless you and give you everything for what you're doing for me." I told Grandfather that it was my joy to reciprocate. When I was a child, I couldn't do anything for myself. He and his daughter, Godmama Verona, took time to guide me down the right path. Now it was my distinct pleasure to be here to help him. I quite my job to be at home with Grandfather to make sure he would be safe.

Grandfather was the first man in my life who really loved me for me, and the one person who brought Jesus into my life. I smiled at him and assured him that I would be there for him. In his last days, he would tell me to open the cigar box and count the few cigars that were left. He enjoyed smoking El Producto Blunt cigars, and he requested them often. He would say that after the last cigar in the box was smoked, he would die. That would be his way of having me keep his cigar supply stocked. I would go and buy two boxes of fifty each so he would have more than enough to hold on to life. I would tell him, "You now have a hundred cigars, so you have at least a hundred more days of living." It gave me much pleasure to see him smile. I was happy even though the smell of his cigars was awful. Grandfather died suddenly when he was ninety-six-and-a-half years old. I thank God for all those precious years.

Making a Way Out of No Way

Cannon and I had broken off our relationship as lovers. The next time I spoke to him, he tried to explain to me about the long-distance love affair that eventually broke us up. His sister had shared with me her concerns about Cannon's infidelity. He tried to justify and belittle his sister by telling me she had a reputation of hitting one where it would hurt. As I meditated over the negative words he expressed about her, I thought to myself, this must be his way of covering up his dirt. I remember when I first met Cannon's sister. My impression of her was that she was friendly. She extended a hug to me when we met. She was very sociable and full of laughter. She knew how to tell funny, clean jokes. This slander from him told me those were his feelings about me also. I've gotten older, and looking back, I thank God for regulating my feelings and not allowing these unkind words from this man to upset me. I must forgive him because I am a believer that one should look beyond others' faults and forgive them. I have had to set the example for my children by being a loving, respectful, forgiving, and caring mother. It did not mean that because I forgave Cannon that I had to stay in an unhealthy relationship. I had to teach my sons how to do the right thing. If you are a reader of the Bible, you have read the words Jesus said as he hung on the cross. Perhaps you are not a reader, but maybe you saw the movie The Passion of the Christ. His words to God in Luke 23:34 were, "Father forgive them, for they do not know what they do."

Angels in My Life

I shared this situation with the twins and they suggested that I let him go. I used to hate him for going to Mississippi, but I had to let go of my selfish ways because he had a mother and other family members there, too. Once he did include me, because I had insisted. I always had a suspicion that an old town sweetheart was there. I questioned him several times. Of course, he denied it. I felt like I was reliving the past. Different man, but the feeling of hurt was the same, and this love triangle caused me a great deal of heartache, pain, and misery. He told me there was no one in his town who wanted to meet me. What a blow to my mind. I felt like he was piercing my heart. Here I was trapped by this thing called love, and to make matters worse, he was nineteen years older than me.

It was mid-June, and the twins were about to turn thirteen years old. I was planning a big surprise for them. I started searching months ahead of time for the best airplane fare and a five-star hotel package. This would be my sons' first ride on a plane. They were both on the honor roll, and this was my way of showing gratitude to each of them because I was proud of their achievement. My hugs and words of encouragement embraced each of them daily. The twins had to pull and push one another to get where they wanted to go. Victor and his brother shared quite a bond. To watch the twins grow into courteous young men who treated each other with respect and honor was touching to my heart and brought me tears of joy. As they moved toward their teenage years, I could see them developing into young gentlemen. Victor and Verdell were always loving and very attentive to me. They had these playful ways and had started something new to determine which one of them would ride in the front seat. I recall asking the twins to go shopping with me. As we were heading out, I noticed Verdell flipping a coin. As the coin rotated and spun through the air, Victor had his eyes glued to the coin. While it was in mid-air, I heard Victor call heads. This was strange to me. I asked them why they were flipping a coin. They said that heads let us know who will be taking care of you while you're driving. Tails means the other person would have your back. "One of us has got to be like a watch dog, Mama, and see what's coming behind you," Victor said. I was thankful that they were attentive to what I was trying to teach them.

The twins were ambitious and had vowed to each other that they were both going to become businessmen and own their own company one day. They were very sincere and expressive with one another. They made a pact when they were ten years old that they were going to study hard together to be smart. I encouraged them to follow their dreams and to reach for the stars. Mama would do all she could to assist them both. I told them, if you follow your plan, then your academic achievements will show it.

They'd earned a special trip. My mind was made up, and all arrangements had been made, including a complimentary ride to and from the airport. My friend Ted owned his own limo service. I called him to get an estimate of the cost of round-trip service from our house to Midway Airport. He asked, teasingly, if I was going out on a business or pleasure trip. I told him about my sons' achievements in school. Ted suggested this would be a great time for him to show his gratitude toward me for all the people I had referred to him. I was breathless, yet most graciously accepted his offer to take us to the airport. A limo was completely out of my budget, but I learned that it pays to help others. If I had not called him and inquired about the cost, this blessing would not have presented itself. All I did was tell a few people about Ted's Limo. It cost me nothing to promote him. What a blessed way to be driven to the airport.

"Let's celebrate the thirteenth birthday of the honorees Victor and Verdell!" That was the theme as I prepared a family vacation in Los Angeles, California. I had booked a tour of Disneyland in Anaheim, California, as an extra bonus and incentive to keep the twins on the honor roll.

Our time came to take this party on the road. We arrived in sunny California. We were booked at the LAX Hilton Hotel. We did not know anyone. I just picked a place and we went. I had called the hotel in advance so that the shuttle bus would be at the airport when we arrived. The driver had to make other stops. This allowed us to have a little tour of L.A. It was a beautiful sight. The palm trees stole the show. As we rode, I pointed to some of the tall buildings, and the twins were amazed and thrilled. They were continually thanking me and jumping up out of their seats hugging and kissing me. I felt happy. I knew I had selected the right place for our vacation. I could see the hotel and I had not told the twins where we were staying. I pointed to the hotel and asked them to look up ahead at the blinking lights. I told them that's where we would be checking in. It looked fantastic from the outside. We were all in amazement. This was our first big trip, and from the sight of things on our first day, it was mind-blowing.

We stepped off the shuttle. There was someone from the hotel staff to greet us, check us in, and escort us to our adjoining rooms. While walking to the elevator, we could not help but notice how wonderful the appearance of the tropical scenery was in the lobby. Everyone you passed offered a friendly smile and a beautiful greeting of "Hello" or "Hi." We also noticed several restaurants conveniently located for us to use. I was a little tired after settling in my room. I asked the twins if I could have about an hour to rest while they both went and explored. They were happy to go and see more of the sights of this gorgeous hotel. Their first stop was to find the swimming pool. Like most kids, my sons loved to play in the water. This would be their hangout for most of our stay at the Hilton.

Before my hour of rest was up, Victor and Verdell came busting into the room, excited about a lady they had met who worked in the hotel. They both tried to explain, talking at the same time. They were touring, and a lady saw them walking and shouted out,

"Hey, twins!" The boys turned around and the lady waved for them to come to her. When they approached her, she smiled and said, "I knew you were twins by the way you were dressed." They told me that she asked their age and gave them compliments. She said they looked very handsome dressed alike. They kept on raving about this lady. They told me she was standing behind a counter and was representing a car rental place called National Rent-a-Car. She introduced herself to them as Ms. Jackie Davis. The twins assured me I was going to love her because she told them that she had twin girls, Staci and Traci. They were the same age as my boys, but their birthday was in March. Jackie gave my twins her number and asked if they would ask me to call her. My twins told her we were coming down for dinner later. She told them that her shift was about to end and she would go and get her twin daughters and perhaps we could all go for dinner.

I called her as soon as the twins gave me her contact number. From the second she answered the phone, our conversation was full of laughs. We could hardly wait to meet each other and for our twins to make new acquaintances with each other. We decided to meet in a couple of hours in the hotel lobby. After I hung up the phone, Victor and Verdell were asking me if I liked Ms. Davis so far. I told them that our talk went well, and that we definitely had something in common.

Jackie and the twins had arrived in the lobby a little early. We hurried up and caught the elevator to go down to meet them. I had no problems recognizing this lady standing there with her double loves. These young women were identical twins and were dressed in white pant sets with long tunic tops. Their hair was black as coal, long and silky. They were wearing dangly earrings, and I could see their beautiful smiles as we greeted them. I walked slightly ahead of Victor and Verdell. I looked back at the images that were trailing me. They were dressed alike in black denim pants and jackets to match, accented with red body shirts. Each of them was smiling also. As we got closer, Jackie recognized my twins and she led her girls toward us. We greeted one another with handshakes that quickly turned into hugs.

All of us were full of laughter and smiles, adoring each double vision. It was amazing. We were no strangers. It seemed to each of us that we were family. Jackie and I were a match. She was fun and had such a beautiful personality. She was a petite lady who stood about five foot six, with fair brown skin. She wore a short haircut that was very sharp and becoming of her. While we were having dinner, the twins seemed to be in their own world, talking and laughing. Jackie and I started disclosing a little bit of our likes and dislikes, and we established that we were both single. I shared with her how I loved to sing and had been in a singing group called the Brown Sugars. She told me about this great-sounding band that played in the evening in the hotel lounge. She was acquainted with two founders of the group and suggested we hear them that night. She assured me I was going to enjoy the music they played. The twins overheard us talking and were all for that. Staci and Traci asked if they could come back with their mother and go swimming. That sounded like a good plan to my twins.

Our evening was on and everybody was happy. Jackie and I were casually dressed for the evening, and the band was playing when we entered through the doors. They were jamming, and the lounge was crowded with about fifty people enjoying the night. What I loved about this set was that I did not have to be away from my children, nor did Jackie. It was a very relaxing atmosphere, and everybody was friendly. I left the room for about fifteen minutes to go to the ladies' room and check on our kids. When I returned, the band was playing and one of the men was singing a blues song. They smoothly swung into an instrumental groove part, and then they made an announcement: "We have the honor of having a singer from Chicago in the house tonight. We are going to ask her to sing us a song after a short break."

I looked at Jackie, and she smiled and said, "Here's your big break."

I was shocked and repeatedly said, "No, you didn't." My dilemma was, I had not practiced with anyone in years. I had not sung in a couple of years, except in the presence of friends or in the bathroom.

Jackie said, "You just told me today how you love to sing."

I felt shy after I had opened my big mouth. Here I was near Hollywood with a chance to sing like a superstar. I now had the opportunity facing me to be heard and perhaps start singing again. The question running through my head was, what am I going to do, sing or run out of this room? I saw the band coming down off the stage. They were walking and shaking hands with their guests. It looked like they were coming straight for our table to confirm with Jackie that I was the lady who would sing. As the two gentlemen approached our table, they anxiously asked, "Is this her?" Jackie introduced us, and they both had the same first name. One was Bobby Zee and the other was Bobby Zoe. They asked me what I would like to sing. I told them it had been a long time since I sang, and they both encouraged me to sing and told me that I still had it in me.

Jackie smiled at me and said, "What are you going to sing?"

I said, "Respect."

Intermission was over, and Bobby Zee introduced me. I came up and started singing and rocked the house. Bobby Zee led the rest of the band into a groove. He was playing an electric keyboard while Bobby Zoe led on electric guitar. As I sang, I held the mike for each person to come up and sing a bar as we jammed that song for about twenty minutes. We had so much fun that after the set, the two Bobby's asked me if I would come out the next night and meet them at Rubens' Yacht Club in Marina Del Rey. I was overwhelmed. This was unbelievable. I told them I would not mind singing, but I needed a rehearsal. Bobby Zee invited Jackie and me to his home the next day for practice. During our practice, Bobby Zee suggested I sing "Respect," "God Bless the Child," and "Since I Fell for You." I was on a roll and was glad to be a part of all of this. It was very exciting to me. Jackie was overjoyed and said, "As long as I have been in L.A., I have never had this much fun." After a great soulful practice, the guys encouraged me by telling me that Frank Sinatra had a yacht docked at this marina, and if we were lucky, he might hear us. We could all become famous. I was grateful for such confidence in me. The idea that I would be an asset to such a great and well-known group was mind-blowing to me.

Jackie made arrangements with her sister to keep our twins at her house while she and I went out on the town that evening. It was like I was a celebrity. I had just made a wonderful connection with some celebrities in a short time. These two wonderful gentlemen and Jackie became very dear to me, and I prayed the feeling would be mutual. We had a very successful night. The songs Bobby chose for me were a hit and touched many people's hearts. We were treated royally, and I was asked to come back to California with an open invitation from one of the managers of the supper club. He said that I could sing my heart out anytime with the two Bobby's. Since then, Bobby Zee has formed a company called Morpheus Music, and I have a standing invitation to come out and sing with them anytime.

A few days passed. Jackie, her children, and my sons were inseparable. Our day had come to go to Disneyland, and Jackie decided to take her girls. We had a great family day. It was like we came to be with them. I feel our connection was ordered and ordained. The next day was Sunday, and Jackie invited us to attend City of Refuge Church, where the Bishop Noel Jones is the shepherd. It was a lovely spirit-filled day at that church service, and I looked forward to seeing him on his broadcast service.

Our vacation came to an end, but it was the beginning of another beautiful friendship with Jackie and her girls. We met so many wonderful "angels" on our trip.

The twins and I wished we could have stayed on this trip forever, but we had to face reality. The time had come to say goodbye for now. We had to return home from our fantastic trip. The fact that we were leaving was very emotional for all of us. So we decided to end as we began, with dinner in the same restaurant where we met for the first time. While dining, I promised Jackie and the girls that we would call them as soon we landed. Jackie wanted to come back the next morning. She and her twins would take us to the airport. I tried to discourage her because of the hassle of traffic. She would not hear of it. They were at the hotel bright and early and stayed at the airport until we boarded the plane. When our boarding numbers were called, all of us started reaching for each other to hug, saying how we were going to miss one another. All of our eyes were glossy as though tears would fall at any given moment. I heard a second announcement, and we hurriedly said goodbye and entered the boarding ramp.

As we stepped on board, Victor and Verdell began thanking me for such a wonderful time. I encouraged them to keep up the great work in school and that we would have many vacations to come. We were all tired from our trip and slept through the flight attendant passing out the peanuts and soft drinks. What woke us up was when we felt the plane descending. When we landed, I flipped out my cell phone and immediately called Jackie to let her know of our safe arrival. As the phone rang, the excitement of meeting her and the twins had me needing to talk with them about our miraculous connection again. When we talked, Jackie and I both shared with one another how honored we were to have met. Jackie and I and even the twins had daily conversations after that. We encouraged each other and wished each other well.

Jackie and I began to feel we could tell each other anything. We always ended our talk with the words, "I love you." We both had a sense of humor about things and would playfully close our conversation at times with "See you later, alligator," "After a while, crocodile."

Jackie and I continued to be friends. We started calling each other "Sister" after a few months. We made sure that we kept our communication lines open. Our twins grew fond of each other, and we all became truly connected.

I was in the Laundromat one Thursday in September. I was sitting patiently waiting for my clothes to dry. I noticed, lying on the chair next to me, a Park Lane jewelry book. I picked it up and began to turn the pages. I was fascinated by the dazzling rhinestones glistening on each page. On the back of the book was a phone number. I wrote the number down and called the next day. Later that evening, I received a call from one of Park Lane's top recruiters, Mrs. Sheilier Stokes. She had a firm voice, yet spoke softly. She identified the company she was with. I wanted to earn some of the beautiful jewels to add to my collection. I explained that I was a part time model and assistant commentator for Shamoné Fashions. I also told her I was involved with a social club called the Jolly Ladies. Their weekend dinner party was coming up in the month of November. Connie Jones, the secretary, had already introduced me to Marguerite Pearson who was the president of the Odd Seven Social. Connie was certain that she could get me into their party as a vendor. Connie wanted me to be on the lookout for Helen Alford, the president of the Kiski Social Club. I told Mrs. Stokes that I planned to display some of my father's fashion apparel at these events, and that I would love to accessorize some of the apparel with this wonderful jewelry.

Mrs. Stokes thought I had a great marketing idea. We had agreed to meet in person that next week for lunch. I arrived thirty minutes early in order to collect my thoughts and relax a moment. When she arrived fifteen minutes later, she looked as though she had just stepped out of a glamour magazine. She wore a beautiful simple two-piece black dress and a loose jacket. It had three-quarter-length pockets that fell right past her hips. Jewelry dangled from her ears and there were layers of rhinestone necklaces around her neck. Her hands were well manicured. She wore three rings on each finger and only 1 was cubic zirconia. She explained the other rings were diamonds that she had won through Park Lane. The fine fashion jewelry blended in with the real stuff and it was amazing to me. I could not tell the difference from the fine fashion jewelry and the diamonds because of the high quality of the Park Lane jewelry. This lady was very well put together, and I can truly say she looked like a dream girl. I wanted to look like that as a young woman. We embraced one another and were seated. She began to tell me all about the company she worked for. She had two months of her check stubs to show her earnings, and those stubs were very impressive to me. She testified to the way working for this company had changed her life, and the lives of so many others. Mrs. Stokes made me want to instantly become a hostess and begin a career with this growing company. Mrs. Stokes had convinced me to allow my first party to lead me to my first paycheck and earn possibly five hundred dollars in fashion jewelry and a bonus for recruiting others.

This was a perfect enterprise for me. I started planning where I would go each day to show my jewelry. I made plans that on Saturday morning, I would target the beauty shops. I had gotten as far as 111th street on Halsted and started to feel hungry. I noticed a restaurant with a beauty shop attached. I thought maybe I could eat and afterward show my beautiful pieces of jewelry. I entered through the restaurant door, and there was a lady standing in front of me. From the back, she looked sharply dressed. She was placing an order and asking if they would deliver it to the beauty shop on the other side. I was glancing over the menu when this lady turned and said to me, "You sure look sharp, and you know, you're wearing some beautiful jewelry." I told her that I sold these lovely pieces. I told her my name. In turn, I asked her name and she said, "Christine Gilmore." I asked if she would like to look at one of my books featuring all of the lovely jewelry. She said, "Yes." She asked if I would like to come on the other side when I was finished eating. I told her yes and thanked her for the invite. She told me there were lots of ladies over there who might be interested in purchasing jewelry. As soon as I finished eating, I stepped on the other side where the beauty shop was. I asked for Ms. Christine. She then introduced me to her hair stylist. I had some little tokens of jewelry to give away to show my appreciation. I pulled two gifts out of my bag and gave each of my two new acquaintances a pair of earrings.

From that day to this one, Christine and I have been very close. She started calling me for more jewelry and wanted to know where my next party would be. I invited her to come and work with me setting up the display and told her how she could earn some of these beautiful pieces while listening to the best in entertainment, provided by Mr. Lee Kirksy and company. She and I partied from big shows to little bars. We drank at bars and danced sometimes until the juke joint closed. We partied so hard in our days together, and then our spiritual change came. So, I suggested we go to church.

During this time the twins were freshmen and we lived in Chicago Heights. I went over to Bloom High School and registered them. After registering, I was greeted by a gentleman who was crossing the street as my sons and I were returning to my car. He stated that, when he saw the two of them, he thought his eyesight was fooling him. This man was very soft-spoken as he shared with us how he adored the double image of seeing twins. He swiftly identified himself as Jay Anderson. As he spoke, I was looking at him. He was tall and portly, with a light complexion. He was a very well-dressed gentleman and had a kind spirit. He was wearing a navy blue sports jacket, white shirt, grey slacks, and a pair of black square-toe shoes. I in turn introduced myself and my sons to him. He explained that he worked at the school as a payroll manager. He went on to tell me that he and five other men had just finalized an entertainment contract at a place called the Homewood Manor. He continued to speak highly of each of these gentlemen, letting me know that they were all professional men. They each worked in the corporate world. He explained how each of them loved to dance and had dreamed of having parties. They wanted to target the old-school dancers who loved to step. Their plans to join together as entrepreneurial partners had recently come true, and he thought, since I was new in the area, that this was a great place for me to meet some new people. Jay gave me a leaflet introducing Friday the 13th Production. It welcomed people to come out and join them every second Friday.

I told him I believed that I was in a great position to meet people and to draw others to their sets because of the beautiful jewelry I sell. I briefly explained that I was a representative for a company called Park Lane Jewelry, and that each piece of jewelry was a high quality of fine fashion jewelry and carried a lifetime guarantee. I told him how I would like the opportunity to introduce my product and myself to as many people as possible. I asked Jay if it was possible for his organization to consider me as a vendor at their next party night. Listening to Jay speak, I realized he and I were both lovers of people. I began to visualize myself at the party. I would be dressed real sharp, wearing my attractive jewelry and drawing in ladies who were interested in hosting a jewelry party. Here I was drifting in and out of our conversation. Then I heard him say, "How do I contact you?" I gave him my business card that said, "Consider Me." He smiled and said that I seemed to be very interesting, and that it was very nice to talk with me. He reassured me that he would call each member and have an answer for me within a couple of days. We parted ways, pleasantly.

Jay called me back with good news. His club members welcomed me and suggested that I be at their first club set. Oh, I was so excited. Jay wanted to connect me on a conference call to the vice president of their club, John Thompson. He told me that pre-arrangements on my behalf needed to be set up with security, and Mr. Thompson was the one to clear me. I thanked Jay and I told him to go ahead with the call. After the two men greeted each other, Jay introduced me. Mr. Thompson had a nickname that he asked me to call him—Cheeta. This connection was special to me. It was grand opening night. My display was featured at the main entrance. I was all set up and believed that I looked good from head to toe. As the guests arrived, my face was the first they saw in the place. The sparkle from the jewelry brought a smile to each viewer's face, and mine.

My first customer recognized me as her neighbor. She had seen me coming and going from my apartment, draped in jewelry. She introduced herself as Jazzy Jo, but her real name was Joanne Brodanex. She represented her nickname to a tee and was an extremely sharp dresser. I remember she had on a pair of three-inch heels with a tight-fitting gold metallic dress that showed every curve. I noticed the rings on every finger, even her thumbs, and thought I knew what type of jewelry to sell to her. She was built up like a Coca-Cola bottle. She stood five feet four inches tall, with cinnamon-colored skin, and she displayed a beautiful, friendly, and warm smile. I took to her immediately. She ended up purchasing more rings. I gave her my business card and told her to call me if she wanted to purchase more jewelry. Later, we ended up going to lunch, and she eventually became a very special angel in my life.

At the club, I invited each person to feel free to handle any piece that was attractive to them. I had mirrors all around so that each of them could see how they looked as they tried on each piece. I asked each guest to refrain from trying on the pierced earrings due to health code, but to feel free to try on the clips and any accessories. As they would make purchases, I asked if I could put their selections in the Will Call so they could party hearty and pick them up later. One lady thought that was a great idea and introduced herself as Mary. She stated she was the head manager at a lounge called Larry's North on Halsted in Harvey, Illinois. She asked me if I would come and see her and bring my display. I asked for a way to contact her. She gave me her number. My purpose was being fulfilled. She had a party for me at Larry's Lounge two weeks later. It became a ripple effect. I then met Gloria, the owner of Gloria's Lounge in Harvey.

The ladies continued to crowd around and adore the glitz as they flattered each other over every piece tried on. We were having a gala time—then suddenly a famous basketball player, Craig Hodges, showed up. He was a friend of the club owners. This young man came by their club set to boost their popularity and to assure that their first set was a slamming, jamming success. It's always been my belief that no one is an island. Each person's life needs others to care and help that person move forward. Jay was the angel who led me to a new acquaintance, and Craig was the angel to draw new people to the area by making this stepper set one to mark your calendar for. Mr. Hodges would show up periodically, and he would be very generous to his fans and friends. He would allow chosen people to select a gift from my table as his token of appreciation for their support. He never left the set without making sure he had paid his tab with me.

I ran into Mr. Lee, who was a comedian and exotic dancer. I had known him since my childhood. While shopping in the local grocery store, I saw a flyer inviting everybody to the town's picnic and talent show. It stated that if you were interested in performing, to contact Mr. Lee at the number at the bottom of the page. The idea of performing in the talent show re-ignited the dreams I had for myself. It was refreshing to feel my passion for singing become reborn within me. I truly enjoyed my singing days with the Brown Sugars and the glamorous life. Through this entertainer, the opportunity had presented itself again. Now it was my time to go solo. This was what I was hoping for. I showed up and sang my heart out. Mr. Lee was blown away. I was thrilled to be involved in the entertainment world. Music was a great part of me. I assumed it was all those records I heard as a child. They were embedded in my spirit from the parties at Godmama's.

I was listening to WJPC Radio one night and heard that on-air personality Budder Man would be appearing at a nightclub called The Cotton Club, in Chicago. I had this dream of mixing and mingling with the stars. I had heard they played karaoke on certain nights. That was one thing that drew me to the famous club. I believed this would be a great way for me to be heard and possibly discovered. I had seen the movie *The Cotton Club*. I dreamed of going there. So I started to prepare for a night out. I went alone and did not mind traveling by myself.

I knew I had to look my best. My thoughts drifted back to how Mr. Lee dressed. I decided it was sparkle time. This was my chance to get elegantly dressed from head to toe. Wearing my glitzy jewelry and my fancy clothes was exciting. I was dressed in an off white, three-piece rhinestone pant suit with a long fox fling fur draped across my left shoulder. It was fascinating to me that celebrities would stop by this famous club. When I left home, I stopped by Mama Love Joy's and she told me, "You look drop dead gorgeous."

When I stepped through the doors, I could hear the music rocking. I was greeted by the doorman, and he said, "You look marvelous."

I was flattered and nodded my head at the man. I smiled and said, "Thank you."

As I glanced around the room, I noticed that there was an empty seat at the bar. I walked slowly, strutting my stuff, and took the seat. The bartender said, "A gentleman at the end of the bar would like to send you a bottle of champagne." I could tell my first night was going to be fun.

I started following the station's night out at The Cotton Club and became familiar with the on-air personalities. The third night I went there, I had the opportunity to meet the legendary Pop Staples, father of the singing group the Staple Singers. I remember taking a picture with Pop, and I saw him there on several occasions. At the time, my sons were involved in a talent search at the Regal Theater in Chicago. Pop Staples and I had talked enough and discovered we had something in common. Here I was, Mama May to my sons, standing with Pop Staple. We both had talented children and had dreams for their success. His dreams were being fulfilled. I invited him to attend my sons' performance at the Regal. He arrived a half-hour late and missed their performance. But he was impressed that they had performed at such a famous theater.

Also, WJPC on-air personalities Emily McKendall and Budder Man were doing promotions for their stations at the Taste of Chicago. I was invited to be in their booth. As I watched them greet the listeners, my dream became more real. I had thoughts of enhancing my speaking ability after hearing their smooth and sensational voices. I visualized a microphone in my hand and people loving my sultry voice. Mama Love Joy encouraged me wholeheartedly. I decided to enroll in Columbia School of Broadcasting. I began to dream of opening up shows as a Mistress of Ceremony.

At the same time, I decided to take a night course at Moraine Valley Community College in travel-agency management. I began working as an outside salesperson at Deerpath Travel in Summit, Illinois. I attended the same grammar and high schools with the lady who hired me. We were not strangers and were amazed at each other's interest in the travel world. I had twin sons relying on me, and I was doing everything possible to reach my destiny. I also found the time to take a series of courses in communication at Triton College. I was doing well in school and added radio announcer to my curriculum. I attended Columbia School of Broadcasting and got my FCC license. I was given my appointment time in the recording studio and arrived early on a muggy hot Monday afternoon. I was eager to get started and excited because I had been promoted to the recording studio and was due to make my first DJ demo. I stepped into the cool air-conditioned studio with my briefcase filled with a variety of music. Mostly, I had slow jams and down-home blues targeting a mature audience. I also needed to set the scene behind the radio screen with a smooth, easy, soft, and mellow speaking voice.

Suddenly, Columbia school of Broadcasting went bankrupt, and I could no longer use their recording studio to make my DJ demos. I told Bea about it and she introduced me to Mr. Charles Mootry. He was the vice president of radio station WJPC/WLNR. He became my beloved friend. The station was owned by Mr. John H. Johnson, who also owned *Ebony* and *Jet* magazines. Mr. Mootry heard my demo tape and allowed me to make my very own commercial, with radio personality Budder Man, for my summer lake jam on the Spirit of Chicago.

After completing all of those courses, I thought about one more thing that I would like to do. Since I couldn't afford to go to the nail salon and my hands were the first things people would see, I decided to go to John Amico School for nails. This was not too far from Summit, and my sons were very supportive while I was in school. They had extracurricular activities after school, and night school was the best time for me to attend. After we would all arrive home, we all studied at the same time. I believe my desire to go to school made the twins focus on achieving the honor roll.

I was a devoted viewer of Oprah Winfrey, who was then the host of the *AM Chicago* show. One day, when she took a station break, there was an announcement that the show was looking for "Single Mothers by Choice." I ran to the telephone and called the number. I wanted to be on television and tell about my young motherhood struggles and accomplishments. Some people would say I should have been ashamed, but I never felt disgraced by anything I did, right or wrong. My Godmama Verona taught me to always forgive myself and, if others were involved, forgive them also. You have to move on with your life. She would say the only way you are going to learn is to make mistakes. So don't be afraid to try in life. I know she was not referring to having a baby at fifteen, but this was what happened. She and Grandfather forgave me, and I had to forgive myself. I am grateful for the double encouragement in my life. Then there was Grandfather Brown, who was so powerful and spiritual in my life. He was truly well connected with the Lord's word, and his knowledge of repentance was great. His guidance also led me to confront any problem without shame or blame. In other words, I had to forgive and try to forget.

When I made the call to get on Oprah's show, I was called back by a representative named Alice McGee. She instructed me as to when to come to the taping of the show. I called Mama Love Joy to tell her that I had been chosen to be on the show. Mama was a lover of Oprah from the first time she saw the show. I remember her telling me how brilliant she thought Oprah was. She never wanted to miss her show. When she or I would have to go out, she would tell me to leave my television tuned in to Oprah's show, so we would be a part of her rating for the day. I was excited because this was going to be my first time on TV. I had asked Ms. McGee if I would be on the panel and was told they had already selected their guest speakers and needed to fill their audience. I had no idea if I would get to speak. When we arrived, we were taken in a room to fill out some forms. There was a representative from the show in the room with us. She was asking questions about how we felt about being single and having children. She was trying to find the talkers in the room. This was her way of selecting the people who would be placed on the end seats. I noticed she placed each of us who had been aggressive talkers in a seat near the aisle, in reach of Oprah as she walked down the center row. If Oprah needed an opinion from her audience, my chances were great.

As the taping began, I was trembling all over. I remembered that Aunt Lorenza Porter was in show business. I recalled asking her, seconds before a show, if she was nervous. She replied that nervousness was a sign that the turn-out would be grand. She told me that movie stars say, "Break a leg" for assurance the performance would be spectacular. I was so excited and feeling overwhelmed when I heard the director say, "Quiet on the set." I was asked to sit on the last seat of an inside row. I thought, oh, God, thank you for where I am seated. As the show progressed, Oprah spoke with her guest panelists and weaved through her audience asking questions. One of the ladies in the audience asked the panelists if they would be willing to have a baby with birth defects. Oprah thought that was a great inquiry. While this question was being addressed, I was thinking about all three of my children and their fight coming into the world. All of them had unexpected health challenges also. While my thoughts were racing, I heard a lady say that she could not justify abortion. I could relate. I could never forget how Vaughn was almost aborted. As this lady finished speaking, I raised my hand. Oprah walked past me.

Before she could touch the lady ahead of me, she suddenly decided to double back to me. She looked toward them and said, "I'll get to you guys in a minute." Oprah came to me and touched me on my left shoulder. She held the mike in front of me and I began to tell a short story of how my first son Vaughn was born asthmatic and became a diabetic at eight years old. With my second pregnancy the doctors talked about the birth defects that my baby would have. There was even a possibility that the infant would die at birth. That pregnancy culminated with the birth of healthy identical twin boys.

I told Oprah that the twins were "A" students. Oprah said, "That's great, that's a great story." Later in the show, a lady in the audience pointed out that after hearing all of our views, she was happy that we could handle the responsibility alone. But she felt that it might be a different story when these kids turned sixteen. She felt that we would not be as happy raising these children alone when they became teenagers. She spoke very compassionately, but in a very soft tone. Her views gave me something to think about. She was concerned that the challenges a child goes through to become an adult required two parents to carry the load.

After hearing this point of view, Oprah said, "We will bring some of them back sixteen years from now." Well, in my case, it has been twenty-three years later and I truly could not have imagined all the difficulties in each of my sons' lives that were affected by my life as a single mother.

During the same time period, the twins' academic achievements were continuously excelling. Victor was listed in the National Honor Society's *Who's Who* Publication, a nationwide listing of outstanding students. Verdell was a strong "B" student, but had begun to experience seizures that affected his grades a bit. They were both great students and excelled throughout their academic careers. They were definitely college-bound black males.

At the age of seventeen Victor and his twin brother, Verdell, would sing all the time. I encouraged them by singing to them. They became very good duet singers. I would sing "Getting to Know You" from the movie *The King and I*. The twins were very, very talented. They had developed into ambitious, thoughtful, and courteous young men. They eventually developed a singing group called IMAGE, which was an acronym for Intelligent Men Are

Going Everywhere. I was their manager and my sons suggested that the young men call me Mama May instead of Mama Mathell.

As a mother, I understood the Lord's gift of their beautiful singing voices. I began to expose them to the field of entertainment. I scheduled assignments for them to perform at different social clubs, cruises, and special events. They began to participate in talent shows and were booked to perform at the Regal Theater in Chicago and on *Showtime at the Apollo*. This event was hosted by comedian Steve Harvey in New York City. We didn't have money to send the boys to New York, so they borrowed a car from their manager, Brian, and drove from Illinois to New York, sleeping in the car until audition time. At the audition, they tied for first place with an original song, "Handing in My Players Card." We were all on cloud nine. It was looking very promising for my twins. After the twins had been seen on *Showtime at the Apollo*, they were asked to appear on the July Fourth celebration at Chicago Heights' third annual city-sponsored CrossRoads Fest. Fireworks were bursting and IMAGE was rocking the stage.

A month later, the twins were asked to return to New York City to perform on Ricki Lake's talk show. Her segment was entitled "My Son Is a Star." Chris Rock, Phil Hartman, and LL Cool J's mothers were judges for the competition. This was an exciting time for all of us, even though Victor and Verdell won second place. Unfortunately, I became very ill during the performance and was taken by ambulance to the nearest hospital immediately after the contest. I had suffered an acute asthma attack.

My girlfriend Faye, who had watched my sons perform on TV, remembered that she had a few famous singers in her family—the famous Williams Brothers and Brandy and her brother Ray J. They all were from McComb, Mississippi. Faye had an idea and ran it by me that perhaps one of them could help the twins get established in the music world. She went so far as to have a third party listen to a recording to make sure she wasn't being partial about the twins' talents. Faye took a press kit to her sister Peggy. She knew how to reach Brandy's manager on behalf of my twins' IMAGE organization. Unfortunately, nothing happened, and the manager never returned Peggy's calls. Faye was disappointed because she knew that the twins were great vocalists.

With all my sons' successes, they had to get back to reality. Victor had secretly had a one-night affair, and the young woman informed him by telephone that she was three months pregnant. Verdell and I were in shock. We thought none of us had any secrets from each other. Victor could not get over how a one-night affair could lead to a baby. I always told my sons the same thing that Godmama Verona would tell me: "What goes on in the dark will surely come to light." As the three of us were family, we supported the young lady and attended prenatal care appointments with her. When the baby was born and a blood test was ordered, the findings were that he was Victor's son. They named the baby Ricky.

Two days before their high-school graduation ceremony, their father gave notice that he would not be attending their ceremony. This hurt the twins because they were very proud of their achievements. This man's reasons were ridiculous. He explained that he wanted to come back and live with us, but I refused him. My denials made him decide to return to Mississippi, and rekindle his relationship with a woman he had had for all the years that we were together. I found this out from some old friends who use to work with us. They had called to congratulate the twins on their high school graduation. They asked me if I had heard that Cannon was still in the baby making business. They said they heard he had a new baby on the way. I wanted to lash out at them but, before I could I became so upset that I felt like I wanted to scream. However, the twins were very excited about their career plans for college. Victor was planning to major in elementary education and focus on math, history, and communication. Verdell planned to major in administration justice, political science, and communication. The twins were escorted by me and a dear friend to Southern Illinois University in Carbondale, Illinois, because their father had fled the scene.

When All Else Fails, Pray

The twins had been living in Carbondale and attending Southern Illinois University for about a year. I began having acute asthma attacks frequently, but I kept on working in spite of the fact that I could hardly breathe. I would go to the doctor or would have to take myself in the middle of the night to the emergency room. I had no insurance. There were times I would go to the nearest hospital and the doctors would prescribe medication that I could not afford. I would remain very ill and would be taken within hours back to the emergency room. I explained to my attending nurse why I was in an acute state and not getting better after a few hours of being released. I could never buy the medicine. She referred me to a social worker at the hospital who submitted an application to public aid for medical assistance. She also referred me to a clinic affiliated with Cook County Hospital. I would have to go through their emergency room and be reevaluated. Once seen, they would prescribe the proper medicine, and it would be ready for pick up the same day. Because I did not have a steady job, there was a strong possibility that there would be no charge for the medicine. In the meantime, the application the nurse had helped me fill out was pending. After many severe attacks and being hospitalized, I noticed my hands shaking, and I was experiencing a lot of sleepless nights.

I finally was granted my medical card. On my next appointment

I was informed by the receptionist that my former doctor would be retiring. To hear that she was retiring saddened my heart. I cried out when I heard the news, "Oh, no, she can't." My emotions started to flow. When I look back on it, I was being selfish. I didn't want the doctor to retire, I wanted her to stay. I believed that without my doctor, who knew me well, I would be unable to make it.

I had to stop for a moment to tell myself that people are not always assigned to you for a lifetime. People come and go for various reasons, even people who are the closest to you. My former doctor knew my life story and would sometimes console me over my problems. I was terrified to think about changing doctors. In my mind, all I could think about was that I had to retell my life story all over again to a new doctor.

With all these fears I was entertaining, I realized my steps were being ordered. When your steps are ordered, you follow your inner voice. You'll be guided right to your blessing. It was then I decided to step out of my comfort zone. I would have no fear and walk by faith. I knew that God would bless me with an excellent new doctor. So I listened to my heart and chose to go to the new medical facility.

I telephoned the new facility to make my appointment. The receptionist asked me, "What would you be seeing the doctor for?" I explained my illness. The receptionist then repeated the names of the doctors who were specialists for my condition. When she named Dr. J. Payne, I chose her.

To me, Dr. Payne's first initial stood for Joy. Her last name was Payne. Of course, I thought her name was spelled Pain. With her first initial starting with the letter J and last name Payne, her name seemed to provide a balance for me. I could feel God as I spoke her name. I started to believe that my steps had been ordered toward this doctor, without a doubt. Her name gave me encouragement to hold on. Joy and Payne, I thought—this has to be the doctor for me. I had to wait two weeks for my appointment with Dr. Payne. I was anxious to meet her. I could hear my inner voice say, "Hold on and know that change is good." I didn't have a close-knit family, and the true loves in my life were my sons.

I was hurting from my head to the soles of my feet when I arrived for the appointment. Dr. Payne was compassionate, prayerful and soft-spoken, but firm. She looked over my medical records while I described my pain. She explained that we would have to work on one of the most important issues, and that issue was getting control of my emotions. I wondered how I could take control of my emotions. I was continuously fluctuating in and out of my past experiences.

As time progressed, my visits to Dr. Payne's office became a comfort to me. I could feel the same kindness here, at Dr. Payne's office, as I did with my former doctor. The staff was so caring and sensitive to my need for hugs and encouragement. My precious Dr. Payne was full of joy and gave me pain-relieving techniques. I truly thank God for Dr. J. Payne. I knew she would guide me back to health. She was another angel to take care of me!

I would often think of the twins' dilemmas of not being able to find employment during their freshman year of college. When I started going through my health problems, things changed for each of them. I really thought my father was going to change his mind about helping out his grandsons. I was praying for a change of heart when I brought him the program from their high-school graduation listing the twins and others on the honor roll. I had a clip from our local newspaper, the *Des Plaines Valley*. There was a section that had all the kids in the paper who achieved honor roll. Even though he was proud of them, he felt that they should get jobs rather than go to college.

While the twins were at SIU, they began to explore the town and found a church called Praise Out Reach Ministry. Brenda Holder was the senior pastor. They noticed the schedule of services listed on the door of their residence and made plans to attend the church the very next service. I remember them calling me and telling me how they believed they had found a church home to attend that was close to campus. I advised them to go out and make sure they were attending a Good Word church. They asked how they would know if it was a Good Word church? I told the twins that as long as the pastor taught from the Bible and they were willing to turn the pages along with her, it would encourage them to read the word for themselves.

At church, they also met two young ladies, Felecia and Nicki. Felecia was eighteen years old, stood five feet, eight-and-a-half inches, and had hazel eyes that complemented her smooth, caramel skin. She had long dark brown hair with a petite figure, legs that went on for days, and a smile with a hint of mischief. She was smart, friendly, and had a great heart, which is probably why she and Nicki became such good friends. Nicki also had these qualities, and was a twenty-three-year-old whose mixed heritage made her absolutely beautiful. She was five feet tall with green eyes, long brown hair, and a killer smile. Victor and Verdell began dating Felecia and Nicki, respectively. They shared some good and bad times in their relationships over the years. By age twenty, Victor and Verdell had grown up to be such tall, dark, and handsome gentlemen. They had the smoothest dark complexions, with full beards that were always trimmed neatly, goatees, and the classic low fade. Their voices were as smooth as butter, and when they spoke, all the young ladies were in love. Oh yes, my boys were handsome, talented, and charming. But maybe they were a little too charming at times.

The twins called me to pray for my health the Sunday they attended Praise Out Reach Ministry. My sons were telling me that the new church reminded them of their church home, at Antioch

Missionary Baptist. They had decided to join the church and the choir ministry. They had grown up spiritually at Antioch, under the choir director Bishop Simon Gordon. Church had become their hangout. So joining Praise Out Reach Ministry made them happy to be in fellowship again. Since Victor and Verdell could sing, they drew other SIU students to join the church choir.

Pastor Holder became a mentor to my sons in my absence. They'd say the nicest things about her and how joyful they were to be under her leadership. They began to call her Mother Holder toward the end of their first month as members; I knew she must have been a blessing from God. I decided to call and thank her for caring for my sons and keeping them active in church. I also shared with her my illness. Our first conversation was friendly and spiritual. I started to call her Sister Holder, and I looked forward to meeting her.

My health struggles continued as I worked part-time as a nail technician while attending travel agent classes. I could no longer stand to breathe the fumes from the nail paraphernalia, and it triggered my shortness of breath. As I visited Faye one day, she noticed my neck was thumping hard and saw that there was swelling in my throat. I called the clinic I attended and explained my symptoms. I was given an appointment immediately. When the doctor saw the condition of my throat, a thyroid test was ordered. Sure enough, when the test results came back, I was diagnosed with a thyroid condition called Graves' disease. After the doctor confirmed my condition, she told me the healing process was a long journey. As the procedure began, I was in and out of the hospital. I had to take an extensive dose of radiation and my hair began to fall out. At this time of my life I became very depressed.

I contacted the twins and told them what the doctors had said. They were disturbed to hear about my declining health and wanted to come home immediately. I became unable to work and could not afford to send money to them. They decided to quite school. I sincerely believe that this was the beginning of Victor and Verdell's wrong turns in life. I wish they had not leaned on worldly temptations for financial support.

By this time, my oldest son Vaughn had been released from jail. He had been caught selling drugs in California. After several months, he was released to a halfway house, while his wife and children lived in a homeless shelter. He needed to provide the authorities with his forwarding address in Carbondale. He contacted his brothers to discuss his relocation from California to Carbondale. He wanted to live with either of the twins. Since my health had not improved, I could not provide a home for Vaughn and his family. When Verdell was asked to house him, he refused. Victor felt obligated to provide Vaughn and his family with a place to stay.

Vaughn moved into his own apartment approximately five months later. He began selling drugs again in the Carbondale area and enticed the twins with his flashy lifestyle. He had big cars and carried excessive amounts of money. He offered them a way to make big money. The twins began to set goals to accumulate enough resources to develop a music studio. Little did they know that major trouble was about to take root. I certainly did not know how deep the streets had my sons, all of my V-boys.

Vaughn owned a barbecue house and disco lounge. The reputation of the restaurant was evident because they always had a packed house. There were many choices on the menu, but the tender juicy ribs were the best. The sauce had its own fame. It was known to be finger-licking good. Vaughn was smart. He was not using an ordinary sauce. He featured Godmama's old family recipe.

The twins, Victor and Verdell, were the featured act, singing a medley of smooth and easy love songs each weekend. This set was packed with standing room only. Vaughn and his brothers became very well known. Little did they know, I would be drawn to Carbondale for their preliminary hearings. This was one of the biggest tests of my life.

As Verdell and Nicki continued to date, they fell in love and planned to marry. Before they could get to the altar, she found out she was pregnant, and Verdell moved in with her. He dropped out of college to work, and so did Victor. They both were faced with fatherhood, and I was very ill. When Verdell and Nicki lived together, the love between them began to fade, and they did not marry. Verdell and Nicki's child was born and they named him DeSaviour. His nickname was DeDa. He was beautiful. His head was full of black, curly locks of hair. A few years passed and Nicki believed Verdell was cheating on her. Verdell had the same suspicions about her. They found out that each of them had been unfaithful to the other, and they split up. Both of them were mature about their break-up and remained friends. They moved to St. Louis, believing they had a better chance to get a good job there. Nicki and Verdell shared DeSaviour as equally as possible, without going to court. He was a happy little boy and very smart in school. He grew to respect both parents for their maturity as he got older.

In the meantime, I strayed away from church for roughly five years after Grandfather passed. It was all over something I thought wasn't right, and that was a big mistake. Then I met a gentleman named John Webb at a banquet. We exchanged phone numbers and began to meet for dinner every week. Through general conversation, I found out he was a deacon. I truly thank God for him. He asked me one day why I didn't go to church, and I explained to him my experience. He looked at me and started to share words of wisdom. He said that some things in life that hurt you are not meant to hurt and discourage you, but come to help you. Deacon John told me that if we were going to be special friends, then I needed to find a church home. His words were for me to get over whatever happened and get on with what's happening now. "You're my friend," he said, "and you need to get in a Good Word church and allow God to continue the good work he has begun in you."

I sincerely thanked God for being on my side and leading me back to church. I once was lost, and God sent an angel to direct my path back to Him. Being obedient and humble, I decided to join my girlfriend Faye and her husband's church. I attended their church service for about a year before God blessed a prophet to stop by our service. I can't thank God enough for sending Deacon John with words that directed me back to church. It was just in the nick of time to hear the powerful words of God. They were spiritually sent just as trouble was routing its way to me and my family.

Grandmother's Journey

Three weeks had passed since my last visit at my dad's and we had a lot of catching up to do. I wanted to talk about my sweet little granny. I had begun to have thoughts about her the night before. I had dreamed many previous nights of how my grandmother looked. These questions tossed in my mind like popcorn dancing in a hot machine. I thought about if I would ever see her again. I visualized her touching me and holding my children one day. I had only met my grandmother once. I prayed that one day Granny and I would be reunited. We would try to make up for all the lost time when we were not together. I realized that neither one of us had anything to do with our separation in life.

All of my friends would speak about their grandmothers. I spoke about mine casually, but like my dad, I never volunteered any information about her to anyone. In my heart, she was definitely someone our family needed to know. I felt comfortable asking my dad questions and waiting for some answers.

In our conversation, I asked if he was keeping in contact with Grandmother. He said he talked with her every Sunday. He said that she was very well. My father looked at me smiling. His shoulders dropped in a limp position. He stretched his hands out toward the table to grab a cigarette and his lighter. He took a puff, and with a sigh, he said, "It is funny you ask about her today. I have been having special feelings and dreams about my mama. I've been stacking up some money and sending it to her in portions for some things her little heart has wanted and needed." My dad loved to shop for his mother. He would often find beautiful long dresses and nice coats with scarves to match. When he would do his local shopping for food and personal supplies, he would always buy extra to create a goody gift box for his mother.

I had never seen Dad cry. Yet, as he spoke of his precious mother, I witnessed a stream of happy tears flow down his face. I saw a spark of joy and a twinkle in his eyes. To witness the expressions he shared with me brought a big smile of delight to his face and mine. This was a great day to get reacquainted with Nathell. I always envisioned Dad as mean, hard, stiff, and cold-blooded. This man, who seemed to be made of stone, had a channel on the inside of him that was loving, kind and gentle. The love he had in his heart for his mother was a blessing. He looked at her not only as his mother, but as his big sister. They were just babies together, and only fifteen years apart in age. My dad respected how tough his mother's life had been. Grandmother had worked hard, but managed to persevere through it all. Dad felt God had blessed him in many ways. He was her only child. He wanted to be a blessing to her and help supplement her income. He pointed out to me that he had never talked to anyone about how he felt about his mother. Nathell adored her and was very compassionate when speaking about her.

I needed to know about me. I believed I could learn something about my identity by getting to know the two of them. I would never know who I was from my mother's side because she had no inkling of who she was. I thought all my traits came from the angels who raised me. I asked my dad if he had any other family members besides Deloris. He slowly brought up a few cousins and vaguely mentioned uncles and aunts. I noticed Nathell was discreet when I asked about his father. He would say, sadly, "I was just a kid when he died. I do not know anything about my father."

When Nathell would talk about his life, I could feel his sincerity. He wanted his mother to come and live near him. Nathell looked for a house to buy in his neighborhood for his mother. He found a nice place right across the street from his home. He shared that information with Grandmother, and she went into a rage. She was opposed to leaving Shreveport, Louisiana. She had lived there for seventy-eight years. Dad and Grandmother had a bad fight over the telephone. I believe both of them were strong and stood on what they felt. I recall Dad being very disheartened that he and his mother had had such a bad verbal blow-out. After this disagreement between the two of them, he decided to give up on the idea of buying Grandmother a home. I could hear him murmur, "She doesn't want to better herself. Here I am, a loving son, looking out for her, and she's swearing she's going to die in her home." I told Dad he was too quick to give up on a good idea. I explained how patience was needed from him for his mother, and that he must believe that all things come in due time. I tried to reason with him in hopes that he would have a better understanding of Grandmother's fight to stay in the South. I praised God for my dad and his generous spirit.

First, I pointed out to him that her mind was limited, but her heart was rooted in Shreveport. She had to stand in defense of what she had worked for. Grandmother couldn't realize that she was getting on up in age. It was not easy for her to give up her independence or her home. I was convinced that time would bring about a change of mind and heart. Dad was not satisfied with my reasoning, and I heard him say, "It is an old shack, and all my hopes and dreams are to see her in a modern-day home, near me." I knew my dad meant well. I understood the both of them. Grandmother's compassionate love for what she had worked so hard for would not let her depart from her friends and family in the South. Dad needed to remember that she suffered in the burning hot cotton fields where snakes rattled at her feet. She had to swat bees, flies, and mosquitoes nibbling at her lean body as she stood on a fiery dirty ground with a trail of ants crawling up her legs. As I drew this picture for Dad, he could see the dirt roads she had to travel to acquire the little she had to call her own.

Dad began to visualize the labor it took Grandmother to put together such a beautiful yard that caught the eye of everyone who passed by. It was her passion to work in her yard. The fresh smell of potatoes and onions, sprouting up in the front yard, drew the bees in to lie on the yellow flowers and make their honey. The wonderful aroma filled the air from her garden. The smell would lead you to her wooded fence that was covered with green vines, with tree limbs embedded throughout the whole fence. People from all around would come by Rosie Lee's and view her variety of colorful roses and her big gorgeous green garden.

I envisioned the precious times she sat in her rocking chair on the wooden porch, laughing with her neighbors and talking to everyone. She would enjoy watching her chickens stroll and strut in the yard as she prepared to collect the eggs they would have laid. In our conversation, she told me of how she loved to cook, and that everything she cooked was fresh and birthed by her gifted hands.

After we talked, Dad thanked me for helping him to feel better and to understand the justifiable reasons behind his mother's decision. Our day was just about to end when Dad wanted to share one more thought about Grandmother's rebelling spirit, which caused her to want to remain in Shreveport. His idea was that if Grandmother was going to continue to make this her home, then Rosie Lee's boy was going to enhance her property.

He anxiously spoke of how there was no running water in her house. The water she used was located outside in the backyard, deep in the ground. She had to fetch her water in an old wooden bucket that hung in the rough part of the well. It was attached to a release lever being held on by an old rusty nail. She would have to collect her bath water, cleaning, and cooking water from this well. When Dad shared his thoughts about having running water put in her house, I jumped up out of my seat, exceedingly glad, and gave my dad a hug. I told him that his heart was pure as gold. I also believed God would bless him in a mighty way for his kindness toward Grandmother.

After that, my dad started sending money for repairs around Grandmother's house. He would always send extra money for whoever took her to the doctor. Grandmother did not drive, and her eyesight had started to fail her. I recall Dad telling me he was going to buy a used car for Grandmother's friend in order to make it easier to get her around to all of her appointments. Oh, Rosie Lee's boy, Nathell, was kind and thoughtful. Grandmother was pleased and proud of the work her baby had done in her home.

She lived there very happy and content until her world became dark. No matter which light switch she would flip on, her eyes could no longer see the light. I recall hearing of when Grandmother first realized that she couldn't see. The darkness to her was as the nights were on the back rocky roads. There were no street lights, and you could not see anyone walking with you or in front of you. She was used to strolling in the dark. Many nights she walked the side roads and had to run past snake ditches in the pitch dark.

The windows to her soul seemed to be permanently out when she reached to feel for a mirror in a familiar place. Grandmother positioned herself in front of the mirror to see the image usually shown. As she reached up to touch her face, she stretched out her fingers toward the mirror. She was fearful and slowly grabbed the sides of the mirror, because she could no longer see her reflection. Grandmother realized that her eyesight was completely gone. My grandmother professed she had the light of the Lord in her eyes.

Dad received a call from his cousins, Sue and Melvin. These two lived next door to Grandmother in Louisiana. Melvin's mother was Grandmother's sister. She was deceased. Grandmother was born a twin and the youngest child of six, yet she lived longer than all of her siblings. Her nephew expressed how they tried everything to keep her. They explained to Dad that it was getting hard for either of them to look out for their auntie any longer. They explained that each of them worked full-time jobs. Grandmother had been treated for cataracts and warned that her eyesight would soon fail. She had refused to get treatment when she first noticed a problem with her eyes. Sue and Melvin encouraged their auntie by extending every opportunity to her to take her to the doctor. Dad reminded her that her twin had gone blind also. Grandmother soon agreed to let them take her to the doctor. After the examination, the findings were that it was too late to save her eyes. The facts still remained, the complete loss of her sight was near, and that meant she would need twenty-four-hour care.

That was quite an adjustment Grandmother had to make. She knew, inch by inch, every square foot in her home. Grandmother was very independent. I heard that she could get around her place with her eyes closed and never stumble. She dressed herself, kept on cooking, and also attended to all other daily chores. This world of darkness strengthened her trust in the Lord. The more I got to know her, the more I was convinced that she was a woman of faith.

When Dad was called and informed of the changes that had to be made, he began to pray that he would have the strength to care for his wife and also to travel south to pick up his mother. After all, he was seventy-nine years old. When Dad shared his new task, I was excited and reassured him that I was available for him. It became urgent for us to bring his mother from Shreveport, Louisiana to Illinois.

I could foresee the problems of driving down south. I called Victor.

We had to pass where he lived to get to Grandmother's hometown. I explained to my son that I was going to need him to assist us in picking up his great-grandmother. He had never seen her, but had spoken with her on the telephone during many of my calls to her. I told Victor that I was not a long-range driver and that his grandfather thought he could still drive fourteen hours straight. Victor agreed and consented graciously to be a part of such a great move. I told Dad his grandson would be waiting in Carbondale and would escort us all the way to our destination.

We were all set to go. Then Dad called and said Clara, his wife, was crying uncontrollably while he was gathering his personal items to put in his suitcase. I told him to go ahead and pack for her also. I knew there was something medically wrong with her. However, there was a lot that was unknown about her health. I told Dad that we must take her along for the ride. Nathell was all upset. The well-being of Mama Clara was the important factor. She had a doctor's appointment coming up in the next few weeks. I felt that, until we knew what she was suffering with, she was not to be left alone. All of the family decision-making fell on me. I prayed throughout the day to be strong for everyone who needed me. There was no other family member in Summit to watch over her. Mama Clara's people were all in Tennessee.

When we arrived, we all exchanged a lot of hugs. Cousin Sue took us into the bedroom where Grandmother was seated quietly, listening to the television. My dad said softly, "Hey, Mama." There were tears in his eyes.

She said excitedly, "Is that my boy, Sonny?"

He gently replied, "Yes, Mama, it's me."

I then kissed her, grabbed her hand and placed it in mine, and I said, "This is your granddaughter, Mathell."

Oh, my God! What excitement she showed. Tears rushed down

my face. My mind told me that she was not strong enough to take that long drive back to Illinois. I introduced her to her great-grandson. Victor greeted her for the first time. He met her with a song on his lips. Grandmother and the rest of us were astounded by his soulful sound. Love, joy, and laughter filled the room.

Victor stayed in the room with Granny as I beckoned for the others to come out with me to discuss Grandmother's condition. My suggestion to our family was to have Grandmother transported by airplane. We all agreed and designated me to be her companion. My dad left all the arrangements up to me. I called the airport, alerting them to her blindness and my disabilities. We were each blessed with wheelchair assistance. Granny had never been on an airplane. She was actually very calm and thankful to be with her granddaughter. I realized our precious talks had prepared us for this moment in time. She asked me if I would promise her that I would stick with her until God called for her to come home. I promised her that if he allowed me to live, I would be there for her until the end of her time. That was a bond between Grandmother and me. My words of commitment allowed her spirit to rest. We had a very peaceful ride to Chicago's Midway Airport.

I had called back home and made arrangements with my friend Pamela to pick us up at the airport. Grandmother was to stay at my place until Victor could make it back with the rest of the family. In about three days, I would bring Grandmother to her new home. This storm in Grandmother Rosie Lee's life brought her to Summit, Illinois, in February of 2000.

Just as the storm clouds were drifting my way, the power of prayer was increasing because Grandmother was a praying woman. She was almost ninety-four years old when she came to live with her son Nathell and his wife. This was also the year Dad's wife began showing signs of Alzheimer's.

Grandmother was a beautiful lady. I could tell how happy she was to meet me again. Only this time, she had to rely on the vision of me from our first time ever seeing each other's face. This meeting was special. We had bonded by telephone for nineteen years. It had been a long time since I had had Grandmother's hugs and kisses. I was long overdue for some of my grandmother's love. I showed her how to embrace me as she sat in her world of darkness in her room. She stretched out her arms, wiggled her fingers, and opened her arms wide. I told her, "Put the squeeze on me, Granny." I felt very emotional. God had answered my wishes and dreams from very long ago. I wanted to be embraced in my grandmother's arms. It was perfectly conceived that my children, who had never laid eyes on her before, would now have that opportunity. I called each of my sons and told them to come and bring all of their children to meet their great-grandmother and great-great-grandmother. When Grandmother arrived at Dad's, it was a week before her ninety-fourth birthday celebration. I called my sister Deloris and hoped that she would fly up and surprise her grandmother. She quickly answered, "No." I didn't ask for any explanations, trying to avoid a verbal fight, nor did I let anything or anyone deter me from planning this birthday celebration for my grandmother. My sister did send her a beautiful card with money enclosed. I wanted to show my appreciation to Grandmother. There was no stopping me. The party was on, and we had a great time. Grandmother cried tears of joy throughout her party. She couldn't remember ever having a birthday party.

Dad and I had our hands full taking care of his mother and his wife. My dad considered the distance between us. He assessed our needs and bought a brand new Ford Taurus as a second car. He already owned a Cadillac Brougham. I kept the new car at my house and I could come and go freely. Dad was confident that he had provided easy access to me any time of the day or night. It was my pleasure to be all I was sent to be by God in each of their lives.

My children did not live near us. Dad was going to need help getting Grandmother and his wife ready for the day without me. I tried to be there twenty-four hours a day. Health-wise, I was not always able to do so. I had worked for the Community Economic Development Association years prior and had set people up with home-care services before. My old skills were put into action, and I called Community Care on Aging located in LaGrange, Illinois. There was a nurse who came out to evaluate their needs. Soon after, a caretaker and housekeeper were provided. Dad and I had anticipated many appointments with an eye specialist for Grandmother. She had left her false teeth back in Louisiana, and I needed to find a dentist for her. Both women also needed primary-care doctors. A complete mental evaluation was needed for Clara. She had severe signs of deteriorating health. I made their first appointment together at Des Plaines Valley Community Health Care with Dr. Hunter-Smith. It was hard to transport them together. Grandmother had to be coached down twelve stairs. She was afraid of stairs. She would cry loudly and would hold her caretaker and me real tight. I lovingly encouraged her, with a soft tone, to assure her that she was doing well. Several trips had to be made to the doctor with Grandmother. One finding was that she had a thyroid problem. The other finding was reconfirming that she was permanently blind. She had one complaint that her fingers hurt. Dr. Hunter-Smith smiled and said, "If that's her only pain, Rosie will be around until she's one hundred years old." The doctor suggested we give her Tylenol for pain. That was the only medicine she was to take.

In caring for Grandmother, I would call her four nights a week and let her laugh and talk until she became tired. I would bring her all of the delicious meals she loved on Mondays and Thursdays of every week, except holidays. When I would arrive, she would be very happy. I would call ahead of time and ask the caretaker to put Granny in her best lounging outfit. She would be sitting at the dining-room table. As I entered, I put on a gospel CD. Our laughter filled the room. Grandmother and my dad were very prayerful and thankful that I would arrive safely. They had praise on their lips for me. Their kind words thrilled me inside, and the delight brought a smile to my face. Grandmother had recently gotten her new teeth that Dr. Robert Miserendino made for her. Ironically, a girlfriend of mine found him in the newspaper and, to my amazement; he was an old schoolmate of mine. We both attended the same grammar and high school. We were two grades apart. He was very gentle and knew how to care for a woman in her mid nineties. She would cry and say that her teeth hurt her. I had to prepare every soft food I could think of, such as black-eyed peas, mustard greens, turnips, spinach greens, mashed potatoes, and her favorite, bread pudding.

I soon learned that my grandmother loved to sing, and one of her favorite songs was "I Got My Religion in Time." As she would sing, she would clap her hands and tap her feet on the floor to keep with the beat of the song. We would laugh our way to the end of a song, and then start flattering each other about how we each sounded great. Grandmother would say modestly, "Oh baby, I can't sing anymore. I am too old." I would encourage Granny not to think of her age. Just know that the Lord's spirit is in her. She would laugh and give a beautiful smile in return. She would pump me up like I was sounding so good. She needed to hear granddaughter sing one more song. She loved all Gospel songs, but claimed one to be the dearest to her heart. That song was, "I Heard the Voice of Jesus." She would say, "Child if you sing that song to me, I would just love you to the highest." There was no way I could deny her heart's desire. My attempt was great. I did not know all the old words, but I remembered how it had been sung. I declare her request touched my soul, and my spirit led me to sing it with a hum and moan like my grandfather, Deacon Brown, did in the old Baptist church.

Things were going very well in the two years Granny had settled in with us. Mama Clara became very ill with pneumonia and was placed in LaGrange Hospital. Within two weeks' time, she died. Dad and I were right by her side. Joanne was gracious to stay with Grandmother while Dad and I attended to the arrangements and home-going for Mama Clara. Now, I need to be mindful of Dad's feelings in the loss of his dear wife. They had been married for over forty years.

Dad loved it when I would just come and allow him and Grandmother to talk, laugh about old times, eat, and visit half the day. I would find myself sometimes emotionally breaking down from it all. Dad would see the tears falling from my eyes as I began to prepare Grandmother's plate. She could not see my tears as I prepared to sit before her to assist her with her meal. She was very independent when it was time to eat. She picked up her food with her fingers. I just loved to talk with her while she ate. Dad would see tears streaming down my face as I tried very hard to stay upbeat before Grandmother. He would hand me a paper towel and pat me on the back. Dad was a strong man and would always tell me it is better to let it out than to keep these feelings on the inside. I must say, these visits were also very good for me. Their wishes were a joy to me. They kept my mind peaceful.

Dad suggested that we tell Grandmother of the trouble the boys were in. He felt we needed her prayers. Dad explained that she prayed and sang all day in her room. He had monitors in her room and leading to every part of the house. He could hear the prayers she was sending up on behalf of her family. I was afraid it was going to hurt her and possibly take her to her grave, but we did confide in her. I hoped this burden would not be too much for her to bear. Grandmother was a warrior and a true believer that God could do all things. Her words were, "Daughter, do not worry anymore, God will deliver those boys out of darkness and back into the marvelous light." She was a mother and had experienced Nathell when he was a troublesome son. Grandmother knew her prayers and others had covered her son, Nathell. She believed this blessing would also be with her great-grandsons.

I traveled to and from their house knowing that I could be honest with my feelings. Some days, I could not even get out of the car. I would cry all the way out there, and my friend Marguerite and I would cook all night. Joanne would come by and load the food in the car to help out. I no longer had to pretend. Grandmother was there to love me. Nathell was there also. When I had to go away on one of the boys' cases, I did not have to deceive Grandmother any longer. I was free.

Just when I thought I was free, my birth mother was complaining that her back was hurting very badly. I called Joanne and I asked her if she had the time to drive me to pick up my mother and take her to the emergency room. She was always a willing person. She agreed, and we made the trip to Summit. The attending doctor ran a lot of tests, and he diagnosed her with lung cancer. Mama Mildred was put in the hospital that day. I called Penny. When she arrived, her commitment was to stay every night until our mother was released. When Mama Mildred was discharged, the doctors predicted she would live five months. I needed my sister Penny to step in to assist Mama Mildred. I was worn and weak from each of my love ones' tribulations. My sister and I talked on a daily basis, and she explained that she was considering moving from where she was because her lease was expiring. I suggested Penny come live with Mama Mildred. I was stretched like a rubber band, and I felt like I was about to pop. I told my sister she would not have to pay rent or any other bills. Mama Mildred was on a low-income rent subsidy. I explained to Penny that I would take steps with the housing authority to get her secured in the unit with Mama Mildred.

Mama Mildred had put my name on her bankbook to assure that her bills would be paid on time. I truly believe that she was at an early stage of dementia that had not been diagnosed at this point.

Sometimes she would not be aware of her surroundings until the next day. She would recognize that food and other meaningful things were missing. I assured my sister that I would look into home care for Mama and continue to do my part. It was imperative that Mama Mildred had someone to love and care about her all day and all night.

It was too little, too late. Mama Mildred died. I had mixed feelings about her death. Her death didn't seem as traumatic to me as the other women in my life. When Mama Mildred was drinking, she could get very evil with her tongue. She would say the most hateful and hurtful things to me. I heard someone say, "A drunk speaks their sober thoughts." Mildred's words began to hurt me worse than ever before. I didn't want to believe my birth mother would say such vile things to me. Believe it or not, it made me stronger. I was with her at her deathbed. She apologized to me for the hateful things she had said to me when I was growing up. I had forgiven her a long time ago, but it made me feel good that closure was brought to the negative side of our relationship. I was sorry it happened so late in the game, especially since Nathell and I had already brought closure to our past. I was able to understand why my parents really gave me away. I love them for it. They both learned to love me in my adult life, and that is all that matters.

I was called, after Mama Mildred died, by the new owners of her building and made aware that Mama Mildred was behind in her rent. This was a sign of forgetfulness and not at all like Mama Mildred. She always paid her bills and made sure she had groceries. She was a very free-hearted person. However, as she became older, she hung around people who were heavy smokers, drinkers, and sometimes drug abusers. She was in love with a man twenty years younger than her. Joe was his name. He served and stood beside her. This man was very much the same as Mama Mildred. She kept him close and let it be known that she loved her man. Joe was there to help Penny on Mama's last days. He made her happy, and that's what matters.

At this time, Victor's case was waiting to be heard. He had been out of jail on his own recognizance. I wrote the judge and included supportive documents from two hospital doctors about Victor's grandmother's condition. I described how the physicians explained to me that the cancer in both of her lungs would likely smother her heart. It was possible that she would have a massive heart attack or she would likely have another stroke and die soon. My request was to please allow the grieving grandson to attend the home-going of his grandmother, and my request was granted. I thanked the judge for his graciousness in allowing Victor to leave while waiting on his sentencing. I will always be thankful for the favor of God present in the judge. He granted Victor a trip to his grandmother's memorial service. I truly believe that in any situation, if you humble yourself and just pray, many times your prayers will be answered. God determines if it shall be done. I made sure Victor was back in the Carbondale area on time, and sent the judge a thank-you letter.

I made all of the necessary arrangements and called in my uncle Claude to help me with the obituary. This was a sad occasion, but it was the first time I had spent quality time with my uncle. I used this opportunity to share all my pain. I was having a tough time with Penny and my nieces. They each thought I personally had a lot of money because of the way I carried myself. Mama Mildred did not have a current insurance policy. When going through her papers at home, Penny and I discovered every policy had expired. I was left with no choice but to have her cremated. I was in much pain about my helpless decision, but I had to give my mother a decent burial. My uncle knew my position. He gave me comfort by expressing his thoughts in a very compassionate way. He said, "Mathell, forgive your siblings for the things that they are saying about you. As long as you and I know the situation, let what they say go in one ear and out the other." After the funeral, Penny and her daughters stopped communicating with me for about a year. Then Penny would check in with me concerning my sons. She would never leave a number so that I could call her back. I had to keep things in my life moving. Dad and Grandmother still were depending on me, while my sons' cases were being heard.

Time moved on, and suddenly a virus plagued Grandmother's little frail body. My dad called me to let me know that she was not feeling well at all. Dad explained how he had warmed up some of her favorite foods that I had cooked. He said, "Baby, she left everything on her plate." I knew how she loved my old-fashioned bread pudding. I told Dad to warm up a slice of bread pudding and put it before her while I waited on the other end of the phone. Dad soon came back to the phone and said, "Baby, I told your Grandmother that Granddaughter says she must eat a little to keep up her strength." I could hear the concern in Dad's voice as he explained to me that he had tried to get her to eat. I needed to relieve Dad's mind, so I told him not to worry, because his daughter was on her way. I started praying that my strength would hold up. I believed that God would supply my needs to care for both of them. I would be of help to Dad by being there and holding his hand through it all. Dad always let me do all the talking. As I was driving, I felt a sense of peace. I would lean on God, and he would supply what each of my family members and I needed. When I got there, Dad was sitting in his rocking chair. I could see how relieved he was that I had arrived. I know that it was not me, but the spirit of the Lord in me that assured him that things were going to be all right.

Dad and I suspected that grandmother's end was near. I went straight to her bedroom and saw that my poor grandmother was very ill. I screamed into the next room, "Dad, telephone the paramedics." The team arrived in a timely manner. They came in and took her vitals. They brought in a stretcher and drove her to La

Grange Hospital. Upon arrival, she was diagnosed by an attending physician. She had had a stroke and a severe bowel obstruction. She appeared to have the flu and was admitted.

Hearing those words, my dad and I became saddened. I have found that no matter how old one is, we as humans never want to let go. She stayed in the hospital for about two weeks, and it was suggested she be admitted to a nursing home. My dad and I did not want to part with her, but it was too hard for my father and me to take care of Grandmother. So we listened to the directions of Dr. Hunter-Smith and put her in a nursing home. The nursing home was located in La Grange. Godmama Verona's friend, Ms. Louise Gary, had a daughter, Debra Gary Johnson. She was an aide attending the elderly at the nursing facility.

My grandmother was one hundred years old when she went on to glory. She was born the youngest of a set of twins on February 3, 1906, and died on my twin sons' birthday, July 5, 2006. She was a feisty woman and extremely spiritual. While Grandmother lived with my father, she had grown to know and love my children.

Grandmother had been praying and waiting for Victor to get out of prison. She called prison "the army" or "the pit." She remained prayerful waiting for his return. She would put her arms around me and let me cry in her arms. She would say to me at the moments that hurt me the most, "Baby, everything is going to be all right." Her words would soothe my soul. She would say, "He's gonna come home. He's gonna come out of that army." She waited patiently for his arrival. I had come to really love my grandmother and cherish her sweet talk.

Grandmother loved to hear Victor sing. Victor would sing everything to her. "Good morning" or whatever conversation he had with her. She would know him by his voice, because Grandmother had become totally blind. When Victor was released from the pit/army, he walked into Grandmother's nursing-home room and began to sing. She said to him, "You the one I've been waiting for. Baby, are you out that army now?"

Victor told her, "Yes, Great-Grandmother, I'm out that army now."

Victor's original thirty year sentence had been reduced down to two years. Because of time served, and along with good behavior, he was released before the two years were completed. I believe the Lord arranged Victor's visit home to reconnect with his great-grandmother before her transition. It was an amazing thing to see Victor walk into that room and start singing. I witnessed Grandmother's connection to the Lord and to her great-grandson. I was in the room with Victor's wife, Felecia; their two sons, Ricky and Aaron; my father; and a dear friend of ours who Grandmother affectionately called "The Baby." The nurse came in and announced she would take Grandmother's roommate out of the room so we could spread out. Victor moved his seat next to his great-grandmother. He began to sing some old time hymns. Grandmother began to sing right along with him. We all began to sing in Grandmother's room at her bedside. We will always remember that day.

The nurses came into the room and said, "We have never heard such singing."

Grandmother said, "Yeah, he done made it out the army."

Victor replied, "Yeah, and I've come to sing all the songs you want me to sing."

Grandmother said, "Sing, baby, sing." He sang her favorites, like "Wade in the Water," "Trouble's Not Going to Last Always," and "I Got My Religion in Time." Grandmother said, "Listen to the music going on up in here." I experienced some powerful moments at my grandmother's dying bed.

Grandmother was a very gracious, loving, and patient woman. We sang and visited, and when it was time to go, she had special words to say to all of us. She said to The Baby, "Thank you for being so good to my family." We began to file out of the room. I was the last one, and she called my name, "Granddaughter." I looked directly in her eyes.

She said, "I can hardly talk no more."

I said, "That's all right, Grandmother, go on and talk it over with the father, because our father has his arms wide open for you."

She replied, "Yeah, granddaughter, I think I'm going on in now. You keep on keeping on."

As I was leaving the room, I touched her toes, and she said, "Thank you granddaughter, thank you."

I said "You welcome, Sweetie Pie. I'll see you there."

She whispered, "I can hardly talk."

As I left the room, I watched my father and the rest of the family and friends walk down the hall. I looked back at the room and said, "God, take her on home." It was the Fourth of July, Independence Day.

The next day, the nursing home called us and said, "If you want to get to see her, you must come now, because her blood pressure is dropping." We decided she should rest in the arms of Jesus. We would remember her just the way we saw her the day before. The nurse replied, "Okay, we will let you know when it is over." While I was discussing the situation with my father, the hospital called to inform us that Grandmother had gone to glory. Debra and a team of wonderful nurses were there to see her through her last day. That very same day, the twins turned thirty-two years old.

What a wonderful blessing for all of us to take part in caring for our blind grandmother in her golden years. Witnessing her make one hundred years old was a historical blessing, a bonus. There were six generations at Grandmother's one-hundredth birthday celebration, and she had the opportunity to hold all the babies. As I watched, Grandmother had maneuvered through her family, sightless and visibly determined to meet all her kin by touch. I don't believe she realized she was bonding a broken family by emitting great love into the family environment. It was then I realized that I was the next matriarch in line to lead my family. I was the next oldest female. I would be the one bonding the family together when Grandmother was gone. Watching Grandmother at her last birthday celebration made me wish she'd been in my life a whole lot longer. It also made me realize I had to help stop the destructive patterns our family kept experiencing. The early pregnancies, the multiple mothers and fathers, and being incarcerated were ruining the moral fiber of the family.

My father wanted to have Grandmother cremated because we had spent so much money attempting to keep the family together and assisting the V-boys in their expensive plight. Her memorial service was the next day, which was also my fifty-fourth birthday.

Have you ever had the thought of defeat and surrendered to the idea that all hope was gone? To those who answer yes, I have also. Especially after going down many one-way streets and losing my sense of direction. I depended on the everlasting word of God, while in my spiritual storm, to guide me and these boys to wherever our destination was. I had to walk by faith and not by fear of things unknown. I could see evidence of how the problems were increasing for my children. I was convinced in my heart and soul of the strong word I had heard prophesized over me and my family's lives. This prophecy encouraged me and strengthened my faith. It seemed that there was nothing else to hold on to.

The Prophecy

I was a new member of Colony All Nations church, where Bishop Carter and his wife, Faye, were the angels of the house. It was April when I attended a Sunday morning service in which a visiting prophet, George Davis, sat at the rear of the storefront church. When Bishop Carter spotted him in the congregation, he invited him to the pulpit. I had never seen or met this man before, but I thought he had a special spirit as he walked passed me. Bishop Carter asked the visitor if he had a word for us, and he said that he did. He said he wanted to give a word to a couple of new preachers who were just starting out with a new church. He wanted them to be encouraged and pray over them. The prophet walked up to the couple and asked them if they were new preachers. They said yes. They were visiting different congregations throughout the city and decided to visit Colony All Nations that particular Sunday. I was amazed. I had never been to a church service where this type of activity took place.

After praying for them, the prophet looked to the right side of the sanctuary where Christine and I sat. He pointed directly at me and announced that there were dark clouds hovering over my head. I could feel Christine tense up as she sat next to me. I looked around thinking maybe he was talking to someone behind me. He continued to point in my direction, saying, "You, the lady in the pink and blue dress. There is a spiritual storm brewing, and the enemy is out to kill, steal, and destroy you and your family."

Faye looked over at me. She realized that I was the one in blue and pink and said, "Mathell, it's you."

Still in denial, I whispered to Christine that there must be another Mathell behind me. I looked around again, but in my soul I knew it was me the prophet was speaking to. My life was about to make a drastic change. A terrible storm was coming in my direction. Our storefront church had no windows, so at first I thought maybe it had begun to storm outside. Christine and I were just babes in Christ, and we didn't know anything about a spiritual storm. Sister Faye had begun to walk toward me when the prophet mentioned the color of my clothing. She escorted me out of my seat. Faye began to cry out, "It's you, Mathell, it's you."

I said, "What storm? I don't know anything about a storm!" I stood up to walk with Faye, but couldn't visualize or comprehend the words of the prophet. My friend, the First Lady of the church, understood the impact of the prophet's revelations and was standing by me for support. Christine was left in her seat, crying and spiritually touched.

As I walked with my four-pronged cane toward the prophet, he said, "God says to tell you he loves you very much. Are you feeling unloved?" I said I was, and he said, "God said you are going to make it through, but there is a terrible storm ahead." The prophet then said, "You have children, but not many births."

I was so overwhelmed. It was difficult to answer him immediately, but his question made me think to myself, I have three sons, but only two births. So, I replied, "Yes."

He said, "They are boys, aren't they?"

My voice rose as I said, "Yeah," in disbelief. I now realized the storm was related to my boys, and I needed to concentrate and hear all he had to say about them.

He said, "You are going to go through something with those boys, and it is going to be so bad that you will feel that it might kill you. But, God says for you to hold on, faint not, for you will reap and he will give you one hundredfold. As a matter of fact, you are going to come across like a ball of fire. Have you ever seen a ball of fire? Have you ever seen a burning bush roll down the street?"

Through my tears, I said, "No."

He ran to the other side of the room, hunched up, and began charging toward me, saying, "You are going to come across like a ball of fire, and the Lord is going to restore your soul, and all of your boys are going to make it to the cross. Faint not, for you are going to reap." This is when I hit the floor.

I was knocked out. I was told by Faye that Christine tipped up to where I was lying on the floor and said to her, "Is Mathell dead?"

Faye chuckled and said, "No, baby, she is under the power of the Lord." Christine broke down and cried with relief, once she saw me move. Faye instructed two gentlemen to help me off the floor, and they sat me in the first pew. Faye allowed me to lie in her arms, and had her personal nurse assist me with the mucous running from my mouth.

I was asking Faye, "What happened to me?"

She said, "The Lord has had his way with you."

I asked that she help me get back to my seat. Faye summoned for the two gentlemen to help me again. At this point, the prophet was on the other side of the room revealing God's word to another saint. When the men positioned themselves on either side of my seat to lift me up, Prophet George shouted as he ran toward me,

"No, no, don't move her. She's got to understand! Bishop, she's gonna need you. First Lady, she's going to need you, too! This storm is going to be so bad that she is going to drop down and want to die, but the Lord says to her that she is going to employ many and she is going to have the top of the line of everything. You are going to travel and people will be coming from afar to see you." He said, "Know that God is God and He will be with you and those boys through it all." Then he instructed the gentlemen to take me back to my seat. As I walked back to my seat, I was leaning on Jesus. I still didn't understand what was happening, but I continued to lean on my Father's words that everything, in the end, was going to be all right.

Faye later told me that she had known Prophet George for over twenty years, and he had never put her in his prophetic word, or better yet, he had never put her over anyone in his prophetic sessions. She said, "He didn't know we were girlfriends," and she was a bit surprised by the situation. Even though she was taken aback by it all, she, too, believed a terrible storm was coming in my direction, and she felt sorry for what was about to happen in my life.

Multiple Situations

Mama Love Joy and I had plans to attend a gala at Marguerite's social club called the Odd Seven. It was a three-day event, and we participated in all the festivities. Mama Love Joy's friend, Frank, who I called Big Daddy, flew in town to celebrate the new millennium with us. The gala was held at the Sheraton Suites in Elk Grove, Illinois. Big Daddy, Mama Love Joy, and I were looking forward to attending a pool party later that evening in the hotel.

I'd persuaded Mama Love Joy to purchase some swimming suits. She brought three of them with matching skirts. Big Daddy had never seen her in swimwear. The suit she decided to wear was a leopard print with a matching long skirt, scarf, slippers, and a beach bag. Mama Love Joy looked stunning. My swimsuit was red and trimmed in leopard. I, too, had a matching bag and slippers.

We both looked like Nubian queens at the dinner dance. We had on our jewels and a variety of fashions to style in. Frank strutted like a peacock with the two of us on his arms and didn't care about any expense. We were chauffeured each and every time we went to special events. He made sure we always traveled first class.

On Mother's Day of that year, I spent the evening taking Mama Love Joy out for dinner. I called Christine and Marguerite and included them in on our dinner outing. For this particular Mother's Day, May 14, 2000, I received a brochure in the mail advertising a spectacular live blues show and dinner dance at the legendary Martinique Drury Lane in Evergreen Park, Illinois. Upon receiving it, I did a conference call to my two girlfriends and read the contents of the brochure to them. I told them about the appearance of J. Blackfoot, who had worked with B.B. King, Bobby Bland, and Gladys Knight. Also featured was Theresa Griffin, who had worked with Aretha Franklin and Anita Baker. It also listed that she had performed at The Cotton Club in Chicago. Just reading about these artists was sweet music to our souls. We were down-home blues lovers. The background on these artists excited each of us.

The place was well-known and fabulous. We were excited about having this great place to attend and, most of all, about wearing our best threads and stepping in style on our day. All of us were fond of the blues, and we loved dining out. We looked forward to an enchanting evening. Each ticket included a four-hour open bar with unlimited soft drinks and cocktails. Dinner was also included, and it featured prime rib or chicken Kiev prepared to our taste. There were other delicious sides, such as baked potatoes, vegetables, homemade soup, tossed garden salad, dessert, and coffee or tea.

This great day had arrived, and Mama Love Joy was to drive Mama Mildred. Christine and Marguerite would come in from Chicago together. I would be coming in from the far south and would meet all of them there.

As I approached the area, I could see the name of this magnificent establishment blinking and flashing in front of the building. There was the convenience of valet parking. I thought, it doesn't get any better than this.

By the time I registered and was escorted to the dining area, my guests were already seated. I greeted each of them with a kiss and each of my mothers with roses and a card. Our night was a groove and full of fun and laughter.

The night was just about to come to an end. Mama Love Joy told me that I should get a head start on traffic and call her when I got home. She only lived about twenty minutes away. I smiled at her and told her that I was going to walk her to her car. She had a way of reminding me who the mama was. She used her tone of voice with authority and directed me to go now and be a sweet baby girl. "Do what your mama says and call me as soon as you get home." I leaned over and gave her a kiss. She lovingly said, "I love you more."

On my drive home, I was listening to some smooth jazz on the radio. I had been driving for about forty minutes when my cell phone rang. I answered and the caller regretfully advised me hurry to the hospital down the street from Drury Lane, because something had happened to Mama Love Joy. All she could tell me was she really didn't know what happened, but to get to the hospital as soon as I could. I panicked, not knowing what could be wrong.

I called my beautician, Gloria, to tell her about the call I had just received. She suggested that I come and get her, and she would drive me to the hospital. I was very appreciative of her kind gesture. On my way to get Gloria, I contacted Christine and explained what little I had been told about my precious Mama Love Joy. Christine started to cry, and she said, "I will be there when you get there." She lived fifteen minutes away from the hospital. When I picked up Gloria, we both broke down and cried. Gloria was Mama Love Joy's hairstylist also, and she was very fond of her. I did not know anyone who did not love her.

We arrived, and I saw Christine standing in the hallway crying. When I was in reach of her, she fell into my arms. I embraced her because she was hysterical. I tried to hold myself together and comfort Christine. Gloria searched for a nurse and asked where Ms. Love Joy was. I was pointed in the direction of Mama Love Joy's room. Gloria took over as support for Christine while I went down the hall to ICU. I found Mama Love Joy unconscious and on life support. There were intravenous tubes in her. As I stood with my mouth open wide, I began to think about the prophetic word of Prophet George. I felt he must have been wrong. The storm wasn't my boys, it was Mama Love Joy. It hurt my heart to think such a thought. My heart began to pound, and I became weak at the knees. I had to support myself on Mama Love Joy's bed rail, so I wouldn't fall to the floor. My wounded mind questioned what had happened. I thought back to that day in church when I was forewarned that a storm was coming. This must be what he was talking about. My tears were flowing and my hand clenched Mama Love Joy's hand. She was cold. I could hear my prayers for her echo in the room. One of the attending doctors came in the room, and I identified myself as her goddaughter. I had a flashback of Godmama Verona and how she died.

While I was thinking, a nurse entered the room to check Mama Love Joy's vitals. The doctor told me that he was going to order more tests. He told me it looked as though she had had a massive heart attack and stroke. She was in a coma. I excused myself and looked for the waiting room. When I entered the waiting room, it was packed with relatives and friends. It was a very emotional time for all of us. I asked them what had happened. But, no one seemed to know.

We stayed almost all night. Each doctor we spoke with could not promise us any hope. We all decided to go home and get some rest and pray for her health. When I arrived home, I called Mama's dear friend Frank in California and told him the sad story. He reacted spontaneously by telling me to get off the phone. He needed to make reservations to get here the next day. He did, and he stayed by Mama's side every day. There was still no change in her condition. Finally, he had to leave. Frank was brokenhearted, but yet prayerful. He had extended all the love and care possible. He had to trust and believe that God makes no mistakes.

Days and weeks had passed, and we were told Mama was not making any progress. Her closest relative had to make other arrangements for long-term care at another facility.

This was very disheartening. It was just three weeks before Victor and Felecia's wedding. I had no idea how I could make it through this crisis and celebrate my son's marriage. Mama Love Joy was supposed to be there and sit in the front row with me. Our cruise was three months away, and at this point Mama Love Joy was having difficulty breathing on her own. Her condition was getting worse. It was very hard for me. I used to talk to her every day, anytime of the day. We would sometimes go to sleep while talking to one another on the phone. When we would wake up, we would start talking and laughing all over again. We always included each other in our daily lives. We kept planning to be with one another. We would sleep at each other's houses. I would get up and prepare meals for her. She loved hot bread pudding, salmon croquettes, biscuits buttered with grape jelly, and hot rice. It was my pleasure to cook all the things she loved. We were inseparable. I truly enjoyed our mother-daughter relationship.

She was scheduled to be transferred within two weeks to the new facility. It was located far north. She was still in a coma, and her condition was severely critical. My prayers were always with her. I would pray, "Lord, whatever thy will is for her, let it be done. Please, Father, do not let her suffer much longer." I began to thank God for her being a part of my family's life. She was loved by many.

Several Sundays had passed. I returned to church, and I was feeling a bit off-center. Christine had begun to talk about things that began to annoy me, and it vexed my spirit. When it came time for tithe and offering, I could hear my inner spirit say for me to leave the sanctuary. I submitted my tithe and left the church abruptly. The prophet had already told me what would happen, and I needed to get a handle on things. I cried all the way home. I was confused. Mama Love Joy was in a coma, and I thought maybe that was the storm, but I couldn't get the storm involving my sons out of my mind. I couldn't get my mind to wrap around what the prophet meant by the storm, and Christine's conversation was not shedding any light on the situation. When I got in my car, I called Bishop Carter on his private line and left a message. I told him I was feeling extremely emotional and needed to speak with him. I asked him if he would please contact me when he had a moment, to help me understand this situation. While driving and waiting for the bishop to return my call, I decided to visit my friend Deacon John. I was feeling faint and needed a person to communicate with.

Two weeks passed before I received a call from Sister Faye on my answering machine. She said that she missed me and was calling to check on me. When I returned her call, Bishop Carter answered the telephone. When I heard his voice, I immediately wanted him to know how I felt about him not returning my call. I said, "Bishop, I was wondering, why you didn't return my call?"

He said that he had received my message, but thought I had made up my mind not to return to the church.

I was perplexed and said, "Bishop, what about the lost sheep?"

He replied in an authoritative voice, "All right now."

I took his statement to mean I was out of line to question him. I replied, "Well okay, I guess I will just stay gone." I asked if Faye was there and he replied that she wasn't. So that ended the conversation. I was extremely hurt by the conversation with Bishop Carter. The prophet had told Bishop Carter and Faye that

I would need them. Bishop Carter, Faye and I had been friends for twenty-five years, and I didn't let this situation destroy the love between us or our friendship. I continued to share with her the steps of my spiritual journey. This included the storm that was destined to come.

When Bishop said these words I began to feel sensitive. But, I quickly became encouraged as I remembered that these were my friends for many years. A heavenly voice I heard reminded me that I would face a spiritual storm. Prophetic word had been released out of the month of someone the Carters knew most of their lives. Mind you, I never saw this man of God before. I am grateful that God blessed me with a discerning spirit and stabilized my thinking. I realize as family, friends or spouses we are not going to see things the same way all the time.

I believe that God has a way of pushing you out of a situation and placing you in a more powerful place. He sometimes brings you right back to where you started. I've always been drawn by spirit to call Faye from time to time and keep her abreast of what God was doing in my life and check in on her family. She and Bishop always welcomed me with open arms. We would share our ups and downs; have a few laughs as though we had never separated. I believe that God wanted me to keep communicating because they were my lifetime friends.

However, I decided to put some distance between us for a while. I stopped attending church, again.

After a few months without attending church, I was told by my son Verdell that I should get back to church. I knew he was right I needed to get back on track.

I was a pain-filled mother in need of spiritual guidance. I was hoping for a spiritual leader. I did know I was to hold on and not give up. I knew I was not to lean on my own understanding, but to rely on God's amazing grace. The Bible says trust no man.

Everything Prophet George had revealed to me was coming to pass, and I had no doubt I was going to make it through and my boys were going to make it to the cross. I felt compelled to receive the word the Lord wanted me to hear.

I realized that my storms have blessed me with wisdom and a spiritual insightfulness. I wanted to love and show compassion to others. I believed we each were born with a choice to love or not to love. I looked for ways to forgive a person. I knew if I offended someone, if given another chance, I would rectify my wrong. I would take into consideration the other person's emotional needs. It comes from the experiences I've had in my life. My way doesn't have to be the way for everyone. A person may not be thinking clearly due to overwhelming circumstances. It was easy to quit, run away, and give up. But, to be able to face your mountains and valleys represents humility and courage. Yet, I pray a prayer just as Jesus prayed on the cross to our Father Who Art in Heaven. I pray that he will forgive anyone who has hurt me or anyone who I might have hurt. With integrity and love, I trust that it is my duty to let a person know when he has hurt me, so we can work it out. We are each needed to carry out the Lord's will. We need one another. We are just like the characters in *The Wizard of Oz*, trying to get to our Spiritual Father. We must follow the yellow brick road. I believe stumbling blocks are placed for reasons, and my stumbling blocks have made me a better person. We must remember the battle is not ours, it's the Lord's.

As I continued to walk by faith, I looked forward to going to church on Sundays. That was my time, and I never let my feelings or my family problems stop me from going to worship. My, oh my, did I get blessed when I went to church one Sunday. An apostle, who could not speak English, was the guest speaker that day. However, there was an interpreter who translated his words into English. I was listening to the words being preached. It was amazing to hear about the resurrection power that God had in Moses, in another language. It truly touched our hearts. Then, suddenly, the preacher felt he needed to prophesy, and the translator spoke as fast as she could. She translated with a feeling for what was being preached. Many words were shared in the prophecy, but I must share a selection of words that touched my spirit. The words of God in Elijah were true, he said. "If the word of God is not true in my mouth, I want God to kill me." The apostle continued to prophesy as he walked the floor. He said, "In this moment, I am going to pray for you. The spirit of God has told me that there is a mama here whose son is in prison. God is going to change the life of your son." I screamed and he said, "Hallelujah! Come here, I am going to pray for you, sister." That "sister" was me. I was escorted by two gentlemen to the preacher. I could barely walk, convinced that the spirit of the Lord was on the move to help me. I felt broken and knew that God was repairing me and strengthening me for his mission. I could vaguely hear the Apostle say, the devil said, "You have lost your children." The years my three boys faced were telling me that the devil was trying to destroy them. The apostle said, "God has seen your pain, tears, and suffering." By this time, my whole body started shaking and trembling. I felt my legs were about to give out. Then he said, "You are in a desert of loneliness, but the Lord is telling you the time is over."

After those words, I became dizzy, and the next thing I knew I was waking up on the floor. I had passed out completely when the prophetic words from the visionary, George Davis, were spoken over my life: "The storm is coming." Now, I was blessed to hear "The time is over." I thank God for such blessed words. The mighty words from the apostle reminded me that my steps had been ordered. When I shared my situation with my friend Bea, she encouraged me to keep praying. We had been prayer partners for thirty years, and what had begun to happen in my life and with my children was unbelievable to her. Yet Bea was there with me through it all. When I told her that my sons were facing prison sentences of twenty years, thirty years, and sixty years respectively,

Bea screamed. She told me she couldn't imagine the gut-wrenching pain I must be going through. She made arrangements to come visit me in Chicago Heights to provide moral support.

When Bea arrived, she was detoured by surprise events preplanned by her immediate family members who lived in the Chicago area. This prevented Bea from having an opportunity to visit with me as she had planned. Bea tried to arrange for some visiting time between us, but her plans just didn't work out. So, before she left, she told me she was going to plan a surprise for me. I couldn't imagine what kind of surprise. After approximately three days had passed, Bea called me on the phone and suggested I come to visit her in Florida. That was a great idea. But I told Bea that I didn't have the money to splurge on a vacation. She said, "You don't need any money." What an angel.

I could see the Lord continually sending me an encouraging word. My friend Marguerite was invited to a church banquet by her mentors from True Way of Life World Ministry, Pastor Evvie Swansey and Senior Pastor Willie Benson III. She invited me to go with her. We arrived and were escorted to our assigned table. The speaker was Prophet Apostle Dr. Lloyd Benson Sr. from Baton Rouge, Louisiana. He began to speak words of encouragement and then announced Esther was in the room. He said he was looking for twelve women to come forward. He continually and emphatically stated Esther was in the house and summoned more women to come to the front of the banquet hall. I found myself in amazement and my stomach began to quiver. The water in our glasses began to move. When the speaker announced he needed three more women, he hollered, "Esther." Marguerite recognized the glasses of water and saw me hold my stomach and said, "It's you, Mathell." She instructed me to get into the Esther line. I jumped out of my seat uncontrollably and ran to the end of the line. That made me the twelfth woman.

The prophet announced he felt an anointing in the room, and that the spirit of Esther was in the house. He touched the shoulders of the first three women in line. He said that someone was next in line for a real big blessing. People were going to know her all around the world. My stomach really quivered when he said this. My mind went to the words Prophet George had said to me a few months earlier. The Louisiana prophet said, "Esther is in this room, and I can feel her presence." The first three women were told God loved them and ordered to step out of line. The next three women were told that they had done well in God's eyes. God loved them and they were to step out of line. The next three women were told special words from God through the prophet and were told to step out of line. Then he reached for the last three women, with me being the last one in line. The prophet told the first two women in my group that God loved them and was pleased with their work and to step out of line. When he got to me, he yelled, "Esther, you are in line for a big old blessing from God!" It took a minute for his words to register in my mind, because I was stuck on him calling me Esther. I really wasn't shocked, though, because this is exactly what Prophet George had said I would experience. My stomach was feeling like it did at Bishop Carter's church that fateful Sunday. The Louisiana prophet revealed that my blessing would be one the whole world would know about. As he prayed over me, I jumped for joy. I ended up breaking the heel off my shoe, but I didn't care at all. All I could do was cry for joy. I knew I was trying to live my life the way the Lord wanted me to. I believed God was going to bestow blessings upon me and my family, and the sky was going to be the limit. When the program was over, people began to walk up to me and touch me in admiration and awe. I knew my suffering was not in vain, and it would be over soon.

As the prophet spoke, I envisioned Esther as a young woman, a risk-taker, full of courage, with a kind spirit. She had a special love for people. She was blessed to encourage others and was a great reader. Esther was playful and dynamically royal. She was a woman of faith, and her trust in God was genuine. She had her mind set to save the Jews. She was able to walk under the auspices of God. Esther married a king. She had purpose and was prepared to die for what she believed.

After the dinner was over, I could hardly wait to get home and read the story of Esther in the Bible again. I needed to understand the prophet's premonition and guidance. Before going to the banquet, I was feeling weak and downhearted. I believe until this day that the words spoken truly came from God. His promises were re-established in my core. I knew that he would renew my strength and make me whole. After reading, I lay awake all night. I thanked the Lord for sending another powerful, prophetic word. The storm had just begun and I would have to face it.

Cruising with a Blind Man

The time had come to go on the cruise. I had to put my feelings behind me. Christine was my down-home buddy. We called each other sisters. We had planned our dream vacation almost a year prior and many situations had arisen. We had to count this as a perfect plan in spite of things. The feeling of excitement was jumping in each of us, and the fact that we were cabin mates was the best arrangement for two sisters in Christ who were facing both foreseen and unforeseen circumstances.

We had arranged to go first class all the way. The best means of transportation was arranged, limousine service to and from each of our homes. We were riding in style to catch our plane at Midway Airport. As we were riding, my thoughts wandered and singled out the memory that Mama Love Joy was supposed to be with us. She had been so excited about us going on a cruise. She could hardly wait to see her baby girl, Mathell, "float that boat." However, her motto was, "The show must go on." So I proceeded as she would have expected me to. I mentioned my thoughts to Christine. She leaned over to embrace me and she whispered softly, "God had another plan for her, baby, relax and enjoy this ride." Upon our arrival at the airport, I had prearranged a wheelchair escort. I was torn, worn, and weak in spirit. My body ached with pain, while my mind drifted in and out of thinking of my Mama Love Joy.

Our group flew out of Midway Airport to San Juan, Puerto Rico. Once we arrived in Puerto Rico, there was a welcoming team, and tour buses were awaiting our arrival. Reservations had been made for us at a fabulous hotel with an awesome view of a bridge that had lights twinkling at night. This bridge ran for miles over a body of water that fascinated me. As I looked out of our bedroom window, I could feel a calm spirit soothing my soul. The night we arrived, there was a jam session planned for our group in the hotel ballroom. I was not feeling up to a party, but I encouraged Christine to attend and enjoy herself. There were plenty of people for her to mix and mingle with in our group. There were eight hundred people from various parts of the world. I knew it was hard for her to leave me, even upon my request. She knew how brokenhearted I was. It was important to me that I get some time to be alone. In between her coming and going, I would cry out to God. I prayed for his comfort and his healing power over Mama Love Joy, her immediate family, friends, and all those who loved her. I prayed to accept the Lord's will over this matter. I asked God for His joy to come upon me so that I could enjoy this cruise. We were scheduled to board the Carnival Cruise Ship the next day, Saturday. I made a call to my son Victor and his wife, Felecia, at about six o'clock in the morning. Felecia told me that Victor had gone out to jog. It did not seem strange to me, since many people jog early in the morning. I told her we were getting ready to board the ship, and I was calling to extend my love to each of them. After boarding the cruise ship, we decided to sit on the lounge chairs on the outer deck, feel the warm breeze, and stare into the ocean. I consciously decided to enjoy the cruise and let happiness take over. While back at the hotel, I shared with Christine some of the precious requests that I had asked God for. I trusted that He truly knew how much I could endure. As I spoke softly, Christine reached slowly into her beach bag and grabbed a handful of tissues for me. Suddenly, I could hear myself sniffling and feel the tears streaming down my face. Christine said, "Your eyes look blood red like your blood pressure is up." She smiled at me and said, "Sister, do not make yourself sick. Believe in God, for everything is going to be all right."

I did have a serious eye problem developing and was diagnosed before this cruise by ophthalmologist Dr. Yuri Kim Kern; I just hadn't told Christine. I did not want her to worry and thought I would share my eye problem after the cruise. After a series of tests, the doctor's findings were that I had thyroid eyes. High pressure in my eyes was occurring and could cause blindness. I explained to the doctor all the trouble my family and I were facing, and that it caused me heartache and many sleepless nights. I am thankful that sharing my inner feelings brought about tender loving care in Dr. Kern's office. The first time I visited her office, she was very compassionate and promised to remember me and my family in her special time of meditation. During my trials, tears, and tests, Dr. Yuri Kim Kern and her staff were always professional. She was filled with words of encouragement every time I saw her. When she entered my room, she showed love with a cheerful greeting, a hug, and a big smile. At the end of each appointment, her assistant, Michelle, was just as delightful and caring. I thanked God for angels in many places.

I convinced myself that joy was coming to me in due time, but I could only feel what was happening in the moment. I knew my prayers were being heard by God, but I was still enthralled by sadness. I had to stand on what I believed, and that was that God makes no mistakes. One of my prayers was for me to be blessed with His good spirit. I felt free and renewed. After this time alone, I was ready to walk with my head up and enjoy this cruise. I was feeling thankful to be surrounded by a multitude of kind people.

My girlfriend, Christine, and I went to our cabin just before dinner and got dressed for the evening. We were dressed to kill in our fancy attire. Christine was draped in a black sequined dress with three layers of gold chains circling her neck. Her ears and her wrist were covered with gold. As she turned, the neckline in the back of her dress had a V-cut and was trimmed in gold beads. The bottom of her dress had a fluted tail. My girlfriend wore a pair of black beaded three-inch heels trimmed in gold sequins, with a handbag to match. Her hair was styled beautifully. She had finger waves on the right side of her head and a waterfall look with loose wavy curls on the other side. I was dressed in a black three-piece chiffon skirt set with a long black duster. The lapel was trimmed in gold all the way down to my ankles. I wore matching flat black sequin step-ins accessorized with a matching black and gold-beaded handbag. My hair was in a large ponytail with a wavy bang in front. Some said that I resembled Star Jones, the talk-show host. Christine and I were two of a kind when it came to dressing up. We loved the same colors, and we loved to go through the motions of putting on the Ritz. That was fun for us, and it also lifted our spirits. We went to the dining room for dinner and had a nice time, in spite of the circumstances. After dinner, we returned to our cabin and channel-surfed until we found a good TV movie. We fell asleep watching the movie.

I awakened from a dream at about five AM. I had a dream that my daughter-in-law Felecia was crying. She had great big tears drop from her eyes. When her tears fell to the cabin floor, they stretched out long and thin. They pierced a hole in the floor. I screamed, "Oh God, Victor. Oh God, what is wrong with Victor?" I yelled, "Christine, wake up girl, something is wrong with Victor." I explained to her in a panicked voice that something was wrong with Victor, and I needed to call his wife immediately. Christine warned me that the call would cost me an arm and a leg. I did not care. I had to call Victor's wife. Christine attempted to explain my dream to me. She said, "Baby girl, we are on water and you were probably dreaming as the waves were striking against the ship. I am sure Victor is all right." I could not be deterred. I picked up the phone and dialed the ship's operator. I hurriedly gave the operator my credit-card information and anxiously awaited my connection.

Felecia's sister answered the phone. I greeted her thinking that she was Felecia. I did not expect anyone else to answer her phone at five AM. The voice on the phone identified herself as Felecia's sister. I knew that Felecia's sister lived in Chicago, but she was answering the phone in Carbondale. There had to be a reason for her unexpected visit. When Felecia came to the phone, her voice sounded as though she had been crying. When I asked her if she had been crying, she replied, "No, my sinuses are acting up." I asked to speak to my son Victor. She told me that Victor had gone to Atlanta, Georgia. I knew better. I knew that Victor would not go to Atlanta without sharing that information with me ahead of time. Victor was not the son who would make a move without his mother's knowledge. Victor was the only son who wanted all my contact information so that he could reach me if he needed me while I was on the cruise. Consequently, I knew that if he had gone to Atlanta suddenly, he would have contacted me directly and in advance.

Victor was a singer and I knew he was expecting a call from the music industry any day. Therefore, he would have called me if he had received some news. I had a suspicious feeling that something was mighty wrong. I asked Felecia if she would try to shield my feelings or tell me the truth, if there was a problem. She said that she would shield my feelings. I explained to Felecia that I had just awakened from a nightmarish dream. In the dream, she was crying very hard. Now I was certain that my dream was true. Something was wrong with Victor. "Is Victor dead?" I asked.

She replied, "No."

I explained that I would return from the cruise within seven days. When I arrived, I would expect some truthful answers.

Victor had told Felecia not to tell me that he had been arrested until I returned home to Chicago. More importantly, he wanted someone to be there to comfort me. The remarkable vision of Felecia crying and Victor's trouble had come to me in a dream on the first night of the cruise. My friend, Christine, looked at me in amazement because the whole dream phenomenon was in the prophecy that had occurred while she and I attended church at the Colony All Nations Church in Chicago. This happened five months prior to the dream I had during the cruise. At that time, a prophet, a man of God, informed that there was a bad personal and spiritual storm coming my way. He conveyed that it was important to God that I be ready and know that God would be with me.

At seven AM, Christine suggested that we go to breakfast and try to regroup. I was still quite depressed, because I began thinking of how Mama Love Joy was lying in a coma and had experienced a massive stroke. Now I had to worry about the situation that was occurring with Victor in Carbondale. I was teary-eyed, but trying to smile. Everyone asked about Mama Love Joy when we entered the dining room. They were all aware of her condition as a result of our previous conversations on the plane. I was trying to laugh and not cry, because only God and Christine knew that I was headed for a new storm.

I had to be patient for the next six days on the cruise. I was constantly reminded of the words the prophet had predicted, "A storm is coming." I wondered how big the storm would be. Today, we are familiar with the terminology of storms. The weather forecasters alert us and provide warnings when a storm is approaching. They have the ability to predict the degree of devastation that we may expect in the aftermath of a storm. The forecasters classify the storms by categories. If the storm has hurricane force, we are told to prepare for a category one or two. With a hurricane category five, you will hear the warning, "Emergency, board up and relocate." I wondered what category of storm, in the spirit, I was facing.

Later, in the afternoon, Christine asked if I had seen them bring a blind man aboard the ship. I had not seen the blind man boarding. Christine showed me where he was being seated as we were approaching the outer deck. The gentleman had been seated in a shaded area in one of the deck chairs. He appeared to be a middle age man sitting all alone. He was just chilling. He had a brown complexion. From a sitting view, he looked to be about average height, medium build, and very well-manicured. He was holding a cane in his hand. He was wearing dark glasses, a nice cool shirt, a pair of shorts, and sandals. Christine and I had to pass him as we headed for our appointment in the spa. Christine's mind was just racing. She whispered to me, "Why is this blind man on this cruise? What can he see? If I were blind, I would not have wasted my money on a cruise if I could not see." As we approached the area where he was sitting, we realized that he was all alone. My voice became loud as I spoke to him. I did not want to pass by him without speaking. I said, "Hi, I'm Mathell."

He replied, "Hello, my sister. My name is Glenn."

I said, "How are you today?"

He responded, "Very well."

I explained there was another sister with me named Christine. Christine began squeezing my arm and holding me tightly. My inner voice was telling me to take a minute with Glenn. I wanted to let him express himself and let us know why he didn't board the ship with us in San Juan. Glenn had boarded when we arrived in St. Thomas.

Glenn and I met at a time when many storms were raging in my life. My thoughts were drawn to the spiritual song "Amazing Grace." In the song, there is a line that says, "I once was blind, but now I see." I can't begin to tell you the comfort Glenn brought to me. Oh, what a day! I have never been so touched while talking to anyone, and I have talked with many exciting people. But this talk really touched my heart, mind, body, and soul. This was a day of discovery for me. I learned my reasons for meeting the Blind Man on the cruise ship, September 4, 2000. This encounter touched me deep within. I came to realize that it was intended for me to learn to walk by faith and not by sight. This man had not been born blind. When I met him, he could not see through his natural eyes, but he could see from within his soul. He knew he was being led by God.

I had my camcorder with me, and I asked him if he would mind me filming his testimony. He replied, "Have it your way." This gentleman was most kind and seemed very sincere and anxious to tell about the spiritual road he had traveled. Glenn began by relating the dilemmas he had faced in getting to the ship. He was traveling without a companion, with a determined mind, blind and committed to testing his own faith. He believed that he could do all things through Christ. He believed that he could board a huge cruise ship, with assistance from the crew. He could walk by faith, if not by sight. He was walking as a blind man leaning solely on his faith in God.

I was intrigued by Glenn's presence. I was eager to hear what he had to say. I was certain that he had a wonderful message to share. Glenn invited us to take a seat near him on the deck. He began speaking freely and with no inhibitions. Glenn explained that he became blind while in jail awaiting trial. He was facing five to ten years in prison, if found guilty. Glenn startled us as he told of a violent attack that was made upon his life in his jail cell. A prisoner, who was assigned to his cell, jumped him suddenly during the night and stabbed him with an ice pick while he was sleeping. This attacker caught him off guard. Glenn woke up struggling in a panicked state, gasping and fighting for his life. During the awful attack, he was struck in his jugular vein. The vicious attack resulted in his blindness. Glenn explained that, after one is stabbed with an ice pick, the puncture closes and you bleed internally. He was rushed to the hospital. It was determined he was hemorrhaging internally.

After Glenn was stabilized, he realized that he could no longer see. He underwent shock treatments and psychological evaluations. This traumatic experience almost destroyed him mentally. The final outcome of this whole episode was that Glenn was declared legally blind. He continued his recovery and returned to jail sightless. He was not able to defend himself in unfamiliar surroundings, nor could he see to protect himself from any other attacker. Upon his return, he was blessed beyond belief. He received a pardon from the judge. Glenn gives all credit to almighty God. Glenn responded to me regarding that storm in his life by saying, "The Lord's word prevailed—even in a court room, I am the judge." Glenn realized that only God could release and pardon him from his chaos. He had gone from turmoil to serenity in God's performance of a miracle. He was blessed and set free. God activated "Footprints in the Sand" for Glenn. He had set Glenn free from all of his prisons to make a journey on a cruise ship, where he would ultimately meet me.

Glenn went on to explain that he was from Oakland, California. As he set out for this journey, he had budgeted four hundred dollars for his cruise expenses. He hired a prepaid cab service to take him to the airport. The cab broke down. He was advised that there were no other cabs available at that time. Determined to solve the problem, Glenn contacted another cab service and was informed that there would be a fifty-five dollar fee.

Glenn had hoped to arrive in San Juan with plenty of time to board the cruise ship. He thought to himself, maybe I should not go on this trip. He thought, "Oh well, I'm here at the airport and nothing else can happen." But there was a surprise awaiting Glenn. When he arrived at the airport check-in counter, he realized that he had arrived on Sunday, September 4, and his flight was scheduled for Saturday, September 3. He was a day late. At this juncture, he had two strikes of disappointment. He really started to believe that Satan was trying to block him. He began to wonder if a blind man could travel alone. The ticket agent informed him that she could book him on the next flight available to San Juan, where the cruise ship would depart. However, there would be an additional fee of $75 to purchase a ticket. Again, Glenn refused to turn around. Remember, he started out with only $400. He thought, I've already spent $55 for a cab that broke down before I could reach my destination. What next? He found out what was next, sooner than he thought.

As the agent began preparing the ticket, she was informed that the cruise ship had already departed San Juan, on its way to St. Thomas. Now, Glenn needed to purchase a ticket to fly into St. Thomas. This ticket would cost $125. Glenn thought, I really won't have any spending money when I get there, but thank God that this cruise is all-inclusive. Glenn would not need any money when he finally boarded the cruise ship. For that reason, he booked the flight to St. Thomas. Glenn believed that there was a spiritual blessing waiting for him on this cruise.

Glenn did not know that he would meet me on the cruise ship. Nor did I know that there was a man, led by God, moving toward me. His arrival would help me with my walk through my storms. I, too, was walking by faith and not by sight. I was walking by things unseen and yet unheard regarding my son Victor. Only God knew what I would be facing after this cruise was over.

As Glenn and I sat on the outer deck conversing, I had a confirmation that it was in divine order that he and I would meet in the middle of the ocean. The storm clouds were raging in my life. I could not determine how much the storm was raging. I realized how blessed I was after hearing the dilemmas Glenn had faced. As I heard Glenn tell his story, I began to wonder, "Who is this man?" He was speaking from his heart. He was so pleased that he had pursued his journey. He told me that it was a blessing for him to meet me. I felt so close to Glenn. He was such a warm person, laid-back and smooth. You could feel the peace within him. Glenn had been through so much. His words confirmed his belief that he could not have made it without the Lord on his side.

When Glenn finished his story, I began to tell him some of my heartfelt problems. I started with my Mama Love Joy. I told him of how she was lying in a coma. I explained that she had had a massive stroke. He spoke to me in a compassionate voice, "Oh, my sister." I went on to tell him of my grandmother Rosie Lee, who was also blind. She had come to Chicago for the first time in her life in February. I had only met her one time in 1981. However, I spoke with her by phone on every other weekend until she moved to Chicago.

I told Glenn how I began assisting my dad; his wife, Clara; and Grandmother Rosie Lee. Clara was diagnosed with Alzheimer's disease. All this was new to me. I had never been around my dad and his wife for any length of time. Suddenly, I was needed in that household to help my dad. He was a man who, back in the day, said he would never need me. He once asked me, "What would I need you for?" I began to feel weary as I shared my story with Glenn.

I told Glenn the story of the prophet who came to visit my church that April. This was a man who I had never seen before. This man delivered an urgent message directly to me from the Lord God Almighty. He told tell me that a storm was coming my way. He shouted, "Hear this and let the word of God lead you as you face your personal storm. Hold on and don't let go." I told Glenn everything, and you could just see that he was awestruck. I started to feel weak and out of breath as I began to tell about the dream I had early in the morning of September 4. I told Glenn that I believed in my mind and my heart that something was terribly wrong back home with my son, Victor. After our stories had been shared, it seemed as though there was a deep connection between the two of us.

The time had gotten away from us during our conversation. My girlfriend had sat wordless. My roommate, Christine, and I had to reschedule our appointment at the spa. Glenn asked if we were going ashore to shop. He said that he would like to go ashore because he wanted to purchase a cross of Jesus. I told him that we would take him with us. Christine and I went to our cabin to change out of our workout clothes. Once inside the cabin, Christine said, "You're always volunteering to help somebody. I don't know how you are going to enjoy yourself on this trip. Now you have taken on this man." I knew that spending time with Glenn would keep my mind off what really had me burdened down. Now Christine and I were preparing to do something we had never done before. We were going to take a blind man shopping.

We proceeded to go ashore and hail a cab. I began describing the beautiful sights to Glenn as we rode through St. Thomas. Our first stop was the jewelry store. It was so fascinating. I had never seen so much jewelry in all my life. Christine and I were Glenn's eyes. He wanted to purchase a cross, and we found the perfect cross for him. Then I suggested that it would be a wonderful keepsake if Christine and I each purchased a cross as well. We each found one that we loved. I told them that we have three crosses, one for our Father in Heaven, one for the Son of God, and one for the Holy Ghost. We were all happy as we left the jewelry store. My sentiment was that if I could help somebody in need, then my living surely was not in vain. I also felt fulfilled that my eyes were being used for someone who could not see. What a blessing for me.

When we returned to the ship, we were informed that our cruise director had planned a beach party ashore. I didn't really want to go ashore again. I was having difficulty walking. I was having difficulty with my sinuses, and my asthma had flared up. I really preferred to remain on the air-conditioned ship. My friend Christine told me that she was not going to stay aboard the ship. She wanted to go to the beach party. I told her to go and enjoy herself.

I called Glenn to see if he would like to enjoy an activity on the ship. Glenn was not a member of our tour group. He was an independent traveler. Before she left for the beach party, Christine encouraged me to help all the people I wanted to help. Glenn and I decided to change our clothes. I suggested to him to call and get an escort when he was ready, and meet me on the outer deck within the hour. When we both arrived at our designated area, we ordered refreshments and relaxed by the pool while we listened to some jams. I had my CD player and my camcorder with me. I suggested that we get in the beautiful pool. I ordered some tropical fruit drinks, and Glenn replied, "This is living."

After we entered the pool, we laughed, talked, and told jokes. I asked a passerby to use my camcorder to film us. It was just fantastic. My mind was suddenly free. People passing us thought that Glenn and I were a loving couple, or that we had been lifetime friends. We really were becoming friends, in the spirit. We were destined to meet at this time, and I knew that we would remain friends for a lifetime. We stayed on the deck for three hours. Christine had gone to the beach party and returned, but we were still living it up.

Glenn and I decided we would take a break and meet for dinner later that evening. I called for an escort to take him back to his cabin. Christine and I returned to our cabin to freshen up. When we all arrived at the dining-room area, we were really dressed to kill. Glenn had on a black tuxedo, and I mean, he was sharp. We had so much fun. Oh, what a night! After dinner, we escorted him back to his cabin. I put his card in the door, and I felt for his light switch. I did not feel it, and I asked Glenn where the light switch was. He laughed and said, "Do you think I can see with the lights on?" I had to hold on to the wall and laugh. The rest of our days were full of laughter and joy. We partied together all night the last night of our cruise. We exchanged phone numbers and addresses, and the next morning we prepared to disembark. I arranged for a wheelchair for both Glenn and myself to get off the ship and at the airport. Glenn's flight was scheduled to leave before our flight, so we stayed with him at his gate until his plane departed.

After Glenn had boarded his plane, Christine and I located our gate and our tour group. People from our group were asking, "Who was the blind man? Was that your relative?"

I wanted to say yes, but Christine and I just looked at each other and smiled. We knew we had entertained a total stranger. The Bible says, "Be careful how you entertain a stranger, for it might be an angel." We explained how we met Glenn on the cruise. No one could believe that we had met him for the first time.

One man said he had seen us shopping. "I saw you, miss, in the pool with the man," he replied.

One lady said she couldn't believe we had just met the man. "Wow, talk about being nice to someone. You two certainly were very kind to that blind man."

Another person followed with, "I wouldn't mind meeting you two anywhere."

Christine replied, "You mean meeting *her* anywhere. My girlfriend Mathell is the one. She just loves everybody."

We boarded the plane, and Christine was my seat partner. We fastened our seatbelts, held hands, and prayed for our safe arrival back home. The airplane backed out of the terminal and headed toward the runway. Up, up, and away. We were headed to Chicago, the Windy City. I was going back to face my personal storms. I pondered, "Oh God, what is up ahead?"

The Storms and the V-Boys

We landed safely in Chicago, and the limousine was there to take us to our respective homes. My mind drifted back to Mama Love Joy's condition, as the fun on the ocean was over. My heart started pounding when I thought about my son Victor. I wondered what it was that couldn't be shared with me while I was on my cruise. When I arrived home, Victor's twin, Verdell, was there to greet me. I knew the situation was serious, because Verdell put his arms around me and told me that he loved me. I told him that I loved him also, and asked what the situation was regarding his brother. Verdell held me tightly as he told me that Victor was in jail and in need of $200,000 for bail. Verdell explained that his older brother, Vaughn, had been stopped by the police in Texas. A search of his car revealed Vaughn was transporting one hundred and seventy-five pounds of marijuana. It was his intent to deliver the drugs to his superior in Carbondale. In concern for his own freedom, Vaughn agreed to identify his superior. Vaughn did not know that this individual had already left the United States. When the Drug Enforcement Agency (DEA) attempted to serve the warrant, that person was nowhere to be found. Suddenly, Vaughn was whipped into a stormy situation.

This arrest would require Vaughn to face the three-strikes penalty. Vaughn knew that he could not accept responsibility for the marijuana. Therefore, Vaughn devised a plot to deliver the drugs to his brother Victor. A new warrant was issued for Victor. This conversation with my son Verdell explained the significance of my dream aboard the ship. The prophetic word had come true.

With this news, I felt faint. "No! No! No! Not my baby. Oh, God, what I am I going to do?" I fell across the bed. I kicked and I screamed. I called out to Jesus and cried like a baby.

Verdell held me and gently patted my back. He rubbed my head and prayed, "Help my mama, Jesus." Verdell continued to comfort me until I fell asleep. When I awoke, I asked Verdell when all of this happened. It had occurred on the evening of September 3. My frightful dream about Victor had occurred in the early morning, aboard the ship, on September 4.

Verdell had to travel back to his home in Carbondale. Before leaving, he explained that nothing could be accomplished until Victor's court date. He suggested that I come to Carbondale, a week before Victor's hearing, to meet with his lawyer. I would hear all the facts at that time. He also told me that Victor would be giving me a call as soon as possible. Verdell assured me that Victor was strong, and that he believed in God. He also reminded me of the divine word, which proclaimed we would all be caught in a terrible storm, but that we would all make it through the storm.

My thoughts returned to Glenn. I picked up the telephone and called him. I related the whole story of what I had faced when I arrived back in Chicago. I also told him that Mama Love Joy's suffering was over and that she had died. He told me to believe the word that was spoken to me before these raging storms began. He reminded me that this storm was going to pass. He assured me that I could rely on him at any time. I asked him for his address and his last name. He told me that his last name was Benton. Little did I know at the time that my sons would go on trial in a small town by the name of Benton, Illinois.

Before our conversation ended, Glenn thanked me for all of the kindnesses I had extended to him during the cruise. He gave me the assurance that God was going to help me through the raging storms. He prayed that the comfort of the Lord would be upon me for the loss of Mama Love Joy, and that the Lord would strengthen me to hold out. This man's faith in God had truly been a comfort to me.

At this point in my life, I was going through some pretty dramatic stuff. I was told I would be entering into a terrible storm, and dark clouds would be over my life, but I was to hold on. The prophet was crystal clear about the storm hitting my three boys, and he was right. The storm hit Vaughn first. My oldest son needed to point the finger at someone, for he was approaching his third strike in the penal system. His health was bad. He was so fearful that he pointed to his brother Victor as the culprit, and Victor was arrested. This was the beginning of the storm.

I wanted to hear another word from Prophet George, but I wanted it to be appointed by the Lord, like the first time. After returning from the cruise I attended another Sunday service at Colony All Nations Church and arrived early in order to sit up front. After getting situated, I looked around and there was Prophet George sitting in one of the back pews. I didn't get up and say anything to him because I wasn't sure that was the direction the Lord wanted me to go. During the service, First Lady Faye came to me and said, "Your preacher is here."

For a moment I had forgotten he was there, because the sermon was so powerful. I said, "Who?"

She responded, "Prophet George," and I smiled. A few moments passed. Then, Prophet George walked up and spoke to Faye and me.

I said, "Hello, Prophet George, do you remember me? I am the woman with the three boys, and the storm has hit."

He kindly turned around to look at me and said, "Yes, I remember you." I said, "My oldest son set up one of my twins and he is incarcerated."

Faye walked away, giving Prophet George and me a little privacy. He had the most peculiar look on his face as he held up his hand—like the motion to "talk to the hand"—and said, "Storm ain't over, storm ain't over yet!" He began to back away from me.

I said, "The storm ain't over?"

He repeated the four-word phrase and said, "Remember everything I said." He backed away out of my sight.

I called for Christine, who was down the hall. I painfully yelled, "Christine, he said my storm ain't over."

I thought back on all Prophet George Davis had said to me on the Sunday he prophesied my storm was coming. He said the storm was going to be terrible, but I was to faint not. God was going to bring all four of us to the cross, but something terrible was going to happen to all my boys. He said to hold on, and I would reap what God had for me. I wasn't looking forward to the storm that was hovering over the heads of my sons. I had to save my V-boys through prayer. My relationship with God began to grow more and more by the second.

Many of life's tests and challenges had begun to attack my family, but I had been spiritually promised that everything was going to be all right.

I arrived two days before the hearing and motion of discovery. There was an appointment made by Victor's lawyer to go over the prosecutor's findings with Felecia and me. His lawyer explained to us how Vaughn was brought back to the Carbondale area by five task enforcement agents from the DEA. These agents boarded an airplane with one hundred seventy-five pounds of marijuana.

There also was a warrant issued for the delivery of these drugs to a man who resided in Carbondale, but had fled the country before the airplane Vaughn and the agents were on could land. The lawyer who was representing Victor wanted me to talk to Vaughn and see if he would tell me the truth about Victor's involvement. I had Felecia take me straight to Vaughn's house, which was about twelve minutes away. When we arrived, I asked my daughter-in-law to stay in the car. I told her I wanted to talk to my son alone. Persistence is what I do best. I began holding on to the rail of the stairway leading to Vaughn's front door. With what little strength I had, I needed to find the right words and to speak in a calm voice to get the answers I needed to understand what happened to Victor. I came in reaching for Vaughn to hold on to. I asked him, "Baby, tell Mama what happened." He was speechless, and I needed some answers. I was asking in a louder tone when his telephone rang. He looked at his caller ID and said, "This is one of the agents I've been working with." Vaughn answered the call and was informed that I had just gotten off the train. My son clearly stated to the caller, "I know, she is standing here with me."

I was stunned. I asked Vaughn, "Who knew of my arrival? Am I being followed?"

He did not answer me directly. He let the caller know he needed to talk with his mother. I started to become hysterical. I asked, "Who is that questioning you, Vaughn?" My son hit his fist on the desktop and said, "This is an Agent from DEA Task Enforcement." Vaughn looked at me while on the telephone and said, "The agent would like to meet with you, Mama."

I plainly said, "No, I am not meeting with anybody but who I am supposed to meet with." I was to meet with Paul Christenson, Victor's lawyer. I heard Vaughn say to the caller that this was not supposed to go this way for his kid brother. Vaughn told the agent that he needed to talk to his mother. He said he would call back later.

I was standing in front of my son with tears falling out of my eyes. I demanded Vaughn tell me the story of how he had placed all these drugs on Victor. He was speechless as he stood before me repeating himself over and over again. "It was not supposed to go like this, Mama." My questions were not being addressed. Vaughn suddenly fell onto the couch in front of me crying, "Mama, I just don't know what went wrong. I am deeply sorry for this trouble we face, Mama. Please stay strong and pray this saga will end in Victor's favor."

I could not stand to be in his company any longer. I began to ease my way toward the side door. As I was walking out, I shouted out loud and screamed uncontrollably, "Help me, Lord, save my baby. Help this child who is corrupt. Hold me up, Lord." I turned and looked at Vaughn breathlessly and said, "You better get Victor out of this trouble, or you might as well shoot me in my back." I walked through the side door. I did not believe I was strong enough to make it through this trial. After I had made it outside of Vaughn's house, Felecia came up the stairway to assist my limp, worn, broken-down body to the car. I knew God's word covered me and these boys. My daughter-in-law sat behind the steering wheel and drove us to her house. Felecia put me to bed. This is where I prayed my best. While resting, I prayed that God would divinely intervene. I had to trust my beliefs that if the almighty was for me, who could be against me.

I felt for Vaughn. He was trapped by the enemy's plan with no way out at this point. This scene had to be played out, and my hope was for the best for Victor. I told Felecia I was torn between the feelings of both sons, not to mention how Victor's twin must feel. I knew the pressure of this nightmare would get to Vaughn and worsen his medical condition. I believed that with this kind of pressure, he would be thrown into a seizure or diabetic coma and suffer with out-of-control high blood pressure.

The blame and the shame were on Vaughn. He had been in the

hospital while the trial had been going on with Victor. I was concerned that Vaughn's health had failed him, but I learned he had shot himself near the rear end. I was told that Vaughn had given a statement to the police that his first thoughts were to shoot his own brains out for what his brother Victor was going through. He knew it was his fault. Vaughn was truly blessed that God turned that aim from his head to his tail. He was a sorry man. He was feeling misunderstood.

Vaughn was the prosecutor's witness. These suicidal actions had proved him not creditable, and he was unavailable to testify. I was called to the witness stand by the defense attorney to tell of Vaughn and Victor's character. I had to testify. My mind was in a spin, and my heart was pounding through the walls of my chest. I could feel the thumping. My walk to the witness stand was like the most frightening of dreams. I was walking slowly with a cane in my right hand and limping. I was praying within my soul as I raised my right hand to swear and tell the truth, so help me God. I began to speak, not to hurt either son, but to be as clear as possible in hopes that Victor would be blessed out of facing a sixty-year sentence. The judge recessed for lunch. As the bailiff and the marshals escorted Victor out of the side door, I went into the corridor. I was followed by Verdell, Felecia, and Brian. I saw the security team walking my son to a private elevator. They were taking him to a holding cell. I belted out, "Victor, I love you. Marshals, let my son go."

When my words came out, Victor threw me a kiss and said, "Keep the faith, Mama."

Suddenly, I felt a pair of hands touch me on the shoulders. As I turned, it was Verdell. He looked me in my eyes and said, "Mama, are you all right?"

My response was, "Yes. I am just fine." I was speaking from my heart and soul. After a week of viewing the evidence and approximately three hours of deliberation, the jury found Victor not guilty. The words, that Victor was free, answered and relieved many people who were praying with us. The news of this miraculous release spread as fast as the wind could blow. Victor was out of trouble. Everyone was saying how wonderful it was that this son could be found not guilty, and the case dismissed in a week-and-a-half. I was so grateful that the trouble between my two sons had ceased.

Victor was released after spending four months in jail. Once released, Victor realized that all he had accumulated was gone. The wedding gifts and money that were confiscated were never returned. By the time Victor returned home, his bank accounts were depleted, and his car had been repossessed. This placed great hardship on Victor and his new wife. He felt desperate to regain his posture and needed to recoup his losses. So in desperation, he made a call to get back into business. This is when Victor learned his real lesson in life. He could not handle the fall. He had lost so much so quickly. He had just gotten married, and his new wife didn't deserve the poverty they were facing. Neither Felecia nor I knew of Victor's decision to begin selling drugs.

God had given several people the task to warn Victor of trouble ahead, but he didn't heed the warning. Victor would say later that he was forced back into the business for survival. Victor told me that trouble never seems like trouble because it is so easy to get into. It is a road we sometimes like to walk and dance on; however, it is a road that is not easy to exit.

Victor had a bad feeling when he got on the road with his business partner. It was his first drug delivery after his release from jail. He heard God talking to him, "Let those who have ears hear, and those who have eyes see." Not only did Victor not listen to God, he didn't try to understand what God meant. All he knew was that he had to deliver twenty pounds of marijuana that was in the car he was riding in. For a fleeting moment, Victor thought of not making the delivery. And then he dismissed that thought. Victor shared a spiritual lesson that I had taught him with the driver, "Cuz." Victor showed him a hundred-dollar bill and asked if he wanted it. Cuz said "Yes." Victor folded the bill in half and asked him if he still wanted it after it was folded. Cuz said "Yes." Victor crumpled the bill and threw it on the floor of the car and asked him if he still wanted it. And Cuz said in an exasperated voice, "Yes, man, I want the C-note."

Victor then told him, "God wants you to know he will take you if you are crumpled, folded, or thrown on the ground. He still wants you to keep the faith in his ability to work through your life."

Victor always liked to share this spiritual story. Now he was feeling the reality of what he was saying to Cuz. He had a compelling and overwhelming feeling that the trip he was making would not be completed. Minutes later, they were stopped by the police. Cuz had a good driving record, and all plates and stickers on the vehicle were current. When the police commanded them to open the trunk, Victor indicated the entire stash was his. He made sure Cuz was not involved. This too was a set-up, but not directed by Vaughn this time.

Victor again faced major prison time. This left his wife and son destitute. With the first jail arrest on his record, this arrest made Victor look like a marijuana kingpin. In actuality, he was only a middleman.

I had heard Bishop Noel Jones preach at the City of Refuge Church and I had been watching him ever since. My dad had also started tuning in and watching. He became a TV member. He had not attended church since he was a boy. The bishop's anointed words arrested his attention, and my dad became a faithful viewer. Through watching Bishop Jones, Dad saw a clip of Bishop T.D. Jakes teaching and preaching. He grew spiritually hungry to hear him speak. I was happy to see my dad seek the Lord's words of encouragement. I thanked God over and over for drawing Dad close to him at this time in his life. When I was a baby, I needed my father the most and he was not there. In my life's journey thus far, I was blessed to have had the Browns and others in my life and my children's lives. It was now my dad's time to learn to become all he could be to his family.

My problems started to feel overwhelming to me. I attended church somewhere every Sunday. I attempted to go to Bible class on Wednesday nights. As the problems escalated, my finances deteriorated. I truly needed encouraging. I wept and sang unto the Lord, night after night, for weeks and years. I shed so many tears for such a long time that I had to go to an eye specialist. I was having severe headaches that were diagnosed as high pressure in my eyes, and the existing thyroid problems caused them to always be very red. I was not that well and, at one point, I had injured my leg and was on crutches. I graduated to using a cane to get around. I did not see well at night, and I had been diagnosed with a sleep disorder. I saw no way for me to attend night services, unless someone could drive me. I discussed my feelings with Jackie, and she suggested that we should try to see Bishop Noel Jones.

I often watched Bishop Jones on TV. He captivated my attention and my heart. It seemed as though he was looking straight into my eyes to my soul. He was saying, "I want to pray with you." His invitation was an open invitation and extended to all to fellowship with the family at City of Refuge. Bishop Jones looked very sincere as he asked that we write him and allow him to pray with us. I accepted the words that God had instilled in him to draw me to his church. This was part of the perfect plan to keep me holding on to the promises delivered through Prophet George Davis.

I was making plans to see the Bishop Noel Jones in person. My prayer was to be reassured that I could help everybody in my immediate family. The night before I left for Los Angeles, California, Victor phoned me and wanted to connect with his twin on a three-way conversation. When Verdell answered, he stated he was just about to call me and let me know that he had been called by his pastor, Ramon Jones, to preach that Sunday. I told him to hold that thought while I switched back to Victor. Then we all could rejoice over him delivering the word of God. Both twins were happy knowing that God was truly with us. I had wishful thoughts of how I could be in St. Louis to hear my son carry the word of God before a church congregation. I explained to each son that mama was on a mission to keep receiving the Word and the power to continue to carry on. We ended our talk by rearranging a song and singing it from our hearts, "I Don't Believe God Brought Us This Far to Leave Us."

When Jackie and I arrived at church, it was packed. I was just fussing with Jackie because we were not early, but we were not late. When we entered, the only seats vacant were all the way in the back. We had the last seats inside the sanctuary. I realized that it did not matter where we sat, because I was on a spiritual journey.

His prophetic words were, "Don't Look Back and If You Do, See the Son of God on Your Trail." As he ended the sermon, Bishop Noel Jones began to sing the same song my twins and I sang the night before I arrived in Los Angeles. The song was, "I Don't Believe He's Brought Me This Far to Leave Me." Bishop had two famous singing artists in the house, and he asked them to take over the song. Stevie Wonder jumped in with his vocals and did a duet with Ali Woodson, former singer of the Temptations. They did a holy jam and spiritually rocked the house. In the meantime, we were seated in the back of the room. I was singing right along with them, and there was a man standing by Jackie. He elbowed her and said, "I knew she was somebody, I just don't know her name." He thought he had seen me before on television and that I was a big singer. Another lady came up to me while I was soulfully singing. I was convinced God was with me. I went out to see the bishop and pressed my way to get my envelope to him. I spoke with the head of security after morning service and explained my dilemma. I was told by security that he would radio back where the bishop was and ask if I could come back there. The bishop gave permission for me to be brought back to him. He was being filmed, and his armor bearer came out and told me the bishop wanted me to come back for the evening service. I had a big yellow envelope explaining about my sons' problems. I identified myself on the front of the envelope that I had prepared for Bishop Noel Jones. I asked the man if he would give it to the bishop, and he gladly took it. I used a black marker to write in big bold letters, "Bishop, I need your prayers. I am a praying mother of three sons I call the V-boys. I believe them to be the three Hebrew boys. They are in a fiery furnace and the heat just got turned up higher." I did attend the evening service, and he spoke a powerful word. When I left, I was encouraged and felt rejuvenated for my journey.

After my first spiritual journey to meet Bishop Noel Jones, I sent him a thank-you card for taking time to pray for my boys. I also periodically sent updates through the mail in regards to my sons.

When Bishop Jones came to Chicago, I was determined to see him again. I would arrive two hours early each time. I once heard my Godmama Verona say the early bird gets all the worms. Sure enough, when I entered through the door of the church, there was a lady dressed in a nurse's uniform. We greeted each other with a hello and a smile. I told her I had an urgent matter and began telling her my situation. She noticed my hands were shaking, and then she touched me by the hand. She said, "Everything is going to be all right for your children." She put her loving arms around me. She was a compassionate sister who could feel my pain. I graciously thanked her for the embrace and the care shown. This lady reached for my envelope and told me not to worry. "When one of the armor bearers comes in, I will give it to him personally," she told me. "I will find you in the church and let you know that it has been delivered." The bishop acknowledged me by raising the envelope up high as he prayed and said, "They will find their way back home."

After my envelope had been delivered to the bishop, I felt I could go on with the other pressing matters in my life.

Felecia and I would attend every scheduled court date. She would go to the court hearings and we would pray together. She was threatened with eviction, experienced repossessions, and was stripped of her finances. Felecia worked a job, but it could not handle all the expensive things that fast money had accrued. Before long, Felecia had to move again and try to hold things together. Ultimately, the stress became too overwhelming for her. She began to drink alcohol and party to get away from the daily stresses she encountered. The pain of missing her husband and feeling loved prompted her to mentally run away from her troubles. She ran into a lover's arms because she thought it would help her hold on to her sanity. Victor began to sense a change in Felecia during her jail visits. I noticed the change, too, plus she wasn't as loving and caring of me anymore. I believed the more she attended the court sessions, the more she became convinced that the evidence was greater than the word of God over Victor's life. On one of their visits, Victor asked Felecia how she was handling their situation. She said okay, but Victor felt like that was not the truth. Eventually, she broke down and told her husband that she was having an affair. There were no secrets between my son and me. He truly needed a shoulder to cry on after it appeared that Felecia's faith was fading fast. These were tough times for the newlyweds, but they worked through this very bumpy situation together, with the help of God. Victor understood and still understands the security his wife was stripped of during that critical time. Victor understood how poor decisions create extreme life-altering situations.

Vaughn subleased his apartment to Felecia. He did this in response to Victor's request. It was the least he could do. Unfortunately,

Vaughn did not believe that Felecia could handle the rent or the bills. Although Felecia had a college degree, there were not many doors open to her at the time. Shortly thereafter, Vaughn evicted Felecia from the apartment so that he no longer would have to worry if the rent would be paid or not. Now Victor could fully appreciate what Felecia was going through and forgave her indiscretions. Felecia understood what Victor was going through and forgave his bad decisions. They began to live their lives together until the storm kept getting worse. Then, another blow came to take all three of the boys at once.

Conspiracy Hits

Then, suddenly, conspiracy charges were enforced on each of my sons simultaneously. Everybody wanted to know what they had done. I attempted to explain their problems as best I could. The number of years the boys would receive if found guilty was astronomical for each of them and so overwhelming for me.

Vaughn's trials and terror had him in shock. He was extradited out of Florida on a suppressed indictment. The very next day, May 2, Victor was on his last day of work release after having served two years in prison for possession of drugs. He was served at his job and transported to East St. Louis, Illinois, on the same indictment. Verdell was serving a five-month sentence at a federal penitentiary for structuring and money laundering. He had about four months to go. Now, another slam was in his face. This son was facing the same charges as his two brothers. A notice was given to Verdell with explicit instructions. A new court date for the charges had not been released. Verdell was now facing twenty years imprisonment, if found guilty.

The boys were all incarcerated for conspiracy. I worked with each of their lawyers, one by one. I continued to work relentlessly, with outside resources, to gain Victor's early release from federal prison. I wrote letters with the help of a lady named Blanche Abner. We made phone calls and prayed incessantly together. These letters were directed to local, state, and national political figures. I e-mailed local celebrities and visited the offices of Operation Push. I was told there was nothing they could do for me. I was told that I would need ten thousand dollars just to have someone read the motion of discovery that consisted of twenty-five hundred pages. I could not accept the thought, for a split second, that my sons' cases were hopeless. When I left the meeting and exited through the doors of Operation Push, I screamed in the middle of the street as though I had lost my mind. I was penniless and I felt helpless. I had just been told, by one of the lawyers at Push, to brace myself, because there was a great chance that I would never get my boys free. I prayed out loud to reach the ears and the heart of God Almighty to please remember your promise that they would make it to the cross. I was not in any condition to drive. I had to call my dear friend and angel, Marguerite, to come with an extra driver and drive me home.

Pastor Wheeler Parker was a barber in the town where I grew up. He cut my dad's hair. When each of my sons turned one year old, he gave them their first haircut. He was a friend to our family, a pastor to many, a devoted husband, a very wonderful person, and an awesome man of God. He lived directly across the street from my dad. I had to keep on seeking the Lord and not be discouraged. So, I had to keep on seeking to be ministered to during these storms. I would see Pastor Parker just about every visit to my dad's house, and he always took the time to ask me, from across the street, how things were going. I always thanked Pastor Wheeler Parker for his time and concern. I could feel his prayers and his words of kindness. They brought cheer to my heart. I thank God for another angel.

Reverend Dr. Jimmie Daniels of Summit, Illinois, was my son Vaughn's Aunt Connie's minister. She had told him about me and what I was going through with all three V-boys. He was caring enough to counsel me when I came out to visit one Sunday morning. He asked his members to pray over me. I felt the favor of God.

Reverend Dr. Jimmie Daniels also referred me to Congressman Danny Davis. Reverend Daniels thought that Congressman Davis was familiar with the Southern district. When I phoned the congressman, he told me that I was a constituent of Congressman Jesse L. Jackson Jr. and that he was out of town. Congressman Davis was compassionate and attentive to me in the absence of my congressman. I remember getting a call from Congressman Davis that Christmas. His call expressed comforting words of hope for my sons' return. I knew God was working for me through the kindness he displayed. The objective was to keep hope alive in me. I learned to lean on God and to encourage myself when there was no one else. Senator Barack Obama had just won the election and became senator. I wanted to congratulate him personally and pray into his life that the Lord would continue to order his steps, and we all can see that God did. I had seen his beautiful family on TV and felt that he was a loving father. I wanted to tell him about the wrong turns my three sons had taken in life. They had already done state time for the crime. I just did not understand about federal time. I felt these sons needed to be pardoned, and I was willing to put up a fight for what I believed as their mother. Soon after I sent my letter, I received an envelope from the United States Senate in Washington DC. I gave thanks to God for a reply.

So I hope you can understand why receiving this letter increased my desire to just hold on. That Senator Obama's office had taken the time to answer my letter was a blessing to my life. Sometimes it only takes a word or two for a person not to give up. I was an inexperienced writer, and the letter had been received by a Constituent Service Representative, Office of U.S. Senator Barack Obama, Chicago, IL. I could see that the reader of my letters thought my issues were concerning the Illinois Department of Corrections. I had included, in my package, a letter from a Supervisor of Southern Illinois Adult Transition Center, in regards to Victor. I believed this particular letter threw the reader off. This was a character reference letter. I realized that sometimes you can send too much information. Senator Obama's office only took care of federal concerns, and all of my sons were in federal penitentiary. Things still worked out. Senator Barack Obama's office referred me to State Senator Debbie Halvorson's office. I called and made an appointment. When I walked into her office, a beautiful young lady introduced herself as Toi Hutchinson. Since then she has become state senator and is using that same office. She was very compassionate to my situation as I explained why I was there. She took all of my important papers and put them in a file. She prayed with me and encouraged me in every way to keep the faith. Senator Debbie Halvorson came in and Toi briefed her on my problem. She was lovely and expressed a very sincere concern for my problem. She gave me a big hug. Her kind words soothed my mind and heart. A couple of weeks passed and I stopped by Senator Halvorson's office. Toi informed me that Congressman Jesse Jackson Jr. was who I should see. I smiled and told her that I had already been to him, and his office was working diligently. My contact was Ms. Annette deCaussin. She was a beautiful and loving lady. I remember the day I met with Congressman Jackson. I shared my heartfelt dilemmas with him. Suddenly, I became overwhelmed and burst into tears. I told him about my son, Vaughn, who was close to dying in the penitentiary. Ms. deCaussin reached for me and embraced me. She told me, in a whispered tone, that things would work out for me. She offered me a glass of water and a box of tissues. During this meeting, Congressman Jackson told Ms. deCaussin to gather information concerning the three V-boys and to let him know of her findings. He assured me that after the investigation, he would get back to me, and he did just that. He, Annette deCaussin, and his entire staff gave me the hope I needed to continue my fight.

I then had an idea of bringing a Gospel play to town for a fundraiser. I was sure this play could bring in enough money for many families in need of proper legal representation, like mine. This play had been put together by my goddaughter, Casey. She and her entire team were willing to waive a deposit. But, I had no money to pay for a venue. The name of the play was "Lord knows I've tried". I must say I was truly trying.

The next morning, Bishop Noel Jones, in Los Angeles, California, was being televised where I lived. His words of sincerity touched my heart. I told my dad to look at him one morning, and he did. He felt the same care from him and told me to get a reservation on an airplane. He would put my ticket on his charge card, so I could go out and try to see the bishop. My dad was frightened that one more letdown would kill me. I believed that God led my way to a gracious and encouraging man of God. I felt blessed. The spirit of God in him made me feel like I could keep on pressing to free my boys.

When I returned from California, I attended church with Verdell who was awaiting trial and out on his own recognizance. I was thrilled at what God was doing in his life. He was going to baptize seven people. Oh, what a joy. This was my first time meeting Pastor Ramon Jones Jr. of St. Louis, Missouri. He became my son in Christ. He appointed me to be the mother of his church after he heard me sing, "God Has Been So Good to Me." This was the first time he had met me. I feel this was another one of God's divine connections.

Unfortunately, during this time, there was another storm for Victor, Felecia, and Victor's son Ricky. Two weeks after Victor was sentenced to do two more years in the federal penitentiary, Felecia was notified that Ricky's mom was killed in a car crash on her way home from work. She was burned beyond recognition. It was a horrible time for our family. I had a severe asthma attack shortly after hearing about this trauma. I needed to hear the words of God to soothe my soul. I also leaned on Mother Davis who informed me that she had shared my story with the other mothers of the church. She believed God could move the mountains set before my family. I soon received a call from Mother Valentine and

Mother Hurd extending their helping hands and words of comfort. Felecia managed to contact Victor, who was still in transition, and informed him of the horrendous news. They proceeded with a plan to get Ricky to come with Felecia. Felecia sent legal paperwork to Victor and kept in constant contact with him so that he could talk to his son. This way he could make sure that they were all doing okay.

Victor had spent two years in a state prison and had transitioned back into the community at a halfway house. After spending almost a year at the halfway house, seven days prior to his release date, he was indicted on Federal conspiracy charges. During his time at the transitional center, he and Felecia had a son of their own and had moved into a lovely starter home. Victor became the assistant manager at Burger King, and Felecia was an administrative executive assistant at a private school. When the trouble hit, Felecia had to take a lot of time off of work. It was a blessing that God was strong in her life, and she kept praying for her family. The people at Felecia's job and her friends and some of her family, including my dad, helped them tremendously. Although she missed Victor terribly, she was able to keep pushing, for her sake and the boys'. The boys and Felecia would go to see Victor, and it would make them all feel closer together. I had to keep working on behalf of the storms the other boys faced.

While I worked on getting Victor home, Felecia worked on holding her family together. Victor worked on spreading the Lord's word in prison. He led a powerful prison ministry and sang in the choir there for different events outside of the prison. Victor touched so many people with his positive outlook and humbleness. It truly made a difference in how his time was spent in prison.

I left no stone unturned. My efforts encouraged Congressman Jackson's investigating team to seek additional information regarding Victor's sentencing. Victor's supervisor at Burger King, Donna, attended court appearances with Felecia on his behalf, and he received letters of support from the corporate office. Eventually, after many prayers, phone calls, and follow-up correspondence from the Congressman's office, Victor was released from jail. Every time we went to court, Victor's sentence was reduced. He started with thirty years and ended with two years. He was actually released in a year-and-a-half.

He came out of prison rejoicing about how many people God had sent to help him. Victor returned to Burger King after his release. Subsequently, he has been promoted to general manager in the community in which he now resides. He resumed his music career and began the process of attaining his college degree in education. Victor now believes in God's realities and totally relies on the miracles and grace of the Lord.

I decided to spend some meaningful time with my sons' wives and children. Felecia and Sharetta had to travel five hours to get to my place, and they did not have two coins to rub together between the two of them. So I had to ask some of my friends to help me get them here. I also wanted to have refreshments to serve my family and friends.

As they each arrived they began talking about their trails. Vaughn's wife, Shelia, spoke first. She placed her hands over her eyes as they filled up with tears. Then she said, "My five children sleep on the floor in sleeping bags." She also stated that she had not been able to find a place for six people that she could afford. Having to bunk in other people's homes and trying to stay off the streets had taken a toll on them. The children had a chance to speak. One of them feared living in a homeless shelter again. Shelia could not bring back all the children's clothing or their bedroom furniture. She lost all their belongings in storage due to lack of funds. All she had was what she could carry in her trunk.

Sharetta had just had a newborn baby boy. He did not have diapers or clothes. She told how I had asked one of my friends, Helen

Alford, who was the director of a community center in St. Louis, to help Sharetta and the kids. I told Helen about the situation and she brought gifts and money to accommodate Sharetta for about one month. Sharetta shared how thankful she was to God for all the help. But she didn't know how they were going to continue to make it. My heart was shattered listening. It seemed that God truly was making a way for her. While we were talking, Sharetta received a call from Verdell. We took a break so they could talk. My son told Sharetta to call his very dear friend, Matthew, and Matthew's wife, Tasha. Verdell had spoken to them, and they were going to bless her and the children tremendously. This was another experience of God making a way out of no way.

Again, everyone wanted to know what the boys had done in order to be facing these kinds of sentences. I recall sharing our troubles with my closest friend, Bea, and her reply was, "Did they kill some people, Mathell?" I moved my head from side to side to tell her no. I was speechless and drowning in my own tears. My heart was throbbing, full of sadness for each of my precious sons. My trials and tests taught me to call on God for help. My sons soon learned to call on God, also.

I remember one hot summer night. Vaughn called me on the telephone and said, "Mama, I am going to leave Carbondale and relocate to Florida with my family." I asked him who they were going to live with. He laughed and reminded me that Aunt Penny had left town, leaving everything and everybody. She had heard someone speak of a Christian Center that was a house of hope. She had little hope left, so she decided to leave. Vaughn explained that he had been keeping up with his favorite auntie for the last six months. They had been talking on the telephone every week. My sister shared with him her progress in such a short time. Vaughn told me she had been encouraging him to come there based on her success. Penny had access to a directory of Christian Centers, and she had started looking into a family ministry for Vaughn and his family. I questioned my son as to whether he and his family could stay where Penny was living. He explained the information Aunt Penny shared with him about her unit being for rehabilitating women only. My son was happy for her, and he understood her need to up and leave. He was thankful that they trusted each other, and that he had been keeping close tabs on her. Penny had confided in him a year ago that she needed help and might relocate. These two were always very close, and were around the same age. My sister was only ten years older than Vaughn. When she was a little girl and Mama Mildred would bring her over to my Godmama's house, she was the big auntie and he was her first nephew. There was a strong bond between the two of them.

A few days had passed after Vaughn and I had extensively talked about his move to Florida. Penny called me in reference to Vaughn needing a fresh start. She convinced me that his wanting to leave the old wounds from Carbondale behind was a step in the right direction. She wanted me to understand her blessed steps toward overcoming her drug addiction and leaving old things behind. She was seeking God and a new beginning. She strongly expressed her belief in new establishments for her nephew. I started to see the value of restoration for Vaughn and his family. I listened as Penny talked at a whisper about her itinerary in Florida. She continued to tell of how she flew out to Florida two weeks before. Her mind was totally made up to flee for her life. Her spirit had led her to run and seek a second chance to live. As she began to get deeper into the heart of explaining her bold move, she was called to a meeting that ended our conversation suddenly.

Penny called again. She expressed her gratitude to this Christian Center for a second chance at life. Her trial and deliverance were felt deeply in my heart. Tears of joy were pouring out of my eyes for my baby sister's liberation. I was very grateful. It was important to Penny that I not be angry with her. In our conversation, she expressed how she respected and loved me. Penny would never let me forget that she was my baby sister, and I was her only sibling. She shared her heart's belief that if her big sister understood her reasons for the quick escape, then I would be able to help the rest of the family to understand. She expressed to me that she was hoping each member would continue to love and respect the steps she had to make. Penny was almost breathless at the end of our talk. She cried and thanked God that no one in our family found her deceased. This talk was touching for me, and in my heart, I blessed the Lord for his direction on my baby sister's life. I felt honored that Penny poured out her heart and soul to me. I gave God thanks for blessing her with the awareness of her need to go where she could feel rescued. I was thankful for her being led to run away from death's door into the ark of safety. Penny was truly receiving the teachings of the Bible. Seeing her own deliverance encouraged her to be an inspiration to others, especially to her nephew. I could feel the difference in my sister. Her voice sounded joyful as she talked about how blessed she was, and how she had met Pastor Paula White. She shared all this good news with Vaughn. He was hoping that he would make those same kinds of acquaintances and be blessed, as well, in the ministry.

Vaughn shared with me that relocating to Florida made him dream of a brighter day ahead for his family. I am grateful that Penny was able to leave walking and not be taken out in a casket. My soul was at peace with any decisions made by Penny or Vaughn.

I was ready to continue to help our mother, Mildred, and Penny's youngest daughter, Makee. My niece had told me how difficult it was for her, at the age of seventeen, to watch her mother leave the state. Makee had to make a big adjustment, because she was facing her last year of high school. This abrupt change made her very distraught about leaving all her old school buddies. Plus, she worked very hard to achieve honor status. After high school, her picture of her future was to be a phlebotomist. It was disturbing for her to think that she would not be acquainted with anyone at a new school. Makee had personality plus. As a teenager, she was very friendly and a beautiful young lady with a fantastic smile. Makee was a sweet-talker. She'd always say the words, "I love you, Auntie Mathell. You are very nice." She soon adjusted and realized she had everything she needed to fit right in with her new surroundings. The biggest adjustment was living with her father. This was something she had not done before.

This move was good for her and me in many ways. The distance between us was only about twenty minutes. Makee was relocating from Bellwood, Illinois, to South Holland, Illinois. It was my time to be the best auntie I could be to Makee. I wanted to guide her and help her in any way I could. I had never been very active in my niece's life before. I would call her every day after school and pick her up from her father's house on Saturday nights. I would take her to church with me every Sunday. We would pray together. She loved to eat, and I tried to have all of her favorite foods prepared. Sometimes, after worship, we would stop at a soul-food restaurant. When we would dine out, this gave us quality time and assured us that our meeting was private. She loved to talk about her mother and her progress. Makee would say how she was still adjusting to living with her dad and her stepmother. She felt as though someone was listening to all her telephone conversations at her dad's house. I would drop her off in front of her new home, and we would take a moment to exchange hugs and kisses. Then we parted until the next time.

I continuously prayed to be a blessing and allow the Lord to help me to lift up her spirits. I surprised my little niece with many of the things she needed. She liked going to church, so I had to focus on enhancing her wardrobe with clothing that would be appropriate for a young lady to wear. This was our time to bond, and it was special to me. As Makee started to feel closer to me, her arms would embrace my shoulders and neck. Her head would lie on my chest and in the softest, smoothest voice, I would talk and sing to her.

My mother, Mildred, seemed to adjust, but I noticed mood swings. She would become so brokenhearted about her youngest daughter's disappearance, especially on holidays. About five months passed. The two of them were finally accepting that change was better for Penny. We all started to believe that God was not through using my sister, nor did her mistakes predict her future.

I do believe my son was following the footprints of his Aunt Penny to become a better person. I sincerely believe that my son was seeking to find a better Vaughn; after all of the dealings he had been involved in Carbondale. My sister Penny's dilemmas had convinced Vaughn to come on. God was working it out for her and could do the same for him. I heard her say, "I owe all my elevation to God." Penny was now the new administrator of assistance at Crossroads Ministry and was very thankful and excited for her growth.

Vaughn could visualize himself and his family living in a Christian Center. My son believed that if he could be directed toward a new beginning, he and his family would have a fresh start. Vaughn was seeking a change after all the devastating court problems that he put Victor through. He had his mind set. The journey to Florida began. Vaughn remembered our talks when he was growing up. It had not been promised to any of us that the road to happiness would not have its ups and downs. It was a bumpy road to Florida. My son and his family had five hundred dollars to make this trip. When their tires blew out, there was a couple who witnessed the trouble. These people were traveling along the same road and stopped to help them. My son did not have emergency money. He only had enough money to make the trip.

Vaughn was the lead driver in the U-Haul truck pulling the Trans Am car. His wife and their five children were following him in the Jeep. A big bang happened on the back two tires of the Trans Am. The eruption scared Shelia. She thought Vaughn was going to lose control of the truck and possibly cause a fatality. The Trans Am appeared to be wobbly. The back end of the car was dragging on the ground. She saw sparks of fire as Vaughn wrestled to get control of the truck to make a sudden stop. The couple saw their struggles and offered to give them a hand. Vaughn did not have any spare money, but he had a lot of material things to sell off his truck. He started with offering his thirty-six-inch big-screen TV. My son said the man was very kind and concerned that he and his family were all right. The gentleman offered to buy the TV. He told the man he could have it for two hundred dollars. The man knew that this was a steal, and he was happy to accommodate them. Vaughn needed two new tires and food for his family. He needed a ride back to the broken-down car where his family was waiting. The man helped my son put the tires on his car, got his new TV, and gave them his blessing as he proceeded on his way.

My son was sincere about this move. When he set out on this path, he was on a wing and a prayer. Vaughn persevered, knowing he only had monies calculated for two nights in a motel. He could only afford one room and was praying double beds would be available. The extra money from selling the TV was a blessing and came in handy to feed each of them. There were seven people in his party. Once he got the children settled for the night, he and his wife would call me and tell me all about their day. We would each thank God for protecting them. We believed that the couple who stopped were angels assigned to lend a helping hand. My son wanted me to pray with him that all of them would make a swift exit. He laughed and explained that checking in was a breeze. He parked on the back row. He and his wife went to check in and requested double beds. After they checked in, they got back in their car and drove around to the back area where their assigned room was. I told my son I believed that God had gotten you all in, and I did not believe that he would leave you without a way out. I encouraged him to keep calling me and follow his dream of relocating where he believed life would be better. They were well on their way to their destination. They successfully made it to Florida in three days.

Penny had made arrangements for them to reside in a family Christian Center, but there were some stumbling blocks. Upon their arrival, Vaughn contacted his aunt by telephone to get the address and direction to the assigned property. She requested they come where she was located first. Vaughn was not sure of his surroundings and did not feel comfortable pulling the U-Haul across town. He assured Penny that once he unloaded his personal items and found a return center for the U-Haul, he would locate her.

The directions Penny gave him were exact and led right to the front door of the proper location. Vaughn jumped out of the U-Haul and walked back to the car his wife was driving. He suggested to her that he go in alone. He started making steps toward the main entrance. When he entered, he stopped at the front desk. Vaughn was greeted by a receptionist and instructed to sign in. Someone would be appointed to him shortly. The person assigned to him asked him to fill out a questionnaire that included listing all of their belongings. My son almost had a panic attack when he told me this part. He and the gentleman went outside to assess all of his possessions. He told Vaughn that this facility did not provide a warehouse to store seven rooms of furniture. This young Christian man explained that this was neither a condo nor a private suite. The facility was for people seeking the Lord, who need to be restored in every area of their lives. People came there with nothing but the clothes on their backs.

My son was very disappointed and at a loss for words. His funds did not include staying another night in a hotel. He called his aunt to inform her of all his struggles. She investigated the matter by calling and talking with the person assigned to Vaughn. It was suggested that Vaughn sell everything except their clothes and donate the proceeds to the center. This man was very frank with my sister. He told her that her nephew had a look of a man who had been involved in worldly things. The man did not know that Vaughn was down and out. He was on the road, running for his life. He had hoped to get his family to safety. Vaughn's efforts were great and challenging. My sister did not have this problem when she made her transition. She left with her mind set to return to Bellwood one day. Her bags were packed lightly. She only had a few select pieces of clothing that would fit into one garment bag.

Vaughn was always a good improviser. It was getting dark, and he needed to sell some things quickly and get his family some food and shelter in another motel. He found a spot to park each vehicle near a U-Haul return office. He then opened up the back of the U-Haul and sold a thirteen-inch TV, a stereo, and a couple of end tables. The next day, they went looking for an apartment. My son was calling me about his every move. When he did find an apartment, he called me because he did not have the money for a deposit. He could not sell the children's beds. I notified my dad of the urgency and informed him that we needed to pool together eight hundred dollars to help our family in their desperate situation. When they received the money, they were able to find adequate housing.

They managed to find a church home and were in fellowship with other churches. Vaughn was great in music engineering. He could set up any surround-sound system. While he was sitting in a church one Sunday, the microphone system started making cracking sounds. Suddenly, the microphone lost sound. Vaughn got up after about twenty minutes and went to the sound area. He asked if he could lend a hand. His help was welcomed, and he fixed the sound system. He was asked to come back and check their system in the next two weeks. The church offered to pay

Vaughn for his services. He truly wanted to be a blessing and told the official that there would be no charge.

Vaughn told me that he been under medical care while in Clearwater, Florida. This doctor had Vaughn on several medications for his heart, nerves, hypertension, and cholesterol. He was also on insulin for Type 1 diabetes. Neuropathy, a disease of the nervous system, had plagued his hands and feet. My son told me of ulcers on his feet and legs, and that he was facing possible amputation.

Even with his medical conditions, he and his family were doing well and were very content with their new hometown and their church family. Then, suddenly, another spiritual and personal storm started moving toward them. They had lived there for only nine months and had adjusted very well until the charge of conspiracy hit Vaughn on May 1, 2003.

There was a court order explaining the charges with each of their names on it. I listened to my sons' pleas of innocence. The charges were for all three of my sons. It stated that they knowingly combined, conspired, and agreed with each other and with others, both known and unknown, to distribute diverse quantities of cocaine and cocaine in the form of a cocaine base commonly known as "crack," and diverse amounts of marijuana. The conspiracy alleged that over forty two hundred pounds of marijuana had been sold and distributed by the three brothers during a seven year stretch. These were very heavy charges. I had an opportunity to talk to a law professor about my sons' problems and the charges. I also stated that they were being pressured to proffer, to tell on someone else, in order to get less jail time. He stated that to proffer was a form of torture, and it should not be used in some cases. He suggested that lawmakers should revise this tactic. From that day, I began to seek out lawmakers in order to revise the law and get my sons' releases. It appeared that this was a no-win situation. My son, Vaughn, informed me that he was being processed into the federal system. My dad and I were there to support Vaughn, spiritually and mentally. We were his only contacts, since his wife did not have a phone that could be billed collect. I could tell my son was very disturbed mentally by these sudden charges. His main concern was his wife and children. He had made a promise to his family, before leaving Carbondale that he would never go to jail again. These charges were quite a surprise and almost blew each of my sons' minds. They each thought that maybe Vaughn had committed another crime that they knew nothing about. They had believed Vaughn's word that his life of selling drugs was done. They had been to jail and completed their sentences on state charges, but never thought of serving federal charges for the same crimes.

I allowed Vaughn to call frequently, and that was my way to keep my son holding on. I would talk to him so that he would not get extremely depressed or have a heart attack. Vaughn, who was in a federal holding pen or was traveling by airplane from Florida to Illinois, was being transported by U.S. marshals.

After my son was flown to Illinois, he was taken to Perry County Jail in Pinckneyville to be processed and detained. Vaughn called and expressed his anxiety. He felt he had been given poor care for a man who depended on medicine to live. He was upset because he was not given any medicine and because he felt sick, weak, and shaky.

On May 21 and May 22, Vaughn was in route to Benton, Illinois. He was escorted by U.S. marshals. I took the Amtrak train, and it appeared to be moving at it's own pace. I could hear the whistle blow as the conductor guided the train down the railroad tracks. As I gazed out the window, looking at the soft blue sky, my mind began to drift to one of the puffy white clouds. My prayers were knocking at heaven's door. I had prayed that someone would travel with me on this journey. I asked God, weeks before the first hearing, to please allow someone to be at my side who I could touch. My senses told me that I was definitely going to need someone with me who I could talk to. I noticed no one had the seat beside me. I had to adjust to the fact that there was not an interested person available to be with me. Right about here, I realized that God had sent his word for us to rely on, and the spirit of his only begotten son to be everything to us in the midst of our storms. These problems that we faced came to shake our faith in God.

As I dreamed, I sincerely felt God's presence abiding with me like a shield of protection. I knew the spirit that was guiding us knew the way over every bridge that we faced. He would carry us over all unforeseen danger. I trusted and depended on the prophesy Bishop Davis had given for me and my family. The train hit a rough patch of tracks, and each car weaved and bobbed me into reality. I was interrupted by the movement of the train and my day dreaming was fading. My thoughts were still echoing to me that God know the ins and outs of my family's storms. On that ride to the Carbondale area, I surrendered to his will and put all my trust in the master's words. I was grateful for time alone to be able to talk with the man who created the clouds. I respected this experience and count it as a revelation. Soon, I heard the conductor say "Next stop, Carbondale, ten minutes ahead." I gathered my belongings to exit. As the doors opened, I recall stepping down slowly on my left leg, which was being supported by my cane in my left hand. I held onto the rail with my right hand. The attendant had put a step stool down on the ground because he could see I needed a little assistance. As my foot stepped onto the stool, my inner voice whispered, "Step on in the name of Jesus." I truly believed my steps had been ordered by God. I was confident that he would supply me with the stamina I needed to attend each federal court session. I believed he would lead me the right way. I had a rental car reserved, and my daughter-in-law, Felecia, took me to pick up the car. I was off to see the judge. I was ready to share my presence in the courtroom for Vaughn.

I believed that trouble does not last forever. My soul cried out for strength as I gripped the steering wheel and stared at the exit sign pointing to Benton. I was truly blessed this day. Without my knowledge, Vaughn had called his godfather to come to court. At the same time, my goddaughter, Casey, lived in St. Louis. She and I talked long distance quite frequently, and we did a lot of praying for one another over the telephone. She had plans to drive to Carbondale and ride over to Benton. She was contacted by her assistant a couple of days before I arrived. She had to attend an emergency meeting on the same day as Vaughn's hearing. After she was called, she suggested that her mother, Linda, be there with me. Casey felt my pain, and she knew my heart was shattered into many pieces. She did not want me there alone. My goddaughter was sincere and had spoken of her concerns to her mother, and they both agreed she would drive me over. It was settled that after court, Linda would bring me back to St. Louis. Casey was happy and convinced that her mother would help her godmother remain strong. She knew the love I needed, and felt assured that her mother was sensitive, compassionate, understanding, and would be the perfect one to walk with me. Soon after we arrived at the courthouse, I was surprised to see Vaughn's godfather, Paul, show up. I had prayed that God would send an angel to attend this case. I was very blessed he sent two at the same time.

When we arrived in front of the court building, we circled around and looked for a parking spot. Next to the Franklin County Jail, there was extra parking. Also in this area, right around from the courthouse, was an exhibit of a hangman's noose. I almost blacked out when I saw this awful sight. It was all fenced in with an old Model T Ford beside it. I had only seen this terrible sight on TV. The hanging noose was made out of thick unbreakable rope. I was almost scared to death by the sight of it. I cried until I could hear myself wheezing. I was about to have an asthma attack. I immediately reached for my inhaler. I leaned on the promises of the Almighty's word that he would be the judge over my three sons' cases in a courtroom. As I gathered strength to begin this journey, Vaughn's case was being heard by a judge. Soon after, my son was escorted into the courtroom by a medical team with defibrillator cases. I saw him pass out. It was distressing for me to witness him laying out looking as if he were dead. The judge was very caring and had the medical team take Vaughn to a nearby hospital. He was examined by an emergency-room doctor and admitted to the hospital to get stabilized with the proper medications. Looking straight up at the brick ceiling, I envisioned my very own view of heaven, and I yelled out, "Lord, save my son, don't let him die. He needs you. Please show yourself strong and mighty with your healing power."

Vaughn was permitted to call me a couple of days later. He was discharged and released to the U.S. marshals and taken straight back to jail.

In the meantime, his wife, Shelia, and the children were struggling to move out of their apartment. She no longer had Vaughn's money to depend on. Before the conspiracy charges hit and separated them, my son's forms of income were disability and working a part-time position as the maintenance man around the apartment complex where they lived. This job kept my son on the grounds and allowed him to keep his eyes on the children. Shelia had a full-time job driving a school bus, and they were settled in very well. Once Vaughn was gone, she had to stop working full time to take care of the children. Eventually, she got behind in their rent and was given a notice to move.

My daughter-in-law called her parents and me to inform us of their move to a homeless shelter. I had gone out and purchased a calling card and supplied a way for us to communicate. My daughter-in-law and five of my grandchildren lived in a homeless shelter for about one month. Shelia had a pending application with the low-income housing authority. Her name was placed on a waiting list for emergency housing, but her stay was running out in the shelter. I told her to start looking for an inexpensive motel to move into, and I would make arrangements to pay the bill with my dad's assistance. Shelia tried her best to stay in Florida, but she could not pay the rent where they were and needed an affordable place for her and the children. Shelia and these children were displaced from July 2003 until late 2006. They were living in La Grange, Illinois, with her parents in a two-bedroom apartment. There was no room for them when they arrived on July 3, 2003. Shelia's mother and father shared a bedroom, and one of her sisters was occupying the second bedroom. The blessing was that her parents made them welcome and did the best they could. Her parents' concern was that they would have a roof over their heads, since their three-day journey consisted of living outdoors, washing up in fast-food-restaurant lavatories, and sleeping in the car at truck stops. The good Lord made a way for each of them to have sleeping bags and cots. Their mother would sleep on the couch. My father and I had assisted our children while they were in Florida in hopes they would stay there. However, we sent the little money we had for gas to help them get back to Chicago. It was an enormous move for her and the kids after their thirty-day stay at the shelter.

Prior to Vaughn's heart failure, I spoke with a Lieutenant at the federal medical facility on June 30, 2003. I told him about Vaughn's complaint of not getting medicine. I explained the distress he was having to the lieutenant. Vaughn expressed how important it was not to miss a single dose of his medicine, and somehow the medical facility kept running out of the medicine he needed.

I went on to explain to the Lieutenant that Vaughn's legs and feet were extremely swollen, which indicated possible heart failure, and that his pain was severe. I asked him to please look into this matter, and I said to him, "Please, don't let my son die in there." The Lieutenant replied, "No one is dying in here, miss."

Soon after this incident, my son was taken to another jail called

Franklin County in Benton, Illinois that was in the same area. There was no reason given for the move.

On July 23, 2003, Vaughn once again had complaints of chest pains. He was taken to Heartland Hospital in Marion. My son explained that when he arrived, his blood sugar was 700 and he had to have a procedure done on his heart. Three arteries were blocked and required six stents in order to release the blockage. He was granted the privilege of calling me to let me know of his troubles. I felt very helpless. My cry was louder than ever to Jesus. I asked him to grant my sick child his healing power.

My son kept me informed of his every move and what each doctor would say. He stated that the doctor who attended him at Heartland Hospital was outraged at his medical condition. Vaughn said he told the doctor about the medicines he should have been taking as opposed to what he was given. God had led my son to forward me his list of medicines and his medical records. He was in and out of every hospital in that area, either with the threat of a diabetic coma or a heart attack. It was a nightmare for me.

I was waiting to come back to Benton for the hearing, and I received another call on September 30, 2003. Vaughn told me that he had been taken from Franklin County Jail to St. Joseph Hospital in Murphysboro. Vaughn could not read the doctor's name on his discharge papers. He gave his medical number off the discharge papers so our family would be able to understand his condition. Also, Vaughn was transported over to Heartland Hospital in Marion on the same day. He was in and out of these different hospitals, and I was not allowed to be at my son's sickbed. This was very emotional and disturbing for me. I could imagine how Vaughn felt about all the things that were happening to him.

Again, Vaughn was taken to Jackson County Hospital for heart catheterization. The doctor told Vaughn that his kidneys were failing him, and that the front part of his heart was not getting enough oxygen. The blood was not being pumped properly to this part of the heart, and his blood sugar was very high. He stated that Vaughn should be transferred to a medical facility upon his release.

After hearing what the doctor said, Vaughn explained his condition to me over the phone. He asked me if anyone from the jail or the hospital called me. I said, "No, no son, no one. I never received a phone call about your health failure."

When Vaughn was released from Jackson County Hospital, the doctor gave the U.S. marshals two new prescriptions to be added to Vaughn's medicines. He told the U.S. marshals and Vaughn that he should be taken to a medical facility. Instead of being taken to a medical facility, Vaughn was brought back to jail and placed in a room all alone. He was left for long periods of time before someone would bring food and some of his medicine. I contacted my congressman, Jesse Jackson Jr., about the situation my son was in. One of his staffers told me that if I would send a letter explaining my concerns, his office would forward a letter to the federal penitentiary with my inquiry. While waiting for a response from my congressman's office, I had a churning, on the inside of me, to write President George W. Bush about my sons and, especially, Vaughn. At the medical federal penitentiary, I was having a serious problem getting information about Vaughn's declining health. Other prisoners were calling because my son instructed them to call his mother and inform me of his critical condition. One inmate called me and told me my son had been taken out of his cell unconscious. I called the penitentiary and inquired about my son. I was talked to very badly. One officer told me, "We will only inform you if he dies." That was a sarcastic answer and it led me to write President George W. Bush. I felt we had something in common. He had twin girls, and I had twin boys. When I sent the letter, it had all the details in it about my three sons. I requested that he look into their charges. But my main concern was Vaughn's declining health. I received a letter from the president of the United States instructing the marshals to give me a report on how Vaughn was doing.

Vaughn's situation lasted about forty-eight hours before he was moved to the general population. When he was transferred, he was surprisingly put in the same cell with his brother Verdell. These two brothers were very glad to see one another. Verdell had not seen Vaughn since the conclusion of Victor's trial back in the year 2000. Vaughn was in need of nurturing, and Verdell was blessed to be there for him. Verdell knew God had placed them together. Vaughn was delusional, weak-minded, and very sick. Verdell was strong and ordained to forgive him and supply whatever Vaughn needed. Vaughn's feet had ulcers, his legs were badly swollen, and his diabetes was out of control. He had no money on his books in jail. Verdell did. He bought supplies to help heal Vaughn's condition. He bathed his brother's wounded feet and prayed for Jesus to heal him. Verdell made the right selection in the canteen for Vaughn's diabetic diet. The love and care Verdell showed revitalized Vaughn for his journey through jail. After a short stay in the same jail cell, Vaughn was moved to a federal medical center. I believe that because of the letters that were sent and the concerns of the officers, my son's life may have been saved.

Vaughn was transferred by airplane to the Federal Medical Center in Rochester, Minnesota. My son believed that while he was in a delirious state of mind, he heard the doctor talk about him needing a heart transplant. He was placed in Butner Federal Medical Center near the Mayo Clinic. Vaughn was severely ill throughout his trial. I am sincerely thankful to the judge for his graciousness and concern for Vaughn's medical care.

During his first year of imprisonment, Vaughn experienced sleepless nights and continuous nightmares about never getting out of prison alive. He realized the number of years he was given was absurd for a man in his critical condition. Anxiety was steadily building up while he awaited a court date. In the meantime, he was constantly being rushed to a nearby hospital in a critical state. He was transported by airplane to Benton and assisted by the U.S. marshals. Vaughn started to feel faint in midair. Chest pains started striking him like straight pins being thrown as darts into his chest. There was a sudden change in plans, and an alternate route was needed. It was known to the marshals that he had acute medical problems.

Vaughn was under a lot of stress. He felt that his defense team was not strong enough to fight a good fight. He didn't think he would have a fair chance, and it almost killed him. Vaughn sent me papers to file with the Attorney Registration Disciplinary Commission (ARDC). This organization dealt with lawyers who did not do a good job for their clients. My son had thought about filing a civil suit. He was convinced he had been tried for this crime already and had served his time. Vaughn would plead with me to try and get some help from the outside. He wanted someone to look into this indictment with a deeper discernment. He was sure the word "suppressed" meant "quashed." The indictment was boldly printed with these words centered in the middle of the page: "Suppressed Indictment."

I witnessed, at this hearing, the most pitiful sight: my son shackled at his feet, with his hands cuffed in front of him. I saw my son trembling and saliva dripping out of his mouth. His words were muffled. The judge would say, "Speak up! Sir, I cannot understand you. Can you speak louder?" Anxiety had taken control of my son. He started shaking all over like he might have been having a diabetic attack. The judge determined that he needed to be taken to the hospital. The judge even asked Vaughn if he felt like he needed to be in the hospital. My son said he tried to get the U.S. marshals to take him, but they would not. The judge asked him why, and Vaughn just shrugged his shoulders. I got to talk with him after he was seen by a doctor in the hospital emergency room. He told me that he could not tell on the marshals, because there might be consequences when he returned to his unit. If word got back that he told on the marshals, he might not make it out of jail alive. The night before and the day of court, Vaughn and I had a conversation on the telephone. He did not believe he could stand trial. When he told the marshals that he was ill, they would say that he was faking. I was terrified that my son was going to die there. I told on the marshals.

I involved every official I could think of. I heard from some, "I can't help you, miss. Your son is just going to have to reap what he has sown." I had to believe that God would set my son free. My son's immune system was progressively getting worse, and he appeared to be leaning toward a final severe massive heart attack with each flare-up. Every time I would be informed about his condition, my heart would skip a beat. My health issues would flare up and disable me. Sick or well, I had to be at the hearing to represent love and care for my son. I had heard that when there was no one to show up on your behalf in a courtroom, it was a sign that no one cared about you. In Vaughn's case, it was important to show him support. I thought his wife would attend court appearances with me, but Sheila would not appear at any of the hearings. She had also stopped writing and had begun to fall in love with another man.

I needed to be there to give my son all the support and love he needed. "Hold on, don't give up." I heard these words over and over in my head. I held onto every word that was spoken over our lives. I was not to bend to the wind of destruction, no matter what. I was compelled to lean on the 23rd Psalm. Spiritually, I know who allowed this storm to get started and who would finish it. I could see the vision and the words that God had promised me. No matter how bad this storm got, I knew that all of us were going to make it. My pleas to my son's lawyer and the letters written to the judge were numerous. Vaughn had been found guilty. But he believed that he was an innocent man.

Vaughn was feeling very sick. When Vaughn arrived in the courtroom, he was escorted by two paramedics carrying life-support equipment. The judge saw how sick, weak, and limp Vaughn appeared and that he could not stand up. The honorable judge asked that a microphone be placed where Vaughn could speak from his seat. When the microphone was placed, Vaughn's voice was not strong enough to be heard. He was assisted by two paramedics and one nurse. It was very painful for me to see my son suffer. The judge decided to have him taken to the nearest hospital. As a result, Vaughn had to get a new court date. He never made it back to court, so the judge actually came to his cell and sentenced him to eight years in jail instead of the original sixty year sentence.

Vaughn decided to fight his sentence. He had done all the research that was necessary to get an appeal. A lawyer who was assigned to Vaughn's case contacted me from the United States District Court, Southern District of Illinois. She was an investigator from the federal public defenders' office. She was coming to Chicago and thought she could save me a trip and come to see me while she was there. I was worn out from court appearances. I couldn't believe I didn't have to leave home. She told me that she very seldom came to anybody's house. Usually, the client would come to her office. When she arrived, she looked over most of the papers I had. I made it very clear that neither my son nor I was satisfied with the work from the previous attorney had done on his case. Many times I tried to contact his office, there was no answer. Rumor had it that he had died very suddenly. I showed her the letters from Vaughn to his lawyer. Also, there were papers I had written to the judge at Vaughn's request. Days after her interview with me, she called and told me that she had another client from this same case. It would be a conflict of interest if she took my son's case too. The attorney had another lawyer who could represent Vaughn in his appeal, and his name spiritually struck me like a bolt of lighting: attorney John Abel. His last name was spelled different, but it sounded the same as "able." I told him, "I know you are able because both of your names are from the Bible."

He could hear my despairing cry, and he said, "I am going to give it all I've got." He was very sympathetic to Vaughn's heart problems and other health challenges. Attorney Abel represented Vaughn and filed an appeal. Vaughn had been granted his appeal, and he was wheeled out of the holding cell into the courtroom with an oxygen tank at his side.

Vaughn had written my dad while he was in prison. He asked him if he could stay with him when he got out. When my dad received the letter, he called and read the letter to me. After reading, he was very sure that he was not going to let Vaughn stay at his home. He had decided to just not answer the letter. Well, it left me no choice but to make room for him to stay with me. As I made preparations for my son, I was very distraught thinking about what I had been told about his condition. The possibility of him needing a heart was overwhelming. I began to even feel sorry for myself. I needed reassurance that God had not forgotten me. I was visualizing ulcers on my son's feet and legs. I received a picture through the mail that showed Vaughn not able to walk any more. That sight truly broke my heart. My firstborn sitting in a wheelchair double his size and weight. His hair had grown very long, and it looked as though he had combed it out into the style of an afro. He looked disparaged. I could see signs that his nerves were extremely bad. The dark marks on his arms told me that he had been itching and scratching uncontrollably.

The judge was a compassionate man. He had Vaughn flown to the best hospital for a physical and mental evaluation. Vaughn and I had prayed together over the phone that this would be the last visit to Benton. My son had written me a letter a few days before court. He had learned his lesson and was very sorry for any wrong he may have done. He believed he had made it to the crossroad. He apologized to me for all the pain he might have caused our family.

Vaughn won his appeal. He had been incarcerated for three years. After reviewing all medical findings, the judge asked who was there on his behalf. I could hear my son declare, "My mother, judge." I was sitting alone, and Victor, who was out on his on recognizance, entered the room. I was thankful as he stretched his hand to reach for mine. He took a seat beside me. The judge was very firm with Vaughn. He told Vaughn that he would give him a chance to get his heart evaluated outside the prison walls. But if Vaughn came back through his court, he promised that there wouldn't be anymore releases. He said, "You will die here." The judge ordered the cuffs to be removed and Vaughn to be released. We truly experienced the power of the Lord. I am sincerely grateful for the return of the three V-boys. I know that the precious Holy Spirit was a light unto their way!

I was very grateful for all the steps taken to get Vaughn on his feet, but a letter he had written to me stayed on my mind in regard to his life and his children's lives. Vaughn was an enigma. There were two sides to him: the side you saw and the side he didn't want you to see. Yet he broke free of his own internal struggles long enough to write me a letter from the depths of his heart. It was a profound piece of prose that was almost poetic. As I read it, I wept for my son. It went something like this:

> Dear Mama,
>
> I feel like I live in the Valley of Dry Bones. It is something like in the Bible when God asked Ezekiel, "Can these bones live?" Ezekiel answered, "Lord, you know."
>
> Now that I am an adult, I look back and realize that the

hands of the Lord were always upon me. Some people would laugh at that statement, considering what I have done with my life, but I do not. Mama, I have been to hell and back. I have felt the hot breath of death, but I survived because my time is in his hands. With the time that I have left on this earth, I will try to make it right. Time is a funny thing. The Bible says beauty is fleeting, but so is time. When you are young and dumb, you think that you will live forever. You think you are invincible, like Superman. But, every man who lives in this world has his own kryptonite. Mama, my kryptonite was the love of money. How did I get to the Valley of Dry Bones or Death Valley? I was born there. Mama, I know you loved me and did the best you could. But you were born in the Valley of Dry Bones too. Remember, your mama gave you away. So you did not grow up with an *Ozzie and Harriet* mom who vacuumed her floor in high heels and pearls. Mama, you were raised in part by Godmama and Deacon Brown. You were very young when you had me. I will always remember you that way, so young and beautiful. At a time when many would have considered it, I give you credit for not aborting me. Mama, I am grateful that you gave me life, but I allowed the enemy to abort my dreams. Your perseverance with the lawyers, and prison officials has helped me to dream again.

Mama, you always had what they called "mother wit." You were a survivalist and a realist. Because of that insight, you allowed me to stay with my Godmama Verona and her dad, Deacon Brown. What a pair! They were down-home old-fashioned country people who would give you whatever you needed. The best in our family culture was personified in them. Godmama Verona cooked, and Deacon Brown read the Bible and fished. They loved me and I loved them. Some of my fondest memories are of my

Godmama's collard greens and hot-water cornbread. If I close my eyes, I can still imagine the smell and the taste. My godfather took me to church and fishing on a regular basis. Despite what people believe, there can be happiness when you live in the Valley of Dry Bones. Not everybody in the valley is dead in the literal sense. Everybody had to hustle because public aid and minimum wage were a reality. Mama, I have learned that there are two exit doors to the Valley of Dry Bones. They are death and money.

My biological father showed me that, when he lost control of his car and it crashed into that building. That really hurt me, Mama. That was my first encounter with death. To me, death is a thief who takes the ones you love. My father loved me. He taught me my ABCs. I love him for that. Even now, I sometimes yearn to touch his face and to ask him questions. "Daddy, what would you do?" "Daddy why did you do …" "Daddy can you …" Dad is still bigger than life to me in my dreams, and I replay the memories of him in my mind. Death is an ever-present deterrent to happiness. Death walks around freely in the Valley of Dry Bones seeking whom he may devour. Who is next? Who wants to be next? Mama, you already know this. But one of the most horrifying experiences of my life was when I found my beloved Godmama Verona dead on the porch. My whole world was turned upside down. It felt as if my heart would shrivel up and stop beating. I could not believe that death came and snatched the breath right out of my godmama. My godmama! Why her? She was so loving and kind. Why God, why? A part of me died that day. I will never ever forget what a person looks like when the breath of life is no longer in their body. They appear smaller, empty. She was just a physical shell, like a deflated balloon. Her death seemed like a cruel trick of the devil. I wanted to call her spirit back. I wanted her to live again. "Godmama, talk to me," I said, over and over again. "Godmama, please talk to me!" I tried to commit suicide after that. I just didn't see any way out.

Mama, you know staying in school was difficult for me. I want you to understand what was inside of me. I managed to graduate and play some football. Remember, I was pretty good at football. But I just didn't have the heart to continue. Going to college was a vehicle for getting more money. However, the enemy enticed me with the lust for money. I succumbed to that lust and became an entrepreneur in the number-one American underground franchise, the pharmaceutical business.

I know, now, it was the love of money. Uncontrollable love of anything is dangerous. Mama, have you ever loved something so much that you put it above everything else? Everyone who hears my story probably wants to make me the bad guy. Everybody wants to believe that it was me who caused my brothers' downfall.

But it wasn't me. The Bible says, in the book of James, that every man is tempted when he is drawn away by his own lust and enticed. Everybody says I am a bad dude. I am the big bad older brother. Everybody wants to say that I set them up. Did I? Was it a set-up by someone or something else that destroyed our family? There are a lot dead bones in the Valley of Dry Bones. But when those bones start paying the bills, wearing designer clothes, paying for trips and shelter, nobody cares that you are a dead man. No one cares that you are a walking corpse, because you are a corpse making money. Since I have been in prison, I have gotten the chance to think about my life. I got a chance to think about the wrong choices

I made. I've tried to blame you or my father; I've tried to blame America and its system of injustice. I think about how the rich get richer and the poor go to jail. But I have to accept it myself.

Mama, when the jail doors closed, I was not afraid because I was already dead. When you have lived with death as a constant companion, you are not afraid. When you take a risk to make money knowing that you may die at any moment, you live each second knowing that it may be your last. We all only trade one moment for the next. We trade one risk of dying for the next. After prison, the next threat from the enemy was my health. I needed a heart transplant. Isn't that a cruel fate, to be in prison and need a heart transplant? But, you see, when you are born in the Valley of Dry Bones, everyone is already dead. They just don't know it.

Mama, you may already know this, but one year before I was arrested, I accepted God and got saved. When I read about Peter and how he denied Jesus, I realized that saved people make mistakes too! Mama, I sincerely believe that you prayed for me. My brothers prayed for me, and strangers, who didn't even know me, prayed for me. I knew that I had been given another chance when that judge, who could have put me away, had mercy on me. Mama, not only was it your prayers, but you told the world our story. Mama, I remember something your life has taught me. You worked your faith with everyone. You talked your faith. You made our tragedies real to people. You wrote letters, you made copies of obituaries, and you called dignitaries. The squeaky wheel gets the oil. Thank you, Mama, for being a squeaky wheel. But Mama, I need one more thing from you. I need you to forgive me. I am so sorry for all that I put you through.

Please pray that the shackles of poverty and the stigma of being in prison will be broken. You see, when I got out of jail, I was still in the Valley of Dry Bones, and now my children are there too! My goal is to help them get out. There is a system in ghetto life that makes it seem impossible to do things the right way. When I returned, my wife was in the arms of another man. I don't blame her. My young daughters are sick, unwed, and pregnant. My sons are scattered, and I am an old hustler who has been hustled by the greatest hustler, the lying enemy. I seek the sanctity of church and God. I believe that I am a son of God, and I believe that these bones can live. Mama, I am your last son to get out, and the prophecy came true. I made it to the cross. I am free, and my children have me. I can walk outside when I want to. I can see the sun shining when I want to. I can kiss my kids when I want to. Thank you for being there, and thank you for taking up the slack with my girls. Thank you for taking them to the doctor and for buying them clothes. Thank you for being an example to my children, Mama. Thank you for holding on to me. I can answer the question that was posed to Ezekiel. Can these bones live? My answer is, "Yes!"

Thank you for your love and prayers,

Vaughn

Enclosed in the letter from my son was a carved piece of wood in the shape of cross with his picture attached. I cried. As I folded his letter neatly and put it back in the envelope, I heard the sound of a train whistle. It reminded me of the day I was on the Amtrak. I was recording our story into a tape recorder. I was praying and thanking God that I had not lost my mind through this trial. That whistle reminded me of when I was hoping to live to see my boys free. Now I can tell you that I did not give up, and my boys made it to the cross. You know there are still some obstacles in our family. But I have my faith and some battle scars to prove that these bones will live.

I was overjoyed about Vaughn's miraculous release. My burden was lightened. Yet we had another problem facing us as he was being released. He could not stay with me because I was on a government housing program subsidy. The rules would not allow a felon to live at my place. It hurt my heart that I risked losing my place if I allowed him to stay now. Vaughn had no place to go. Upon release, my son had a portable oxygen tank that was too heavy for him to pick up. He was bloated with fluids and seemed to be about two hundred pounds. Vaughn was on a walker and half of his medications were missing. I knew I was going to have to take him to Oak Forest Hospital in Cook County as soon as he arrived. When we did make it to the hospital, they gave him a referral to Stroger Cook County Hospital in Chicago. There was a team of doctors who got him on the right path to becoming as healthy as possible.

Vaughn had many struggles. His next challenge was to go to the Social Security office and apply for disability. Two of his cousins allowed him to stay with them for about six months because the determination for his benefits was taking so long. I had no money to help with his living expenses. I was already sharing whatever food I could with him until his food stamps kicked in. Without any money coming in, he was asked to leave his cousin's home after a very short stay. His Auntie Connie took him in. Pastor Wheeler Parker was kind enough to give him a bed from his home to sleep on. But that did not last either. His grandfather's heart softened and he allowed Vaughn to live with him for one year. This is when his benefits were finally approved.

He couldn't get a job because of the severity of his health condition. Vaughn's Aunt Janice worked at a secondhand store and was able to get him a few garments when she heard of his need. Vaughn found a landlord who did not do a background check. He overlooked the felony and let Vaughn have a place to stay with his daughter Versharia, who was fourteen years old and pregnant at the time.

Vaughn was also taking care of his seven-year-old daughter, Naya, who had juvenile diabetes. Her mother felt she was better off with my son, since they have the same illness. My son had more responsibilities than he had ever imagined. I believe he learned how to love, care, and have patience for his children from me. He knew that he had to see that each kid would be as healthy as possible. His first priority was to get an insulin pump for Naya. He wanted to preserve her organs with the proper doses of insulin administrated through automatic injections. When Vaughn became insulin dependent, the insulin pump had not yet been perfected. Vaughn was praying to be a better father for all of his children in spite of his mistakes. From the looks of things between my son and his wife, all hope of their marriage rekindling was gone. She was involved with another man, and Vaughn was with another woman. Vaughn had supposedly fathered a child by another young woman who was seventeen years old. Vaughn's wife had left all the responsibilities of enrolling their little daughter in school to him. The insulin pump was new to the nurse at Heritage School. Vaughn contacted the company that made the pump, Animas Corporation, and a nurse came out to the school and helped the school nurse become more familiar with the pump. In the district where Naya was attending school, she was the only child who had the insulin pump. The nurse would take extra precautions and call Vaughn if there was a slight change that she was unsure about. Vaughn did not have gas or a good running vehicle. He couldn't keep going over to the school when Naya would have a reaction from her diabetes. My son told his grandfather about all of his dilemmas, and this one touched Grandfather's heart. He started lending Vaughn his car. I noticed a big change in my dad toward his family. He was the longest-living relative. I am a believer that it is a poor wind that never changes. I bless the Lord for my dad's change. God had allowed him to become a better man than he had ever been before.

It was the night before Thanksgiving when my son, Verdell, called me and told how he had been pulled over by the police. He spoke of how he was told to step out of his car, lie down on the concrete ground, and spread his hands and legs wide open. The police searched him and his car. After this search, he was escorted to the police station for questioning and detained for twenty hours before he was released. Soon after, Verdell called me and informed me of what had taken place. I broke down. I was due in St. Louis the day after Thanksgiving for a social event. My son's encounter with the law had me weak in the knees. I was counting on God to prop me up on all sides. I wanted to know why the police did this to my son. He tried to explain that it was on account of suspicion. He had been detected in the post office, by a security monitor, mailing money under a fictitious name. Learning of this was absolutely disheartening for me.

My son explained that he had been invited to church by his neighbor, but he had not accepted the invitation until after the police had detained him. He had not attended church in about four years. He wanted me to know that he had asked God to forgive him and his brothers for all the hurt and pain they may have caused their mother. His words touched my heart and my spirit. I whispered, "Baby, let the Lord comfort you and guide you. Verdell, Mama has realized that everyone has his own road to travel. There will be high mountains, low valleys, and many unexpected, unbelievable times of trouble. There will also be times of greatness and awesomeness. I believe that it takes something to bring each of us to the Lord. Just remember, respect the road designed for you and believe that Jesus will be with you. We all know the story in the Bible of the three Hebrew boys—Shadrach, Meshach, and Abed-nego. They were cast in the midst of a fiery furnace, but came out unscathed (the book of Daniel, chapter 3). Remember that what God did for them, he will also do for you."

I decided to attend a neighborhood church. The door keeper saw me, as I entered the sanctuary. She asked me what was wrong, and I told her. She embraced me and I cried on her shoulders. As I wept, she began to pray from her soul. Her kind words seemed to lighten the load that was on my mind. She said softly to me, "I am the mother of three children—Kyrne, Stacy, and Spencer, the latter two being twins." I had been visiting this church for about seven months. I don't ever remember meeting this lady before. My mind started feeling comforted and soothed. She was another angel sent to catch me in her arms. I was very grateful to know God and God alone could put an angel in my life whenever I needed one. This beautiful, wonderful woman was filled with all of the love and understanding I would need. Instantly, I believed she was sent to keep me strong. Only God knew that I had three sons, and two of them were twins. As we stood in the door embracing one another I was burdened and had to keep on walking and pressing while on this journey with my boys and their families. My body felt limp, and I could hardly stand. The lady led me back to my seat and eased me onto the bench. As she patted my hands, she stuffed them with Kleenex. Within five minutes, she came to me with her phone number on a piece of paper. In a low voice, she said, "My name is Lou please feel free to call me anytime."

After the church service, I could hardly wait to get home and call her to thank her for her kindness. I truly am grateful for the lifeline that was extended to me. Sometimes a person only needs to feel that somebody cares in order to keep holding on. My heart was filled with love for this special lady. My mind kept a vision of her all day long. I remembered her beautiful smile as she reassured me that whatever my problem was, I had come to the right place for help. She was tall and had a light complexion. Her hair was a sandy color, cut short and sassy. Lou was a full-figured lady. Once I made the phone call, we connected for what seemed like a lifetime of friendship. Since then, there has not been a problem that either one of us has encountered that we did not pray each other through. We spend time with one another at lunch or at dinner. She and I have grown to be great sisters in Christ. Her words of encouragement are always, "Mathell, God is in the background working things out for you and your family."

My son Verdell had shared his story of how he was almost killed in his apartment. After hearing my son express all the details of this traumatic experience, he broke down in tears on the phone. The last thing I heard him say was, "Thank you, Lord, thank you. You sent me an angel to block the bullet." Suddenly, there was a dial tone. I repeatedly redialed Verdell's phone over and over. Either there was a busy tone or the voice mail would pick up the call. I panicked. My thoughts went straight to Lou. She had a way of reassuring me that every bad thing was being worked for our good. Seemingly, I needed to hear Lou's soft soothing voice to reconfirm that the storm was in motion. "But Mathell, you must remember who orchestrated the storm and who the captain of your family's ship is." My thoughts drifted back to Colony All Nations Church, where the word of God had become engraved in my heart.

I proceeded to call Lou. When she answered, my voice was trembling, and she sounded nervous. "Mathell, what's wrong?" Before I started explaining what my son had told me, I alerted her that I was sincerely in need of an ear and would like to know if she had about half an hour to console her sister in Christ. She instructed me to pour out my troubles on her and then she stated, "I am here for you."

I began by telling her that my son Verdell had been through a shocking ordeal today. I explained how he had shared it with me. Visualize him sitting in his living room with two guys that he thought he knew very well. But, soon, my son learned these two men were setting him up to rob him and destroy him. They were about to send him to an early grave. Lou was quiet and breathing hard as I continued to tell her of how Verdell was robbed by people he thought he knew. These young men had even started calling me Mama. My friend Lou hollered, "Shut up, Mathell! This is too much to bear. Is he hurt?" I explained further. Verdell regretted having a lot of women in his "player" days. He shared with me that he met a cutie pie named Tia in the grocery store. He was dazzled by the twist in her walk. He whistled at her and drew her attention. When she turned, she was beautiful to his eyes. I seemed to have drifted off while he was talking about this diva. The words of wisdom rang in my ear that beauty was in the eyes of the beholder, and also that looks are deceiving. I continued listening and I heard my son say that from the way she looked, he simply had to have her. He sort of laughed and said, "I was being a lustful and greedy man. When she smiled at me, it thrilled me. Her voice was sultry and charming. Lust was almost the death of me."

Tia and Verdell had recently broken up. Verdell had run into her one day, and she looked as if she was in need of help. See, Verdell was a good guy underneath it all. He allowed Tia to make some extra money, instead of just giving her cash. He belittled Tia by asking her to cook and clean for guests he was entertaining. The house was full of people who knew she was his ex. Five of them were women who were dying for a chance to be next on the "V" list. Tia saw too much. I just couldn't believe my son wanted her to see he had moved on in a big way, but I told my baby, "Hell hath no fury like a woman scorned." Little did he know, he had created a monster. Evidently, Tia thought he had a lot of money. Verdell always kept a "pimp's" bankroll. That's where you take a fifty- or one-hundred-dollar bill and cover a stack of dollar bills to make it appear that you have a lot of money. He heard of this idea from his grandfather, who was a gambler. I believe what Verdell saw long ago—his grandfather's bankroll—gave him the wrong image. He flashed his fake roll one time too many, and now the game was getting ready to be played on him.

He was entertaining his friend Craig, who had recently gotten married. The phone rang. It was Fred and Eddie, Tia's cousins. Fred had just gotten out of jail. Fred called the house and asked if it was okay for him and Eddie to come by. Verdell told them it was fine, but they had to hurry. He was going to pick up his son from school and would be leaving soon. My son thought nothing of it. He wanted to see them and wanted to help Fred if he could. My son and these two men were sitting on the couch playing a PlayStation game. They were having a conversation about a party that was coming up. One of the guys was the same height and build as Verdell. This young man was not able to buy anything new that would be stylish and sharp enough to appeal to the ladies.

When my son explained the story to me, he surmised that he had been set up. Verdell heard his friend's dilemma and jumped up from playing the game. He told Fred to follow him, while Eddie continued playing. Verdell told of how he compassionately invited Fred to his room and extended his kindness. He gave him the opportunity to pick out anything he wanted to wear, so he would not miss the party. Just as Verdell attempted to turn the closet light on, Fred extended his arm and put the pistol to the back of Verdell's head. He said, "Get on the ground, V." My son refused. Fred hollered to Eddie, "Come on, I've got the drop on him now, but he won't get down." Fred called, "Bring Craig in." Eddie also had a weapon as he rushed into the room. They knew my son wasn't going to die on his knees, but they also knew my son wasn't going to watch his friend pay for something he had nothing to do with. It was Tia's cousins threatening to kill Craig that sent Verdell to his knees. Eddie was instructed by Fred to tie up Verdell with the telephone cord. He knocked him in the head with a hard iron pistol while holding him at gunpoint. As I continued telling Lou this dangerous tale, she was weeping uncontrollably.

My son had me visualize him looking down the nose of a gun. As the two guys stood with two weapons, they told Verdell that he had better tell them where he kept his money. My son said, "I shouted out, 'Take what you like, just don't kill my boy.'" Neither of the men believed him. Verdell tried to convince each of them that the bankroll he was flaunting was a pimp's roll. They said they had never heard of anything like that. My son's thoughts directed him not to waste any more time explaining about what he had learned from his grandfather.

Verdell was duct-taped and tied up with a telephone cord. Some would call it hog-tied. My son explained how he had been stomped across his face till the lenses popped out of his glasses. Lying there in his own blood, he thought about what his family would do without him.

Eddie hollered to Fred, "Let's shoot him now!"

Verdell began to pray, "Lord, please let my mama, my children, and my family forgive me, and forgive these heartless men."

He remembered Fred saying, "You're too calm. You act like you been through this before." He hadn't, but at that time Verdell wasn't afraid to die. He had made peace with his spiritual father.

Fred told him to shut his ass up. He said, "This nigga is praying." That's when Fred dropped the pillow on the back of Verdell's head, cocked the trigger, and turned the television up as loud as it could go. Fred raised his hand up high and came down swiftly, striking my son in his face. He asked Eddie to hurry up and stuff Verdell's mouth, so Fred could shoot his brains out and nobody would hear him scream.

Verdell knew what time it was, but Fred was stuck deliberating with himself. He was talking out loud. He said, "I don't want to kill you, but I know you are not going let this go." Fred was holding the gun. He was raving about how he was about to pull the trigger. As this child of mine spoke, I reminisced about the times I told my twin sons not to claim a person to be your friend as soon as you meet him. I tried to forewarn them that everybody is not your friend. However, a friend that Verdell met long ago was now his roommate and was at work that day. There was a moment of silence. I realized my son was crying from his soul. I called him anxiously by his name, and he called the Lord's name out and said, "Mama, God stopped a bullet from entering my head." He was overwhelmed with thankfulness that God had sent someone to his front door. Rasasa had been friends with Verdell for about thirteen years. They really became friends when they went to college and ultimately became roommates. Verdell said he heard the door open and a voice said, "Hey, man, where are you?" It was a startling surprise to the thieves and attempted murderers.

"It was the voice of my roommate, Rasasa, that saved me," Verdell explained. "He was home half an hour earlier than usual. Fred and Eddie hid behind my bedroom door and Rasasa saw me tied up like a piece of cattle. The two men jumped out at him and beat him with their pistols, and he was knocked unconscious."

Verdell's apartment door was left wide open, and the two men fled from the building. A neighbor noticed the two men and saw Verdell's door open. He came into the apartment. The television was loud as he walked past the living room toward the bedroom. He could see a shoe and someone lying on the floor. The neighbor was carrying a cell phone and called the police to the scene. Then went back to the crime area and pushed the bedroom door open. Rasasa's body was holding the door slightly closed. As the neighbor tried to stick his head into the door, he saw Verdell tied up on the floor. He began to untie my son, and then the police entered and radioed for an ambulance. While on the phone with my son, he said he realized the angel assigned to his life was Rasasa. My son believed God had sent Rasasa home early to stop him from being killed. This was God's plan.

Rasasa was carried out semi-conscious, but he fully recovered. A few days later, both Verdell and Rasasa were asked to come to the police station by investigators who hoped to get more information on why these guys targeted them. A few days passed; and Verdell was in the shopping mall and saw one of the men who had tried to kill him and his roommate. He alerted mall security of what had happened to him. Security apprehended the young man and took him to the police station for questioning.

While being questioned, the young man implicated Verdell as being heavily involved in the drug scene. Suddenly, the situation was reversed, and the police began to question Verdell. Verdell found himself in a world of trouble. He was accused of mailing large sums of money out of state through the postal service. There was supposed to be a sketch in a silhouette of a black man fitting Verdell's description. He had to go to court. He was found guilty and was sentenced to five months in jail. I was told by my son's lawyer that the judge was lenient because there was word from federal prosecutors that another case involving Verdell and his brothers was on its way. This case involved conspiracy to distribute drugs. It would involve high-profile lawyers, and the case was thought to be as big as the movie *Blow*. I was worn out by this time and terrorized about what was coming. As I approached each son about the new case coming, none of them knew what I was taking about. With each case being tried separately, it took several years of constantly being in court before all issues were resolved. Believe me; I had grown very tired of case after case after case. Verdell was a wheeler and dealer when he met Sharetta. This was shortly before he developed a legal issue. Sharetta had one daughter, Mindy, and was pregnant with her second daughter, Holly, when Verdell met her. The father of her unborn child was not supportive during her prenatal care. My son helped her through her pregnancy as a friend, but eventually, they became lovers.

Suddenly, Verdell and Sharetta announced that they were getting married. I had been introduced to this young lady one time before this engagement. Neither he nor she had known each other for any length of time, approximately eight months. As a parent, I thought that this was too soon. Verdell and Sharetta's problems with other relationships, along with his criminal issues, appeared to have them marrying for the wrong reasons.

Sharetta was twenty-five years old and stood five feet one inch tall. Her skin color was caramel. She was born with a beauty mole right below her nose. Verdell's new wife-to-be was well aware of all the trials Verdell was facing. I was puzzled as to why they would confuse the lives of these little girls. How would they explain to the girls that their stepfather would be going to jail in the next few months? My son was dumbfounded at my question, because he had not thought about what effect it would have on the children. For selfish reasons, Verdell had gotten sentimental and compassionate about Sharetta. After his brush with death, my son was uneasy living on the first floor alone. I told my son the children were too young to understand now, but later, they would ask her why she married a man who was headed to jail.

In spite of all the odds, their marriage took place. Sharetta attended every court case and reassured my son that she was with him all the way. She got pregnant with his son while he was awaiting sentencing. Sharetta had knowledge of the battle ahead in court and the great possibilities of jail time that Verdell faced. I believe reality set in and she wanted to back out, but there was nowhere for her to go. She really seemed to be a very nice young woman. I had been there, fighting through the highs and lows of life, a single mother of three. I had to play the field with single men and married men. I knew life. I understood this desperate move to come together as one. I had listened to her tell me how she was being forced out of an apartment by a roof that was leaking and floors that were weak and squeaky. She and the fathers of her children were not getting along. She had not completed high school, and that limited her from securing high-paying jobs. I often encouraged her to go back to school and empower herself. I knew that would have a good impact on her children. I told Sharetta how I stayed in school while my sons were in school, to be inspiring and direct each of them to reach for their dreams. I spoke of how the twins told me that they were proud of their mother for going that extra mile to become an achiever. My son Victor would say, "Mama, keep your mind open to learn, and never believe you have enough knowledge." I would smile at my baby, because hearing those words kept me going. Sharetta would thank me for sharing my stories and for encouraging her to go back to school. She and I would have good talks about her life struggles.

Victor was serving time, and he had never met his twin's wife-to-be. I was not up to a wedding or any other social event. I agreed to be at the wedding because I believed it was the right thing to do as his mother. Divine Word was the name of the church where Verdell was an active licensed certified minister under the leadership of Pastor Ramon Jones Jr. Shortly after Verdell met Sharetta and her girls, they became members of the church. Sharetta also became a praise dancer. They were joined together as man and woman in holy matrimony as planned. It was a very nice, simple wedding with about forty guests attending.

We all were getting along lovingly. I felt like I really had a daughter I could love. I wanted to be there for her, especially with what we were facing with the law.

The time had come to serve the five months. Three months into his sentence, Verdell was notified that another case was on him where he could be tried for conspiracy. He was now facing twenty years. The overwhelming turn of events was too much for all of us, but especially, Sharetta. His new wife moved her daughter's father into their apartment and began discussing divorce proceedings. Pastor Jones gave his support wholeheartedly to my son, because he knew Verdell was carrying way too much on his mind and heart. When I heard this, I called Sharetta to find out if there was any truth to this rumor. She did not deny it. She told me that she had married Verdell for all of the wrong reasons and should have always been with this individual instead. It was soft music to my ears to hear her tell the truth. I told her how I adored her for her honesty. She was my daughter-in-law, and my son honored their marriage. There had been many times when my son would pour out his heartfelt problems and ask me to pray for him and his family. He had confessed that in the past, he had been a lightweight player, and he knew one day he would have to pay for the pain he had caused other women. It was Verdell's time to cry. He was sorry for all the things he had done and had begun to repent. He asked the Lord to walk with him, talk with him, and be his guide. Once incarcerated, he fasted for twenty-one days. When I would come to visit him, he had the special anointed look that Moses had when he came down from being in the presence of God. Verdell looked older, and men would walk up and call him Minister Verdell. He would introduce me, and the kindest words would be expressed by some of the inmates. They would tell me how the Lord was very strong in my son, and how they would not have made it if my son had not been there with them. I recall one young man who said, "I don't mean I am glad he got in trouble, but I am thankful for his journey." This young man told me that he did not believe in the Lord until he met my son. As he was speaking, he put his hands on Verdell's shoulders and said, "Your troubles brought you to me and so many others. It was so that we may know the Lord and be saved." They each gave one another a hug and a hand slap, and we continued our visit. All of a sudden, from the dome above where we were sitting, a dove appeared and landed near my son's feet. To our amazement neither one of us had seen a dove except at a magic show. For me the dove represented God's perfect peace and God's light shining on Verdell.

Verdell was blessed to lead a group of men three times a day in prayer. The group grew weekly as word of mouth got around about a man on the premises who could truly pray. Verdell realized he was ordained to be there in that position. He was very close with the chaplain. He was in prison as Jesus was once in jail. I was taught by many spiritual leaders that the devil can be kept away. Get thee behind me, Satan!

At the same time, I heard a preacher preach a series from the Bible on Joseph. When I heard the prophetic words about Joseph and his brothers, I had a better understanding of my boys and their troubles. I bought and engulfed every word that was preached. I started sending Bible study lessons into the prison to encourage every man I had met. I had heard Pastor Paula White testify on television about her vulnerable situation. She said it took about two or three thousand cassettes and CDs to keep her encouraged. So she surrounded herself with the word. That's exactly what I did. One sermon by Bishop Noel Jones was entitled "I've Got to Win!" It kept me believing we couldn't lose when God was in control.

I decided to seek other ways to enhance my career opportunities, while waiting for court. So I submitted a leather fashion portfolio with eight-by-ten photos to *The View*, a TV show. I thought the horrific hurdles were over and I could pursue my dreams to be a personal shopper for ladies. I believed that it would be a fun job to mix and mingle with all kinds of people. I had recently been involved in a fashion show, and pictures were taken by Moore Video of some of my glitzy and glamorous garments. I felt very proud of my collection. Again, the spirit led me to send a preview of the latest in styles to *The View*, in hopes that I might be selected to be on the show. I was praying and asking God to get me back on my feet again. This seemed like a great opportunity for me. After a few weeks passed, I received the nicest letter from *The View*. It said that they appreciated me providing them with my fashion portfolio, but they couldn't accept my proposal at this time. As I read the words, I felt a sense of thankfulness and encouragement. This letter was uplifting to me. The sentiments behind the letter brought me joy. I was captivated by the thought that one day my fashions might be seen on *The View*. At the end of the letter, they stated that they didn't have the time to address each letter they received, but because mine was so professionally well done, they took the time to send it back to me. Hearing from them was a pivotal part of what helped me to remain strong. I had decided to take a little time and set up a photo shoot with some of Bobbie Ross's models and, in time, I would write *The View* again.

One morning, I was reading the newspapers and found an article in the *Chicago Tribune* entitled, "High Court Voids Mandatory Sentencing in Federal Courts." There was also a header by columnist Mary Mitchell, of the *Chicago Sun Times*, that read, "Harsh Sentencing Guidelines Finally Get Needed Scrutiny." This meant federal guidelines were changing, possibly in our favor. Spiritually, I was encouraged that the prison doors would open and Verdell would be given another chance. After reading these articles, I called Verdell's lawyer, and he had gotten the news also. I was optimistic that my son Verdell could be released. A year and a half had passed, and my son's case was due before the Judge. He had already received his pre sentencing investigation report, (PSI) three days prior to court, stating he had to serve a minimum of fifty five months. It did not look like Verdell was coming home, soon. I made some calls to a few friends asking for prayer. I also called Verdell's oldest son, DeSaviour. He was my prayer partner. He was a praying little boy who attended church every Sunday with his mother. They all were members at the same church at the time. Verdell's son had seen him preach, teach, and sing lead in the church choir. DeDa was DeSaviour's nickname. He adored his father, and my son spent a lot of time with him. They would have weekends together. Every holiday, his mother would make sure they spent time together. DeDa had witnessed his mother opening up church services with prayer. He had seen tears stream from his mother's and father's eyes. My grandson had become a young man with emotions. I had seen him open up church in a three-piece suit, down on his knees, with his head bowed and tears falling while he prayed. Awesome!

Verdell and Nicki had become the best of friends. They did not hold bitter feelings toward one another. They were always lending an ear to each other when there were problems. She was very encouraging to me when Verdell was first incarcerated. She helped me research lawyers in the area who could take Verdell's case. I thanked her for her kindness, and she told me it was her pleasure. She needed to help get her son's father back. After all of her efforts, I couldn't afford any of the lawyers she found. I had to stick with the federal public defenders and rely on the word of God. I had been taught that God would be a lawyer in that courtroom. I believed that his spirit lived within my soul. He calls the shots—or, in this case, the verdict. God Almighty is everything to me. I learned that if I was going to believe, there must not be any doubt. I thank our spiritual father for blessing me with extraordinary faith and belief in his word. I am sincerely grateful that Nicki and my son are very respectful to one another, even to this day. They have set a good example for a child to follow. DeSaviour had both parent show him how to be a Christian and a gentleman. They attend most of their son's games together. Nicki got married and her spouse respected their relationship. When my son was sentenced, Nicki and her husband were quite concerned because of their desire not to see DeDa hurt.

When Verdell and Sharetta were together, she and Nicki were the best of friends. They would have sleepovers at each other's homes. I recall DeDa making a statement of how it was wonderful to have two houses in which to spend time with his parents. He cherished having both of them. The love between them was beautiful. My grandson, at an early age, was very prayerful and powerful for the Lord. He said he would like to preach one day. His love for the Lord is very precious. He is a very delightful person to chat with. The night before court, he had a dream that his dad was free. DeSaviour saw a picture of him and his dad at an old condemned grocery store. In his dream, they had begun to clean the store, and it was looking good. They had started a father-and-son storefront church. After hearing about his dream, all I could do was encourage him by saying dreams do come true. I promised to join him in prayer for his dad's release. This was a prophetic dream coming from a ten-year-old mind. It was awesome to hear. I was encouraged after talking with my grandson. I believed the word of God was true, "He shall set the captive free." I believed that God could do all things.

My time had come to hobble onto the train to get to Carbondale and then to Benton for court. My body was stiff and in pain. I was all alone. Pastor Ramon Jones couldn't make this court date. This was the only one he missed. I knew that spiritually, God was with me. Again, the hangman's noose stood before me. I thought about the positive and negative sides of a hangman's noose. Positive thinking made me feel that the time of hanging people was over. I still had to go forward with a positive attitude that Jesus hung on the cross and suffered, bled and died for us to live.

When I entered the waiting area, Verdell's lawyer appeared and invited me into a conference room. He began talking about a new law established in the United States versus Blakely. The lawyer's expectation was that Verdell stood a great chance of becoming a free man that day. The lawyer explained that the judge now had the authority to use his own discretion instead of going by the guidelines. Suddenly, Verdell's name was called to stand before the judge, and the federal prosecutors presented their case. My son's lawyer brought forth his case, and the judge heard both sides. After weighing both sides, the judge told Verdell, "I am going to let you out."

He asked Verdell who was there for him. Verdell said, "My mother."

I looked up and held my hands tightly I said to God, "How great you are! Thank You, Lord." My prayers had been answered, the law had changed. I am a believer that God is an on time God and He is never late on any problem.

After filling out a lot of papers, Verdell was released. He and I got on a train and headed to my home in Chicago Heights. We rejoiced by singing. A few tears of joy flowed as we continued thanking the Lord for Verdell's deliverance. He wanted to spend a couple of nights with me before traveling to the last place he had called home in St. Louis. He had heard the rumors that another man was staying in his place. Evidently, love did not live there anymore for him and his wife, Sharetta. When Verdell returned to St. Louis, he moved back in with his wife. However, things were not the same, and it didn't look as if they would get any better. He attended a job fair. Later, while shopping at the grocery store, he met his former boss and was blessed to get his old job back. So Verdell moved in with a friend he had met at work named Johnny. Things were beginning to get back on track for him. Verdell had tried everything to keep his family together, but Sharetta just did not want the marriage and was not willing to try. She had called the police on Verdell several times. She wanted the officers to put him out of the house. A felon doesn't need any enemies. The last time the police came to the house, an officer advised Sharetta that the house was as much his as it was hers, and maybe one of them could move to the basement. She let the officer know that she didn't even want Verdell on the premises. The devil was on the move. I was sorry that two beautiful people could not work it out. Neither of them had money to move out. She had been laid off for months. My son had stayed in homeless shelters because he realized she could get him put back in jail on a lie. So he did what was best. He moved on at her request. They planned to get a divorce. After you have done all you can in any situation, consider letting go and letting God fix it.

After all had been said and done, people wanted to know how I saved my boys. Just what did you do? I told them that the release came from the voice of God Almighty through an anointed and appointed prophet. I read, in the King James Version of the Bible, Romans chapter 10, verse 17: "So then faith cometh by hearing, and hearing by the word of God." I remember clearly as each of my sons was born. When it was time to name them, the letter "V" rang in my ears. "V" stands for victorious. The twins were born and they did not have the health challenges that had been predicted. I claimed "Victory" for them. Their deliverance tells me that they were born to make it through the tests and trials of their storms. God says victory shall be mine.

I am grateful that I was spirit-led to lobby Congressman Jesse L. Jackson Jr.; the president of the United States, George W. Bush; and many other officials for the release of my sons. Their letters added to my fight and gave me much hope. This was the most demanding and challenging time of my life. Everything was coming at me, and each new issue was as powerful as the last.

At this time, my dad and I were restoring our relationship. We had become prayer partners. He purchased "Best Friends" and "My Daughter" greeting cards for me at Christmas time. I had forgiven him as he had asked of me. He was the only one left for me and I for him all my other guardian angel parents had died. As I write this, I could see that we were in the same situation. He really needed me, and I really needed him. I had to break it down to him about the power of God, because he wasn't in control like he thought he had been all his life. We soon became a team supporting each other, and it felt right to be taking care of him. He didn't take care of me as a father should, but God placed Grandfather in my life as the perfect substitute. I'm not confused, and I am very thankful. Through my writing, I want to eradicate the cycle of major dysfunction and immoral behaviors in our family. I am prepared to fight to end the cycle of sexual abuse, financial struggle, and the warped sense of family that has developed in our communities. I want to build and strengthen my family ties to ensure that our family lineage can be used as the model for every family that reads this story of my life.

Wanna Be Like Mike

All of the things that were happening in my life were starting to really affect me. I could feel myself bleeding on the inside, as I could hear my heart thump repeatedly. My whole body had started to feel hurt and pain from this bumpy road that I was destined to go down to get to a brighter day ahead.

I remember talking to my friend Pamela about the pain in my body. She quickly interrupted me and said, "You know, I had some of those same pains that you are describing, but I have never incurred the troubles you are bearing, Mathell." She explained to me that her primary doctor referred her to a team of doctors who found the proper medicine to relieve her of her excruciating discomforts. I asked her for the phone number of her doctor. When I called that medical facility and explained the pain I was experiencing, I was referred to Dr. Kathleen Weber. There was a two-week waiting period to see her. I secured the first available opening. This team of doctors was noted for providing care for world-class athletes. Dr. Weber was assigned to me as a sports medicine specialist. I could hardly wait for my first appointment. My body was getting stiff, and my right knee was swollen. My dear friend Joanne chauffeured me to my first visit. When we arrived at the doctor's office, I registered and completed the necessary paperwork. Then the nurse called my name and escorted me to the examining room. After the nurse finished with my vital signs, she told me to get comfortable and that the doctor would be in shortly. Suddenly, the door opened and Dr. Weber stepped inside the room. She introduced herself and extended her hand for a friendly handshake. This young woman was very soft-spoken, but what impressed me most was her beautiful smile. She was very attractive and somewhat young to be a doctor. I told her that I loved her haircut and the color of her hair, which was two tones of light and dark brown. Our hair colors were almost the same. Dr. Weber was a small-built lady and short in height. She had a great sense of humor, very warm and sincere. Her greeting made it easy for me to relax and let her be my doctor.

She evaluated my body reflexes and sent me for x-rays of my knee and my lower back. She found a tear in my right knee, and arthritis in various parts of my lower back. Her consensus was that the tear did not require surgery. Therefore, she did a referral for physical therapy and made an appointment for me to see her again. Before our visit ended, we talked and laughed some more. She allotted time for me to reminisce a little bit about the old wise tales my godmama would share with me when I was a teenager. I explained to Dr. Weber that I would hear my godmama talk about how old "Arthur" was hurting her so badly. I didn't know what she was talking about, and I knew I hadn't met anyone in her life named Arthur. I would ask, "Who is old Arthur?" She would reply, "He is kin to the Ritis brothers." Godmama would then laugh and say, "You'll know him soon enough, baby." I smiled at Dr. Weber and acknowledged that I had finally made an acquaintance today with old "Arthur."

In between physical therapy sessions, I made return visits to the doctor. On one visit, I was hurting all over my body. You had better believe old "Arthur" attacked my body throughout my shoulder bones, arms, knuckles, back, and legs. The flesh around my ankles had swollen to ten and a half inches around. I was in need of a specialist for my arthritis aches and pains.

My follow-up appointments drew me closer to my doctor. I began to feel her inner spirit. I could feel her closeness to me. I felt her compassion on my third visit. She entered the room and greeted me with a handshake, a hello, and a great big hug. That hug was most welcome, and it allowed me to know her as friendly, personable, approachable, and very understanding. I recognized she was filled with love. She shared her love and care with me at the worst time in my life. She was there to embrace me. I managed to put my true feelings away until I could get back to the car. I concealed my true feelings by putting a smile on my face and bellowing out with laughter. I would throw my head back and hope and pray that my laughter would not turn into tears.

I could feel, by spirit, a special bond had developed between Dr. Weber and me. Nothing could hold me back from pouring out all of my troubles now. Tears from within me began to flow. I shared with her some of my heartfelt concerns about my three sons. She reacted by reaching out for me and holding me in her arms. Dr. Weber assisted me through some of my darkest days and nights. Psalms 91:11 states, "God shall give his angels charge over thee, to keep thee in all thy ways."

After several visits, Dr. Weber informed me that my condition was controlled as much as possible and it was important that I focus on losing weight. She empathized with me that stress sometimes causes one not to be aware of an eating disorder. But at this time, she would need to dismiss me from her caseload because I had completed all of my prescribed treatments. She informed me that I should visit her only as needed from now on.

A week later, I had another one of those sleepless nights, and a freak accident occurred in my living room. I was up cooking in the middle of the night. It was a common practice for me because I could not always sleep. I would utilize this time to organize my day and to make out the grocery list for special foods for Grandmother and Dad. With my medical problems, it was too hard for me to try to shop. I would have many choices to select from to prepare the Southern-style dishes that they loved. I had a friend, Marguerite Pearson, who would help me prepare those special meals. I was honored to cook for them and was blessed with a special angel that would travel sixty miles round-trip day or night to assist with this assignment. This particular night, we started cooking and making noise with the pots and pans about eleven thirty. The dinner was almost ready at one thirty in the morning. I told Marguerite I could handle everything now. I was very grateful to have her in the kitchen, and I appreciated her for always being there for me. I prayed traveling grace be with her. I reassured her that everything was in control in the kitchen, as the food was on its last simmer.

It was quiet time for me. I often looked forward to the time to connect with my inner sprit. That time was always special during the wee hours of the morning. I could cry out to the Lord in song, singing and praying without the interruptions of the telephone or the doorbell.

I decided to exercise while waiting for the food to finish cooking. I went to my workout area and grabbed my big blue exercise ball. I began to exercise using the instruction sheet given to me by the physical therapist. I started by sitting on the ball to stabilize my back. Next, I stood up and began dribbling the ball to help slenderize my upper arms. I was having so much fun dribbling that I suddenly felt as though I was a basketball player. I visualized my favorite player, MJ. I felt like a little girl again. I suddenly felt rhythm in my legs and wondered if I could cross my leg over the exercise ball. My athletic curiosity almost killed me. When I tried to pass my right leg over the ball, the ball flipped me. I flipped head over heels into a split position. At the same time, I could hear a loud popping and cracking sound. I screamed out in pain, "Help me, Jesus."

Questions began flowing out of my mouth like a river. "Lord, am I torn up from the floor up? Am I all broken? Lord, will I ever walk again?" I was in great pain, and I couldn't stand up. I cried as I crawled to my bedroom where there was a phone. I tried to raise myself up off the floor by pulling on my bed linens. My leg felt like rubber each time I attempted to stand. The pain was excruciating. The pain was comparable to the pain of giving birth. I could not reach the phone on the table. Therefore, I had to pull the phone down to me by its cord. I dialed my godsister, Joanne, because she had a key to my apartment to be used in emergencies. This was definitely an emergency.

Joanne came immediately. However, she had difficulty in gaining access to my apartment. I heard Joanne stomping the snow off her feet in my hallway. I felt relieved knowing that help was here, but I wondered why it was taking so long for Joanne to open the door. Suddenly, the phone rang. It was Joanne telling me that her key to the deadbolt lock was not opening the door. It was at this moment that I remembered that the lock had been changed. Immediately, I wanted to beat myself up for procrastinating. The lock had been changed weeks before this incident, and I hadn't given her the new key.

I hung up the phone and crawled to the door in severe pain, dragging my right leg. Again, tears began streaming down my face. I screamed out, "Lord, help me," with every inch I crawled. Finally, I made it to the door. I was laying flat on the floor, with my face down. I hardly had anymore strength to crawl. I reached out and pulled up on the door knob and finally unlocked the deadbolt. I fell into Joanne's arms when the door opened. She held me tightly and consoled me and helped me to a chair. My dear friend called the Chicago Heights Paramedics. They soon arrived, but it had snowed about four or five inches, and the walkway and the stairs were covered. It was not safe to try and bring me out on a stretcher. However, there was no way I could stand to walk on that leg. The paramedics were very kind. They asked where the shovel was and started making a path to get me out safe. Joanne helped me get dressed to go to the hospital. When we arrived at

St. James Hospital, the attending physician in the emergency room told me that a fall of this nature could have resulted in a broken neck, a dislocated hip, or a broken leg. A fall of this kind could have been fatal for a woman of my size.

The doctor stated, "You are lucky."

I responded, "No, God caught me in the palms of his hands and protected me. I am most grateful that the Lord spared my life."

I was released from the hospital after being treated for three days. I was instructed by the attending physician to make a follow-up appointment two weeks after my discharge date. I was to call the clinic. But my heart led me back to Dr. Weber.

I was released with home-care assistance. Three days a week, a nurse came out to take my vital signs, and a physical therapist was sent out to rehabilitate my leg. I lay in bed awaiting a follow-up visit with Dr. Weber. I began thinking about writing to a few people who were in vulnerable situations like me. There was one person who I had never met before. I felt the spirit led me to encourage her. That person was Martha Stewart. I wrote her to extend my love and support. I wanted her to know that everything was going to be all right for her. My spirit wanted to be part of a team of people to support her and her family. I truly believe that in times of trouble, God will send angels to support you. I thanked God, through my times of dismay, that I had others, not just my family, that I could count on. I believe that, if I expect God to bless me and my family, I should also expect God would bless others through me. He is able to wipe away our tears and work out our problems.

I, too, was in a vulnerable situation. I was a praying mother with three sons in personal dilemmas. I wanted to share with Martha that I was a mother whose children were in trouble. I introduced my sons to her by sending her a group picture, a card, and a letter that explained the trouble my sons were in. My words to Martha and her family were to be encouraged and be patient. My prayers went out for her mother also. I, too, had a grandmother praying for me and the return of her great-grandchildren.

It was very rewarding and uplifting to me when Martha Stewart had her office send me a thank-you card. I was most grateful. My grandmother was ninety-nine years old at that time, and my dad was eighty-four. We sent Martha a set of light-up champagne glasses with light-up ice cubes and stirs. We thought of these gifts as God's light to show her the way.

My home care service was ending, and it was time for me to see my doctor. I still couldn't walk well, but there was some improvement. The condition I was in was devastating to my mind. Here I was, over two hundred and ninety pounds, needing assistance putting on my clothes and thanking God for Joanne. It was wintertime, cold, late January, and the weather conditions were dry. The car Joanne was driving me to the doctor in was a four-door 2001 Ford Taurus SE. That's not a small car, but she still had to coach me as to how to get in—my left leg first, and then my crutches. We both knew any bending of my right leg would make me want to holler, cry, and throw up both of my hands. I waved my hands in the air and said, "Lord, heal me."

I loved the way God made the connection between me and Dr. Weber. I believe that only God knows what we need and who we need. At any given time, he will supply our needs. I went through turmoil to make this trip to see Dr. Weber. I knew God was doing something special. She was not only sensitive to the recovery of my leg, but she was also a blessing in my life to assist me with the healing of my mind and my spirit. The multiple difficulties with my body drew me to a wonderful and wonder-filled person, Dr. Kathleen M. Weber. She was another angel.

A Miracle on Flight 1483

After the drama of falling in my own house, I needed a vacation. Bea had arthritis and had thoughts of moving to a warmer climate. She had visited Florida, and her mind was set on West Palm Beach. She relocated while I was in the middle of a terrible personal storm with my three sons. I telephoned Bea to share my heartaches. She was the one who was there for me during my long stretches of hysterical moments. Again, she was the first person who showed me love as my friend and sista in my time of trouble.

While I was in the middle of all my issues, including my health challenges, Sista Bea called me and instructed me to pack my bags and come to Florida for some rest and relaxation. I was overjoyed. I couldn't stop thanking her for the invitation. Her thoughtfulness was above and beyond my imagining. I could feel God's love in her. The lamp of God lighted my way directly to a person who was full of God's love. She was not a selfish sista. I was looking forward to the time I would spend with my friend. Bea asked me to select a date to travel to Florida. Selecting a date wasn't easy, due to my many family obligations. Therefore, I enlisted the help of three special ladies, Joanne, Darla Boyd, and Marguerite. Without their assistance, my miracle could not have taken place. These three ladies helped me shop for groceries and cook meals for my grandmother and dad. They delivered the meals to my dad's home. These ladies' kindness allowed me to take advantage of the invitation.

I selected May 12, 2005, for my departure date to Florida. My health challenges required a wheelchair escort to the gate. I boarded Delta Flight 1483 and found my seat. A young lady with long brown hair and thick eyelashes was sitting in the aisle seat, holding a baby who looked to be about eleven months old. The baby had curly brown hair, long lashes, and caramel-colored skin. In the window seat sat a gentleman with brown hair and a gleaming smile. Before taking my seat, I looked at my ticket and asked the flight attendant if she thought the young lady on the aisle would exchange seats with me due to my leg aliment. I did not realize that it was in divine order for me to sit in my assigned seat. I also did not realize that there was a blessing for each of us on that row. Later, I would find out that it was fate, true enough, for the young lady was originally supposed to have flown out with the rest of her family the day before. I would also learn that Jim, the man sitting in the window seat, had been booked for an earlier flight, but a business meeting required him to stay longer than expected. The young lady preferred the aisle seat so she could attend to the baby's needs. Therefore, I took the middle seat. I greeted the passengers on each side of me, including the baby. I said, "This must be the angel row." We all laughed. I didn't know then that we had all been blessed by divine intervention.

I must explain this once-in-a-lifetime experience. It was truly a miracle how I was able to meet my great-grandson for the very first time. He was born on June 13, 2004. His mother, Cara, who I had never met, was sitting right beside me, arm to arm. I had no idea that my great-grandson and his mother were flying with me through the clouds.

I was talking to the gentleman on my right. His name was Jim. We began talking about our families and discovered that we had a lot in common. He had twin sisters, and I had twin sons. He had two sons, and I had three sons. He had a loving mother, and I was a loving mother. This young man seemed so very nice. He was the same age as Vaughn. He was born the same month and year, just three days apart.

I told him I wanted to watch a movie, but the flight attendant had put my DVD player in the overhead compartment. Jim told me, "You don't have to worry about your DVD player; you may use my laptop computer to watch your movie." I thought that this was so very nice of him. He said, "I am going to take this time to relax."

I replied, "Oh my God, this is truly a sweet person, another angel."

Jim laughed and said, "If I were you I wouldn't call me an angel."

He said that he was not a big believer and had just a little faith. I told him that God could work with him. I explained to him that he had the mustard-seed faith. It only takes one seed to create an entire tree. I told him I believed that each one of us in our row was an angel, even the baby. In the past, I had never sat beside a baby who did not require a seatbelt. On this flight the mother, Cara, had to hold the baby on her lap. The baby would not stop playing with me. He started blowing bubbles and smiling. When he pinched me, I thought to myself that this baby was going to be trouble. I said, "Baby, you better not pinch me any more."

The mother of the baby said, "I don't know what's wrong with him. He really doesn't like anyone; he doesn't let anyone touch him without crying."

The baby was playing with me as though he knew me. I asked how old he was. Cara told me that he was eleven months old. I never thought to ask what the baby's name was, but I knew that this baby was special. I expressed to Cara that he could have been one of my babies. He was a precious little one. I said to him, "You can call me Mama May, as all my grand babies do."

While the baby was playing with me, Jim asked the names of my twin sons. "Victor and Verdell," I replied.

The young lady said, "Excuse me, I didn't mean to be listening to your conversation, but did I hear the names Victor and Verdell?"

I responded, "Yes, you heard me correctly. Did you go to school with them?"

"No, I have never met them, but I recognized their names." She then said that she was sure the brothers she knew were not my sons. "The brothers that I know have a brother named Vaughn."

At this point, I was simply astonished. I explained, "Victor, Verdell, and Vaughn are all my sons. I am their mother."

She stared crying, and I asked her what was wrong. She replied, "This baby I'm holding is Vaughn's grandson. This baby is your great-grandson. His name is Triston Jr."

I gasped and said, "Oh, my God!"

Jim heard Cara's remarks, and he became emotional. As the flight attendant was walking past our row, she noticed that we were all in tears. She became concerned. We shared our story with her, and she became emotional, as well.

Passengers in the surrounding rows and across the aisle in front of us and in back of us were tapping us on the shoulders to say that this was fate. Our flight attendant attempted to find a logical explanation for our seating assignments. She asked for our last names to determine whether the computer had assigned our seats together by last name. I was sure that the computer did not put us together, because Baby Triston was carrying my maiden name. No one on this flight knew my maiden name except God.

Angels in My Life

I was high above the clouds meeting my great-grandson and his mother for the first time. I didn't know the young lady's last name. She was an Italian lady, and I am an African American. I took her by the hand and whispered to her, "Could you repeat the name you gave to the flight attendant?" We formerly introduced ourselves while the flight attendant went to check our names on the passenger list. The flight attendant came back to tell us that all of our last names were different. We had not been seated according to last names. "I know that," I replied. "I am Mathell Givens."

The flight attendant looked at me in astonishment and responded, "This has to be fate."

Jim, the passenger on my right, continued to display his emotions. Jim was a Caucasian man who explained that he was not very religious because he believed things just happened. This experience, up in the clouds, had drawn him closer to God. He was anxious to share this experience with others. Jim wanted to know where the baby's grandfather and father were. Why hadn't they brought baby Triston to meet me?

I contemplated for a moment, trying to decide exactly how to explain this very difficult situation. Triston Sr., the baby's father, had not contacted me in the past five years. Triston Sr.'s father—my son Vaughn—was incarcerated and facing conspiracy charges in a federal medical center. I explained that his medical records showed that he was in need of a heart transplant. He could not be placed on a waiting list because he was serving time in a federal prison. Vaughn was currently in the appeal process. I turned to Jim and continued sharing my story. I explained how our family was praying for an appeal in Vaughn's case. The appeal would provide Vaughn's freedom, and then we could find a heart specialist.

I explained to Jim that I believed Vaughn was in the "belly of the whale," as it is stated in the Bible, Jonah Chapter 2:17. God's whale will one day bring Vaughn to safety. Jim looked at me and said, "That's a powerful statement. I wish that I had your story."

As fate would have it, I had written my story prior to getting on the plane. I had e-mailed the story to author and screenwriter Tyler Perry. In the email, I explained how I called his office and was told by a lady who answered that Mr. Perry doesn't do other people's stories. After hearing this, I was still hopeful and said to the lady, "I believe he will consider mine, because I am a Dreamer!" I listened to my heart before leaving home that day and had brought a copy of the email with me. I had read an interview in a magazine of Mr. Perry's amazing journey out of the wilderness into the marvelous light. I could relate to Mr. Perry's story of homelessness because of the conditions Vaughn's five children were living in. Vaughn's family had been displaced as a result of his federal indictment. My son Victor was also incarcerated in January 2005. In February of the same year, the mother of Victor's firstborn child was the victim of a fatal automobile accident. She was driving and her brakes went out. This caused her to plow into a tanker truck. She was burned beyond recognition. This child, Ricky, was suddenly left without a mother or father to raise him.

I had also e-mailed Oprah Winfrey. She had just begun her travels to South Africa, where she motivated and provided encouragement to the South African children. In my e-mail to her, I requested that she help me to encourage my grandchildren, especially my granddaughters. I was so afraid that my granddaughters would fall into an "I think I am in love" trap. This often happens when young girls do not experience enough love and attention in life. Vaughn's wife had to work, and she could only find part-time work as a bus driver. For her part-time job, she was called at all hours of the day or night. She did not spend consistent time with the children. Jim was in tears when he finished reading the copies of the e-mails that I had written to Tyler Perry and Oprah Winfrey. Jim was a scientist who knew a famous author and screenwriter of mystery stories. Jim promised to help get my story to the appropriate parties. In Jim, I had met another angel. I had been waiting for a miracle. Delta Flight 1483 had provided that miracle. Oh, what a blessing to have had the opportunity to meet my great-grandson, his mother, and my new friend, Jim. Jim was my God-sent godson. To this day, Jim calls me Mama May. We talk by phone and e-mail each other on a weekly basis.

I explained to Jim the reason I was taking this trip. I had been invited to come to West Palm Beach to visit my girlfriend Bea. My friend was led by compassion to try and help mend my broken heart. Bea was a blessing to a sista who needed love. As we approached Atlanta, I began crying. Jim was crying, and my great-grandson's mother, Cara, was crying. Baby Triston Jr. was fast asleep on my chest.

I give honor to God Almighty for ordaining this day in the sky on Delta Flight 1483. God had used ordinary people to bless each other. This experience in the sky left me in awe.

When the plane landed in West Palm Beach, my soul was bubbling over with excitement. I told people throughout the airport of the wonderful surprise on my flight. My sista Bea and her husband J.L. met me at the baggage counter. I could hardly speak fast enough to tell them about the miracle in the sky. I was grateful. The Good Lord had used Sista Bea to orchestrate a perfect meeting above the clouds.

We left the airport and headed to their new home. The view was phenomenal as we arrived at the gated community. I could see the swimming pool from the front gate. The pool area was set up with tables and umbrellas. The grounds were neatly manicured, and all of the homes looked fabulous. As we entered Bea's home, I heard a noise. I asked Bea if she heard a noise. She said no. She began to show me around their lovely home. Again, I thought I heard a noise. Suddenly, as we passed the patio, I saw two familiar faces.

The faces belonged to my sisters in Christ, Myra and Shirley from Dallas, Texas. All I could do was slap the hall wall over and over again and stamp my feet. I shouted, "Oh Lord, here we are again, the four musketeers. How many more blessings do you have in store for me?"

I had not seen Myra in twenty years and Shirley in six years. Bea had contacted them and told them about my troubles. Myra and Shirley traveled to Florida to surprise me. They wanted to spend time with a sista in need of much love. They were two more angels.

Life Goes On

Never in my wildest dreams did I believe that I would raise three sons who would graduate from the same elementary school as I did. Nor did I believe that I would sit in that same school office waiting to register my granddaughter Versharia. She was entering the eighth grade. As we waited, I found myself reminiscing about all the wonderful times I had on the school's premises. My fourteen-year-old granddaughter and her dad, Vaughn, had recently moved to Summit, Illinois, where Graves Elementary School is located. There had been quite a bit of remodeling and additions to the school in the forty-one years since I graduated. The school had been divided into a middle school and elementary school. While I was registering Versharia, I thought I would inquire about a trophy I had won forty-one years ago, when I was fourteen years old. The office assistant who enrolled Versharia identified herself as Mrs. Johnstone. I told her that I graduated from Graves Elementary School and shared with her that I had won a trophy for the Most Talented in 1966. Winning that trophy was one of my most exciting experiences, and it had a positive effect on my life.

I explained that I was writing a book. I showed her a picture of Spike Lee, the famous author and movie director, and myself. It had been taken at his book signing. Mrs. Johnstone expressed genuine happiness for me and encouraged me to continue my writing. She took all of the contact information to reach me, and she promised me she would attempt to locate my trophy.

I did get a call, but not from Mrs. Johnstone. The call came from the school principal, Mr. Lewis. He introduced himself and told me that he was holding the trophy for the Most Talented for the Class of 1966 at Graves Elementary School. The trophy had my name engraved on it. He said that I was the last person to receive the Most Talented award at the school. He invited me to pick up the trophy and take some pictures. Mr. Lewis also suggested I come back to the school when my book was completed for a book signing and to make a presentation to the students. I agreed to donate a book to the school to be displayed in the school's showcase. Mr. Lewis explained that he did not recall anyone who had graduated from Graves Elementary School and had written a book. I was filled with gratitude and happiness. We set a date for my next visit to the school.

I called Mr. Adam Bruce, a videographer. Adam agreed to accompany me on the scheduled date. When we arrived at Graves Elementary School, the superintendent, Mr. Dixey, joined Mr. Lewis in welcoming us to the school. The school photographer was also present to take pictures. Adam videotaped the school administrators awarding me my trophy. I felt so proud. I needed this push to keep me stepping toward my future. I could feel the love, pride, and care from Mr. Lewis and Mr. Dixey. They showed great appreciation for my time, work and effort. They appeared to be impressed with me, even though they didn't know the message or subject of my book. This was a spectacular and awesome event for me.

Mr. Lewis gave us a grand tour of the school. We visited the auditorium to see the stage on which I had performed and graduated. I was taken into a room where teachers were meeting. There, I saw Mr. Sullivan. He and I both were raised in Summit,

Illinois, and knew a lot of the same people. Versharia was assigned to one of Mr. Sullivan's classes.

This was an emotional time for me, because I had the opportunity to share the predicament my granddaughter was in with the faculty. She was pregnant and only fourteen years of age. She was also estranged from her biological mother. For that reason, I wanted to be all that I could be for her. I had the complete attention of the people in the room. After I shared Versharia's plight with the faculty, I became so overwhelmed that I had to back out of the room. The faculty and administrators did not know Versharia's father had been in prison or that she had been abandoned by her stepmother. There was so much they didn't know about Versharia.

In the hallway, I fell into Adam's and Mr. Lewis's arms, consumed with emotion. It took a moment for me to regain my composure. Afterward, Mr. Lewis escorted us to some classrooms that had been remodeled. We went into the same classroom I sat in when I was fourteen. Mr. Lewis told the students that I had attended their school and was standing in the same classroom I occupied forty-one years ago. I thought to myself that the children were precious little ones, and so was I when I was their age. Mr. Lewis explained to the students that I was writing a book. He asked me to share a few words of encouragement and motivation with them. As I exited the room, I was touched by the moment. This event would definitely be recorded in my life's journal of precious memories. At the end of the tour, Mr. Lewis asked if the visit had brought back a lot of memories. I responded by belting out the song *Memories*. He then replied, "I can see how you won that trophy." In the future, I hope the school will return to the practice of presenting an award to the most talented student.

I had a wonderful role model and teacher at Graves Elementary School, Mr. Fred Dunleavy. He was a drama and theater instructor. He saw my potential from the very beginning. He had me focus on singing and acting. He motivated me the entire time. I am grateful because Mr. Dunleavy saw my potential and encouraged the development of my creative and professional skills. He was one of the kindest and most outspoken people I have ever met. Mr. Dunleavy taught me to stand up straight, hold my head high, and act as if I owned the place. He was very instrumental in forming the woman I have become. In 1966, I was one of the leading actors in a musical play written by Mr. Dunleavy. It was an awesome play that highlighted my skills and contributed to me winning the trophy for being most talented.

Mr. Dunleavy transferred from Graves Elementary School to Argo High School, where I was enrolled. He wrote and produced a musical at Argo High School. I was selected as one of the leading ladies. I had the opportunity to show off my vocal talents again. My performance enabled me to win yet another trophy. I sang a solo entitled, "I Knew When My Love Came Along." I also did a duet with another young lady entitled "Ohio." The play was a smash hit. Those were the days.

My biological parents missed my grammar-school days. However, when I was in high school, my birth mother, Mildred, became a security guard at the school. She and Mr. Dunleavy became acquainted and that made me quite happy. Mama Mildred had married a great man named Lenny. They lived directly across the street from Argo High. When there was trouble at the school, or when a fight or protest would erupt, I would run out the back door directly to Mama Mildred's house. I learned well in grammar school to stay clear of trouble. Mama Mildred and I had a yo-yo type of relationship, but during this time, we became closer than ever.

I have had many flashbacks since I enrolled my granddaughter into her last year of grammar school. I recalled when I was pregnant at age fifteen. I find myself very sensitive to my granddaughter's difficulties. I understand what Versharia is going through in and out of school. I know it is hard for her. I am very grateful to walk beside my granddaughter and be a blessing to her. I find myself praying and asking others to pray with me as I walk with her. I encourage her to keep her mind on school and her dreams. There are others whom I am indebted to who have blessed Versharia in their special way: Aunt Felecia; Ladrena BoBo; Karen Turner; Catherine Ingram; Aileen Johnson, Pamela, my childhood friend; and Britney Smith, Pamela's daughter. They are a blessing to Versharia, as my godparents were to me. I am compelled to become the same for Versharia. Similarly, I am very fortunate Mr. Dunleavy encouraged me to continue high school. He told me that anyone could make a mistake, but that I must continue my education. I am very proud to say that I did.

On November 16, 2007, my granddaughter Versharia delivered a six pound, fifteen ounce baby girl. I played a major role in the birthing of my great-granddaughter. It was the most wonderful experience of my life being in the delivery room. Versharia's father, Vaughn, assisted also. There was a long wait before the baby entered the birth canal. Dr. Lerch was the attending physician. When he entered the room and examined her, he voiced his concerns that she might need to have a cesarean section. He said that sometimes, at the age of fourteen, the mother's body may not have matured enough for a baby to successfully enter and pass through the canal without getting stuck. So he felt he needed to forewarn us of all possibilities. Immediately after the doctor spoke, I began to pray out loud. I placed my hands on my granddaughter's stomach and called out to Jesus for help. I prayed that Jesus would clear the birth canal and let the baby enter. Versharia did not have any knowledge of what a cesarean was, and I explained to her that I had one with my twin sons. Versharia asked me if it hurt, and I replied yes. I still have the scar to show where I was cut. I pulled up my dress and showed her the cut on my stomach from my C-section.

My granddaughter was in shock. She had a frown on her face. She said softly, "I sure hope I don't have one."

I told Versharia to help me pray for her and the baby. She asked me what to ask God for. I gave her a very simple prayer: "Lord, help me and please supply everything that I need for my baby to come safely."

I prayed some more for myself. I needed to be strong and witty. As I think back to my firstborn, I was just a young girl, fifteen years old. I could feel Versharia's concerns and uncertainties about having a baby. I kept on walking and waving my hands and praying. I was praying and singing, "All of Our Help Comes from the Lord" and "Lord Move in This Room." Versharia was quiet, and I believe, deep in her soul, she was praying with me. In between Dr. Lerch coming in to monitor the progress, the nurses were there constantly. The first shift of nurses would each say that she was making slow progress. The baby was doing well. Her heartbeat was very good, but first babies take time. As the morning shift of nurses ended, the new shift came on and began to do their rounds about four o'clock in the afternoon.

The contractions started to get stronger. Versharia couldn't bear these pains, and when the nurse came into the room, she asked the nurse for an epidural. While the nurse was with her, I slowly walked out of the room and waited for the nurse to come out so she could call for the specialist to administer the medicine in Versharia's back. I stopped the nurse, and I smiled at her. I said, "Can you slow down before making the call?" The nurse looked at me in amazement. I said, "I need my granddaughter to feel these pains for a little while. I don't want her to feel like it was easy having a baby. If she thinks that all you have to do is call for a pain shot and not feel the contraction anymore, then she'll think it's a piece of cake to have a baby." I told the nurse it was very important she remember how painful it was before the epidural was administered.

The nurse smiled at me and said, "I got you."

My granddaughter was very strong and bore down as the pains hit her. She would stretch her hands up high. Her fingers would spread and stiffen out. She would sigh, "Oh, ooo, oh, Mama May." I started to coach her on how to breathe. I wished we had taken classes. However, without the classes, we managed just fine. God coached me, and I started demonstrating. I sucked in air through my nose and slowly exhaled through my mouth. I spoke out firmly, "Breathe, baby girl, breathe. Look at me. Come on, baby; you can do this," and she did.

As the contractions became more and more unbearable, Versharia would holler out. She would turn on her left side and say, "Oh, where is that doctor with the medicine?"

I was tickled inside. I explained to her that when the doctor comes and starts the procedure, it is advisable that you do not move while the needle is being placed in your back. I had heard from a nurse that you could become paralyzed if you moved during this procedure. About forty minutes had passed when the doctor came walking through the door. I can truly tell you she was weary and worn out from pain. She started to become happy because she had heard that with this shot, she would not feel anymore contractions. She had heard from her sister, who had a baby the year before that she would only feel pressure. After the process, Versharia felt much better.

All of the nurses in the birthing center were excellent, but there was one who was extraordinary and connected to my sprit as she entered to take granddaughter's vitals. She introduced herself as Nurse Jenny Stewart. This was the first nurse who introduced herself. She had an accent. I asked her where she was from, and she replied with a smile, "England." She told me that she had heard me praying as she entered the room. When I arrived at the hospital, my granddaughter had already been there for five hours. I never left Versharia's side because her contractions started to increase. It seemed the more I prayed, the greater her contractions became. Nurse Jenny became an integral part of the birth. Along with me, she helped coach my granddaughter to push and to say to herself, "I am wonderful and God is wonderful." I stayed through each shift until the arrival of our new baby girl. What a miraculous moment when I heard her cry. To my surprise, the nurse placed her in my arms first. She was such a beautiful little baby. Times were very hard for me, and my son Vaughn had very little. This baby was born into a sometimes cold and cruel world. But she was here. I had to believe someway, somehow, we were going to make it with our new baby. I prayed God would provide.

In my lifetime, I can never remember my father and I being together on Father's Day. I remember asking my dad, year after year, for at least thirty years, "Let's go to dinner on Father's Day." He would always refuse. But with God in my life, I would humble myself over and over again. I would continue to ask him each Father's Day. I would get the same answer, and I would be so disappointed. I would never get so discouraged that I would not keep coming back, waiting to hear yes from my dad. I had always believed that one day, my dad and I would have this special time together as father and daughter.

Two weeks before Father's Day, I told him that I would not take no for an answer anymore. I said, "Dad, you have used every excuse there is during my lifetime. In the past, you have told me, 'No, baby, I can't leave the house. You know I run a business from home, and I am afraid somebody might try and break in.'" I explained to my dad that he didn't run a business anymore. He didn't have the responsibilities that he had had in the past. He no longer had to care for his beloved wife or his precious mother. "Starting this Father's Day," I stated firmly, "you are going to take my life and your life out of the holding pattern. You must start to enjoy your life with your daughter." I explained to him that at eighty-five years old, he needed to start enjoying life. He tried to rebel, but he realized how adamant I was about this subject. At that moment, my dad agreed to spend Father's Day with me. I was so overjoyed. I reached out to my dad with my arms wide open to give him a big hug. Inside, my spirit was screaming and shouting "Thank you, Lord."

For the first time in my life, at the age of fifty-four, I had a date with my dad for Father's Day. One of my dreams was about to be fulfilled. This dream could make me so very happy. This is one of the days that I had prayed for as long as I could remember, even when I was a little girl. In past years, my dad and I had only attended funerals for family members together. I realized that we were about to experience something that we had never done before. What a blessing to know that patience is a virtue and all things come in the proper time. Finally, our time had come.

My dad and I had been through a lot in the past seven years. We had some sad times and some happy times. I could see clearly the love between us had been on trial. Now, our future looked bright. My dad and I realized that the past was the past, and we could not do anything about it. We were both very happy to be together at this time in our lives. We realized that we had truly been blessed by God to have this opportunity. Many times, people wish they could have, should have, or would have done the right things in their lives. They did not have the chance to make amends with one of their loved ones or a dear friend. I could feel the Lord healing, mending, and restoring a father and a daughter. We were both looking forward to our outing. Well, check this out, our day had finally come. I couldn't even sleep. The night before our planned outing, I tossed and turned all night. I was up at four o'clock in the morning. I was imagining how the day was going to be. I prayed and thanked God for arranging this special day. I walked around the house talking out loud, "I am going to be with my daddy on this Father's Day." I was just like a little girl, because I still have some little girl in me.

The time had finally come for me to travel to my dad's house, which was about one hour away. As I was riding along in my car, I worshipped, I sang, and I had a good sermon in my CD deck that kept my mind in perfect peace. I felt so much joy. Before I knew it, I was about ten minutes away from my dad's house. When I arrived, my dad was all smiles. He asked me, "Daughter, where are we going?"

I said, "Daddy, it's a surprise, but I believe you are going to love it."

He responded with a big chuckle, "Baby, you know all the nice places, and you know Daddy hasn't been anywhere except where you've taken him."

I must tell you that my dad, even in his younger days, didn't go anywhere. It was not that he couldn't afford to, because he had plenty of money. But he just didn't allocate the time. I remember when I was working for a travel agency. I used to bring him brochures to help broaden his interest in travel. He dreamed of retiring one day. In retirement, he planned to take our whole family on a cruise. I remembered the words he had spoken twenty-five years ago. The time for the cruise had arrived. I had planned a brunch cruise, in Chicago, for Father's Day. As we approached our destination, you could see the ramp to the big ship. I said, "Daddy, look over there. Look at that mega ship."

He said, "Baby, are we going over there?"

I answered, "Yes."

His face was glowing. He asked, "Is it really sitting in the water?"

I thought his question was so cute. It made me smile and laugh. I said. "Oh yes, Daddy, it is really sitting in water."

"Are we going sailing?"

I told him, "No. The ship stays docked."

He said, "Daughter, you know how to make somebody happy."

I told him I remembered his dream for our family. I hoped this would make him happy. This was his first step toward his ocean cruise. I said, "Dad, God is so good, and I can't thank him enough for our day. It pleases my heart to be out with you today. I know we are going to have fun." We both agreed that only God could have arranged this day and made it so precious and memorable.

As we approached the valet area, my dad became excited because the car was being parked for us. I smiled when I realized that this was a first-time adventure for him. He said, "Daughter, you know about big-time things. Is it expensive?" I explained that the fee would be waived because of his handicapped parking decal. We used his automatic wheelchair so that he could explore the whole ship in comfort. I am here to tell you, we had a blast! Dad had never seen so many people. He was all smiles and continuously thanked me and enjoyed the view of Lake Michigan from the dining room. We were both dazed by the water and its movement.

I said to him, "I must tell you something about your daughter that you don't know. Your daughter loves the water. I am a water baby."

He smiled and said that he also loved the water. He hadn't been on a ship since he was in the army. But that was a stressful time for him, because it was during WWII. This experience on the water was different, because it was so relaxing and the view of the lake was spectacular. "I am at peace, daughter. I think that looking into the water is soothing my mind. Baby, this is nice." He had a great big old smile on his face. I told him to enjoy himself, because this was our day. We had a fabulous brunch. Dad had never seen so much food. As Dad and I sat dining together, I realized that the best was yet to come. I realized that God was truly at work in our lives. I was overwhelmed with this awesome connection.

What love God has for each of us. I realized that only he can fix what is broken in each of our lives. He made each one of us, and he is the only one who knows everything about us. I sometimes become surprised when I react in a certain way. Yet none of our actions are a surprise to the Almighty. He knows the plan for each of us.

Our day ended with a big hug and kiss. There was so much gratitude expressed between us. I held my head up toward the blue sky and smiled. I knew that heaven was smiling on the two of us. Father's Day 2007 was definitely an unforgettable day for me and is imprinted in my mind as a miracle.

I've always wanted to be Nathell's little girl. But it's funny how things happen. If we fast-forward to today, my dad and I are very close friends. We have been taking care of each other for over seven years now. As I look back, I see how the Lord's spirit guided me to help him with his wife until her death. We also were led by love and compassion to rescue his blind mother. Now, Nathell and I really know what it means to be blood kin.

One Sunday, at church I met Mother Davis. During the time for testimony sharing, Mother Davis testified that she had no cartilage in her knees. A few minutes after her testimony, I had begun to sing along with the choir, "Oh How I Love Jesus." As I sang, Mother Davis asked me what was wrong with me. I replied, "It's my children." She went to the front of the church and got on her bad knees and prayed for me and my family. After church, we talked. Mother Davis was a woman who had had many experiences and had two sons who had been in vulnerable situations and a daughter who had gone astray. We exchanged names and were glad we had met. Yet we never called one another. A year later, after Mama Mildred had died, I went back to see Mother Davis at the church. The choir sang a couple of songs, and then, to my amazement, they began to sing, "Oh How I Love Jesus" again. As I harmonized along with them, she turned and looked back. I was two seats directly behind her. It was as though she could hear the urgency in my voice to reach God. She slowly walked back to where I was sitting and commented on how angelic my voice was. She asked me what was wrong this time. I told her that my mother had died. After church, we talked for a long while and consented to be a mother and daughter to one another. We felt God had sent both of us to comfort each other. I have felt Mother Davis and I were ordained to love one another.

Before I met Aileen, I had a goddaughter who had considered helping me with my book. She decided she wanted to be paid because of financial difficulties she was experiencing. I always tried to make myself available to help her in any way. I could never ask her for money for any reason. She wanted a negotiator to discuss her role in the project. I asked Mother Davis if she would be that person, and she agreed. Three minutes into the conversation, Mother Davis assessed the situation and ended the conversation. She stated that this wasn't a project my goddaughter should be involved in. When it was just us on the line, she said, "Baby, what's the man's name with the '40 Acres and a Mule'?" Just as she asked me the question, her other phone line rang. As I held on, she switched back to me and said, "That was my daughter, Kemmy. While I had her on the phone, I asked her if she knew the man's name, and she said his name was Spike Lee." Mother Davis prophesied that day that Spike Lee and I would meet. She instructed me to keep moving forward. She took me under her wings, as her daughter, and our relationship continued to grow.

Four or five days later, I heard an announcement on television that Spike Lee would be at a book signing at Borders Bookstore in downtown Chicago. The prophetic words spoken from Mother Davis were before me. I began to make plans to meet Spike Lee.

The night before meeting him, I had a set appointment to visit with a very loving, spirit-filled, and beautiful lady named Phyllis Luster. I had recently met her at a spa. While relaxing in the whirlpool, we shared some very heartfelt stories. I told her that my dad was in the clothing business. She invited me to come over and show her some of the fashions. By the time I arrived, I was emotional and needed to talk about my family's situation. She was quite a listener. I wanted to share with her my idea of writing a book and my upcoming visit to see Mr. Spike Lee. I felt this was a divine meeting between Spike Lee and me. I did not want to stumble through it. When I told her, she grabbed me by the hands and began to pray for me and my family. In her prayer, she asked God to open up the windows of heaven and pour out as many blessings as needed. At the end of the prayer, I asked her how I should act when I met Spike. Phyllis smiled at me. She began coaching me on how to approach him and what to say. There was so much laughter between us. I was charged up and ready for this new spiritual journey. I thanked her and commented that she was precious, and she said, "That's my husband's name, Precious Luster, of Luster Hair Care Products." My visit with Phyllis Luster was a blessing. I will always remain grateful for her kindness. She took time out of her busy schedule for me. I believe she was spiritually sent to lift me up. We have remained friends. I feel that she was another angel assigned to me.

The next day Joanne and I went to Borders Bookstore to meet Mr. Spike Lee. He autographed a copy of his book for me. As he was writing, I heard my spirit tell me to mention my grandmother. I began to talk like a poet. I said, "Mr. Lee my grandmother is ninety-nine years old. Her name is Rosie Lee and your name is Spike Lee." I could see the amazement on his face. He replied, "My grandmother is also the same age." I went on to point out that my dad's nickname was Ike just like Spike. He smiled. I asked him to take a picture with me. I gave him an excerpt from my manuscript that I had gift wrapped. He gave me a hug and told me to let him know when my book was completed. It was magical being with such an artistic and successful writer and movie producer.

When I returned home and shared with Grandmother my encounter with Spike Lee, Grandmother wanted to know Mr. Lee's grandmother's name so she could pray for her. A few days later, I learned Mr. Lee would be visiting the Betty Shabazz School in Chicago. So off I went to find out Spike Lee's grandmother's name. Again, I was the third person in line. Mr. Lee recognized me, and I shared with him my grandmother's request. He smiled and said, "Let me write her name in your book," and he wrote the name "Zimmie." The irony of it all is I had a mother figure I called godmama. Her name was Jimmie. This awesome blessing assured me I was going in the right direction.

Meeting Spike Lee

One particular Saturday, I decided to stay at home and take it easy. The moment I took a deep breath, the telephone rang. I glanced at my alarm clock and noticed it was exactly 7:00 AM. I checked the caller ID and noticed that it was Mother Davis. I always looked forward to answering her calls because there was always such delight in her voice. This call was no different, as she greeted me with "Good morning." As in every call, she extended a prayer requesting many blessings for my day and the three V-boys. Mother Davis asked about my plans for the day. I shared with her how I was feeling and what I wanted to attempt to do. She felt my dismay and suggested I come to her place to rest and allow her to console me. I told her that sounded like a great plan. I hurried off the telephone and began to prepare to spend the day with my God-sent Mama and from that day I started calling her Mama Davis. While I was packing a few things to take with me, the doorbell rang. It was Mark Whitman, a gentleman who had been helping me film parts of my life story. He was in a hurry, but stopped by to deliver an envelope with some footage snippets and documents regarding my life's journey. I was anxious about viewing the footage and video snippets, so when Mark left, I finished packing and placed the unopened package in my bag.

When I arrived at Mama Davis's house, my spirits were lifted. I showed her the package I had just received from Mark. She was excited to view the video snippets, and once we got settled in, we put one of the videos in the recorder. It was so much fun to watch Mama Davis jump in her seat and say, "Baby, this is like watching a movie."

Mama Davis was thrilled. She shared her vision of Spike Lee coming back to Chicago. She wanted me to find out when and where he was going to be. She expressed in her soft-toned voice, "Mathell, I can feel him returning and you must find him." She said, "I am convinced he is looking for some new movies, and baby, you certainly have a great one." I was so excited and encouraged to hear Mama Davis profess this to me. I was on a natural high. We had a wonderful day together, and I felt terrific when our day ended. When I got home on Saturday evening, I began to prepare for Sunday morning church service and then went to sleep.

The church service was a lovely spirit-filled fellowship, and it was perfectly matched with my Saturday with Mama Davis. Normally, I treat myself to breakfast after church, but this particular Sunday, I went straight home. After entering the house, I immediately took off my Sunday best and turned on the television. I was starting to prepare my evening dinner when the afternoon news came on announcing the Chicago International Film Festival honoring the movie star Ruby Dee. The newscaster's next announcement floored me. The presenter of Ruby Dee's award was none other than Mr. Spike Lee. I was so overcome, I missed the event details. I immediately called someone who I knew would know about such things, Karen Mayo. I needed information to get to Mr. Lee. Karen was an acquaintance who was involved in all types of special events. She was also a wiz on a computer. Karen needed an hour to research the information. She returned the call within the hour and informed me that Spike Lee would be at Northwestern University's Thorne Auditorium for the forty-second Chicago International Film Festival. She told me how much the tickets were for the program and after-party.

I excitedly called my girl, Joanne, and told her about my evening with Mama Davis and her prophecy about Mr. Spike Lee was coming back to town. Joanne insisted she would go with me and assist me due to my health. She wanted to make sure the parking wasn't too far away from the venue, so I wouldn't have to walk far. My body had become weak and fragile, but I pressed on. She was always there to help me. She was indeed a true friend. My beautiful sista, Joanne believed in my dreams and had much love for me. I shared with her the cost of the ticket to see Mr. Spike Lee give Mrs. Ruby Dee her well-deserved award. I let her know there was an after-party where we could meet some of the celebrities, but that that was an additional cost. She suggested we place the after-party tickets on her credit card. However, I felt that if it was God's will for us to go to the after-party, a way would present itself. I assured Joanne that we were going to go to the affair on faith. We further talked about Mama Davis's premonition. Joanne said, "I stand strong with you, Mathell."

We left home in our red dresses, an hour early, and were among the first guests to arrive. This gave us the opportunity to get a good parking space and choose great seats. The auditorium's seats appeared to be too low. I was afraid I would split my dress at the seams and possibly reinjure my hamstring if I had to squat so low to sit. I thought I would need paramedics to assist me out of the seat, and I wanted to be spared from such embarrassment. As those thoughts entered my mind, I noticed folding chairs in the front of the auditorium on the main floor. I tapped Joanne on her shoulder and pointed to the folding chairs. She and I rushed down to the area to see if the space was reserved. Thank God, it was not. As I approached the folding-chair area, a young lady stepped from behind the curtains onto the stage. I asked if the chairs were for special guests. She replied no. They were for those who were disabled. Those were the words I needed to hear. I sat and patiently waited for Mr. Spike Lee's presentation. I was in the front, so I was sure he would see me when he came on the stage.

Spike Lee was introduced and began the award ceremony by showing a series of movie clips from Mrs. Dee's films. As the clips began, Mr. Lee took a seat in the audience in the front row, seven seats away from me. This was a divine seating arrangement. No one could have planned it better than God. When the program was over, I rushed up the stairs to the lobby. I had hoped to speak with Mr. Spike Lee. I as told by a lady from a cable company that Mr. Lee had just left through another door. Contemplating my next move, I began to browse around the lobby, waiting for Joanne.

When Joanne reached the lobby, we began to discuss the program as we walked outside the auditorium. The second shuttle bus heading for the after-party was filling up. We stepped outside the auditorium, and to my surprise, a man approached me and asked if I had a ticket for the after-party. At first, I thought he needed a ticket and I told him no. The man touched me by the hand and placed a ticket in my hand and walked away. I thanked God for the blessing he had just bestowed upon me. However, I needed two tickets, one for myself and another one for Joanne. As I looked down at the ticket I was just given, I found there were two tickets instead of one. I had told Joanne that if it was meant for us to go to the after-party, a way would present itself. So Joanne and I were blessed to go to the after-party and God did make a way.

Joanne and I were grateful as I held up the special after-party tickets. I believed that, since I didn't see Mr. Lee in the lobby, I would have an opportunity to see him at the after-party. The third shuttle bus was filling up quickly, and I thought about my health when it came to boarding the crowded shuttle. I saw another trolley behind it and mentioned to Joanne that we should wait to get on the next one, so we could sit together. I thought that with me being a plus-size fluffy lady, it would be difficult to have to crawl into a seat and lean on a perfect stranger. I thought it would be best to sit next to Joanne who I could elbow or lean on if I needed to.

All of a sudden, the shuttle bus driver loudly announced, "There are five seats left." I heard a soft rushing voice in my head say, "Get on the trolley, five is a good number." I pushed Joanne toward the crowded bus and said, "Get on the shuttle, Joanne. God is talking to me." My thoughts were how God took his hands to form man. I said, "Joanne, five is a good number. Let's get on this shuttle bus."

We stepped on the bus, and little did I know, there was an angel waiting for me on the shuttle. I made my way up the stairs of the bus. Joanne immediately found a seat and sat down. I silently asked God to direct my path to a seat. As I looked toward the passengers on the bus, a woman raised her hand and summoned me to sit next to her. Her smile was very friendly and inviting, and I followed her motion. She slid into the window seat so I could sit comfortably next to her. She began to tell me that she noticed me standing outside and saw I was having difficulty with my leg. She also said she saw the man give me the tickets for the reception. She asked me to lean on her, so I could stretch my leg in the aisle. It was such a peaceful and smooth arrangement that I didn't mind not sitting next to Joanne. I said, "God bless you, little angel. I asked God for an angel, and he brought me you." Her name was Aileen Johnson. She carried my mother's maiden name.

I needed to attend the after-party because I wanted to speak with Spike Lee. I wanted to share my story about my grandmother, and, also throw in the V-boys' story. I learned that Aileen was a member of the Advisory Board of the Black Perspectives segment of the Chicago International Film Festival. When I shared a little of my story with her, she said that she would be willing to get me to Spike Lee if he was at the after-party. I was so excited to meet her, and knew she was sent by God. I gave her my business card and she gave me hers. The irony of it all was when I saw where she worked; it was at the same place I was getting legal advice for my book. As I was leaning on her, she admired my beautiful jewelry and my red outfit. She said red was her favorite color and asked if I were a Delta Sigma Theta. Mrs. Ruby Dee was a Delta, and because I was dressed in red, they thought I was a Delta too. I told her I wasn't and not to be fooled by what I had on. I told her I was really broke and all the jewelry I wore was given to me from the estates of deceased women. It made me realize how people can look at me and assume I have it all together. They take it for granted that I don't need assistance of any kind. I shared with her that I could not afford a ticket for me and my friend to attend the after-party. It was by the grace of God that the gentleman came up to me and gave me the two tickets. She smiled at me as if to say she was not surprised by God's grace. We shared a lot on that short bus trip. We learned she had recently moved to the same south suburb I lived in. She is a twin sister like my twin boys. When we reached the after-party, we found out Mr. Lee would not be in attendance. We had a great time with Aileen and decided to have lunch in the very near future.

Aileen and I met for lunch a few weeks later and talked for hours. I showed her a snippet of the videos of my life's journey. She was really amazed at how God worked in my life and how I was handling my journey. I asked Aileen if she was a creative writer, and she replied she knew how to write and believed she could be creative. She stated she had taken a class where she went to the Cook County women's prison to write poetry with some of the detainees. She said she believed she was creative. I asked her to help me frame a portion of my book. After some thought, she agreed. I love the way God moves. This angel has become very special to me.

After discussing with Aileen my encounters with Spike Lee, she informed me that she heard Mr. Lee would be in Chicago soon. She investigated and found out when and where. What she found out was that Spike Lee would be visiting two Chicago schools as a mentor to encourage the students. Aileen contacted the first school's assistant principal, only to find that his speaking engagement was a closed campus event. After she told him why she wished to attend the event, he informed Aileen that Spike Lee would be at Cristo Rey Jesuit School located by Chinatown in Chicago. The principal of that school was Ms. Patricia Garrity. We thought if Spike saw us, we could possibly talk a few moments with him. Grandmother had died, and I wanted to tell him that. Aileen helped me compose a letter, and off we went early the next morning to see him.

I was very ill the day we went to see Mr. Lee. I had gone to the doctor the day before we were to go to the school. Acute asthma had attacked my body something fierce. I just knew I would be hospitalized, but by the grace of God, the x-ray machine was malfunctioning. The doctor decided to give me some medicine and several breathing treatments to see if it would help. I was to call the next day to report to the doctor. Even though I was feeling horrible, I was relieved I wasn't hospitalized. That meant I could attempt to get to Mr. Spike Lee. That evening, I prayed and listened to an encouraging CD from Bishop Noel Jones entitled, "After All I've Been Through, It Has to Happen." I called Aileen and told her, "Be encouraged, I believe we will get to see Mr. Spike Lee tomorrow."

The medicine didn't do much good, but I pressed on. I am a believer that there is a blessing in pressing for anything your heart desires. When Aileen got out of the car, she noticed a vehicle with a driver and asked if he was Spike Lee's driver. He told her he was, and we knew we were in the right place. Aileen went in first to see which door would be easier for me to go through. She went in and briefly shared with the receptionist our plight. The receptionist summoned Mr. Peter Beale-Del Vecchio, who came to the front desk to further investigate our undertaking. Aileen expressed to him how sick I was. He was a man full of compassion. He had us sit in a nearby waiting area. Aileen came and assisted me into the building. We watched Mr. Lee talk with Mr. Peter Beale-Del Vecchio, the director of development, and some of the honor students studying film.

It was very hard for me to walk, and climbing stairs was out of the question. There were special provisions made for me and Aileen to ride on the elevator to each floor. We were escorted by Mr. Connors Kendall, who gave us a tour of the school while Spike toured and talked with some of the students. I was very honored and thankful for the kindness extended. We had a picture taken of Aileen, Mr. Connors, and me. When the meeting ended, Mr. Beale-Del Vecchio told Spike Lee of our wish to talk to him. He walked up to me and greeted me with a smile and asked so graciously what I needed. I told Spike my grandmother was so fond of him. I wanted him to know she had gone on to glory. I told him that I had sent him a letter about Grandmother's death and her obituary. I wasn't sure if he had received it. When we had the opportunity to talk, he was very compassionate and sincerely receptive to the news I had given him. I wanted to share with him about the book I was writing. I asked if I could give the envelope I had prepared to his publicist. He gave me his consent with a very warm smile and a hug.

I was hospitalized the next day, but thankful to have accomplished my mission of seeing Spike Lee.

Little Girl Next Door

In early 2008, my landlord sold her building and the new landlord honored my lease agreement. However, when it expired, she wanted the unit I lived in, so I had to move.

I never mentioned in this book that I am easily frightened, but I am. I believe we all have some fears. When I would leave or enter my apartment, I opened and slammed the door a few times to make noise in case there were any critters like raccoons or squirrels lurking on the porch. I had a really tough time when garbage day rolled around. In late spring of 2007, Illinois had an infestation of cicadas. They were absolutely everywhere, and the sound they made terrified me. I would have anxiety attacks merely thinking about going outside and being surrounded by the flying insects. The bugs hide underground, and every so many years millions come from hiding and make a seriously loud sound in unison. Each week, starting the day before garbage pick-up, I had to muster up the courage to prepare for garbage day. One day, before braving the dreaded task, a little girl appeared. I called out to her, "Little girl, little girl." She answered and I immediately said, "Oh, baby, I really would appreciate it if you would empty the garbage for me."

She came right over said, "Yes." I gave her one dollar for her trouble and asked her name. She said her name was Ieacsha Emery. She told me that she lived next door and that she was ten years old. She was a pretty little girl with a loving spirit. I told her she was my angel and how thoughtful she was to assist me. She said for me not to worry, because she would take out the garbage every week, or whenever I needed it. I was delighted and gave her a hug. She said, with a big smile on her face, "You don't have to give me any more money. I just want to be with you."

I told her she was special and also a precious wonderful baby to be so caring to me. She told me that her mother's name was Kathleen Johnson. It occurred to me that she had the same last name as my birth mother. Ieacsha went on to tell me that she had ten other brothers and sisters. Ieacsha asked me if I could be one of her grandmothers and I told her, "No. I don't think so." But I could hear my inner voice say that I could be her God-sent mother and that she could call me Mama May, like all my children. Ieacsha had an agreeable smile on her face, and it seemed as though her big beautiful eyes were even smiling. I felt she was a God-sent daughter in my life. God sent me help through a baby, and in turn I could be there to help her. I often talked with her mother, who they called "Red." Many times, she had expressed her gratefulness to have someone, besides family, show love and concern for one of her children. Her passionate words made me think about when I was a little baby. Verona and Van Brown were blessed from God to take part in loving and structuring my life. Those precious thoughts rested in my heart. I prayed to be a good person and that the spirit of God would allow me to be special in this little girl's life. I believed that God would supply all of our needs. I was grateful to live next door to her. I knew her grandmother, but she had just moved out and left the house to Ieacsha's mother. My apartment lease was up, and I was asked to move by the new owner. However, I did not want to give up my new little friend and angel.

I decided to keep in touch with her no matter where we were. I would cook and invite her to eat with me almost every day after school. Her company delighted me, and it was my pleasure to sit her at the table, serve her, and say our grace together. I was somewhat lonely and troubled, and she filled my void of missing my children and their children. Because I was not able to be with my children and grandchildren, God sent me a baby to love. To me, God was restoring my hope of being with my children again. We had not been together as a family since 1999.

While standing on the back porch thanking God for everything, I began looking up toward the sky and singing "God Has Been So Good to Me." I only knew two lines of this song. Ieacsha was apparently playing in her front yard and heard me singing and ran around to the back. She said, "Mama May, I can sing, too." She said one of her favorite songs was by the gospel singers, Mary Mary, but she only knew two lines of the song. We both laughed and smiled at each other. She began to sing the lyrics. "I've got to get myself together 'cause I am trying to get to heaven," she sang boldly. I stretched my arms open wide for her to come up and stand on the top stair with me. Looking up at the sky, Ieacsha sang her little heart out. I had her do a repeat of the song and held her by the hand, and we both bowed. I applauded her and assured her that God heard her and me, and he was pleased that we had come together as one. I invited her in the house and began playing a variety of music that we could work on and sing to. I had a stack of papers that needed to be shredded, and she loved to be my little singing helper, like I once was to Godmama Verona. We found ourselves serenading one another like Godmama and I did. We bonded and most definitely admired each other. I started going over to talk with her mother and found myself asking if she could spend the night. Next thing I know, she and I were going out for breakfast and then to the movies. She was such a fun baby, and she would always say, "Thank you, Mama May."

One day in school, Ieacsha was given an assignment. She was

asked to write about someone special, and she wrote about me. She came by and read her letter to me. The words about me that she had chosen brought a smile to my eyes and tenderness to my heart. She was very proud of her writing, and she expressed to me that she wanted to be a writer like me. She told me that her teacher thought I was a very wonderful lady. Shortly thereafter, Ieacsha was in summer school and had a part in the school play, just like I once did. I rehearsed with her every day and even on the weekends. She invited me to the presentation. I was so proud of her, and she did an excellent job. She has a kind spirit just like me, and she is the daughter I never had.

Ieacsha went to get some extra help to get me moved. She brought her cousin Tivanni Flood over to help me move to my new residence. He was as gracious as she was. He would not take a dime from me. He just asked if I would be his Mama May also. I could not refuse. Ieacsha was very excited to tell me that he could sing, too. I was surprised and suggested he sing. This young man sang "That's My Dream" smoothly and rocked my soul. I instantly started calling him Superstar and yelled for more.

I am eternally grateful to God for bringing this beautiful little girl and her cousin as angels into my life. My prayers are to be everything that God intends me to be to her and to him.

Divine Inspiration

Mother's Day 2008, Mama Davis shared with me her church experience with her daughter at Family Christian Center located in Munster Indiana. They attended church for a Mother's Day brunch. An announcement was made at the brunch that a prophet would be visiting the church on the upcoming Wednesday, and she invited me to attend. The announcer stated that the month of May was the month of miracles, and my nickname is May. Mama Davis thought she and I should attend the service. She had a wonderful time with her daughter and said the edifice was outstanding. I became excited and told her I would go, because I believed there would be a word especially for me. I shared this conversation with Aileen, and she decided to attend the service with me.

We arrived, not as early as I would have liked to, and wanted to find a seat up front. My friend Lou is now a member of the church and she, Aileen, and I went into the church together. The church was very packed, and as we scouted for three seats, we came upon a row where we would have to climb over five or six people to sit down. The man seated on the aisle had some physical complications, and when we realized his standing would be an imposition, we elected to sit somewhere else. We came upon a row in the section directly in front of the pulpit that had four seats and decided to sit there. The aisle seat had a young woman with a cute little chubby girl seated on her lap. The little girl had an eye issue that was noticeable as we made our way to our seats. When I saw the little girl, I realized that this mom was there to receive healing from God through the prophet we were about to witness. Anxiousness rose in my stomach because I knew I was in the right place, at the right time. The buzz was that an awesome visionary would be delivering the word, and I could hardly wait.

When the service began, the associate pastor suggested we attend every service in the miracle month of May. Immediately, I decided I would follow those instructions. I knew I was developing my miracle story, and it was currently the month of May. Those precious thoughts were enough for me to attend the Wednesday and upcoming Sunday services. I expected a word from the Lord.

The service was extremely powerful. We witnessed the healing powers of the prophet. He touched the man whose row we were initially going to sit in. That man was visibly healed. His mother and sister were sitting next to him, and they cried out and praised the Lord for the prophet's obedience. The prophet also came upon the row we sat in and touched the little girl's eye. He pronounced deliverance over her. He then turned to the mother and touched her stomach and indicated she was having pain in her abdomen. The mother cried out at the accuracy of his declaration, and he prayed over her and told her she was healed. She announced that she felt no more pain, and that was enough for me. I was definitely coming back to this holy place. Before we left the sanctuary, the leader of the church, Pastor Steve Munsey, announced that he would be continuing the word on miracles, and I could hardly wait the four days till Sunday service.

While driving to Pastor Munsey's church I looked at the early morning sky. It was if I was riding into glory. White rays of twinkling sunshine appeared right in front of me. I immediately thanked God for pouring his majestic love all over me. It was almost indescribable. The sky looked like a vibrant diamond drizzling into a handheld fan. It sparkled and glistened as it covered the sky in front of me. The glare of the rays was one of the most beautiful sights I'd ever seen. I had asked the Lord to show me a sign that I was headed in the right direction. In his wonderful way, his light led my path. I prayed for him to show me a sign that only he and I would know. I asked that he allow the words of Pastor Munsey to flow like a river out of his mouth. My, oh my, did he answer my prayers.

Aileen stated that she would be coming back, and I invited another friend, but when Sunday morning arrived, both of them had to cancel. I was disappointed, but I understood. What the Lord has for me was for me, and I had to get the teaching for my life. I realized I was the willing vessel needing to receive the fresh word from God. I pushed on to Pastor Munsey's Sunday morning church service. This time, I arrived early and there were only a few people seated quietly in the sanctuary. I was spiritually guided to sit in the center section, second row. Once I was situated, I closed my eyes and began meditating. A few minutes passed and I was politely interrupted by a lady's soft voice. "Excuse me," stated the kind voice. She asked if the seat was available next to me and I told her it was. She sat and I introduced myself. She told me her name was Linda and asked if I would help her save two seats for her family members. Ten minutes passed and a young girl, about eleven years old, approached our row with a lady. Linda announced that they were the family members she was waiting for, and we directed them to the seats we had saved for them. Once they were seated, Linda made the introductions. To my surprise, all three of them were named Linda. When I realized I was sitting around three Linda's, I was reminded of my miracle flight to Florida. I thought of the three angels (myself included) seated in the same row on my miracle flight. Suddenly, I felt chilled as though I had been touched. I heard in my spirit the words "the Father, the Son and the precious Holy Ghost." I immediately knew I was in for a special moment.

I shared with the three Linda's what I had heard. The little girl's grandmother said, "Guess what, May, my best girlfriend's name is May." I wanted to jump out of my seat and perform a spiritual dance. I knew this meeting was no coincidence, and I could hardly wait to know more.

A gentleman sat down in front of me and turned around to greet us. I spoke and introduced my new friends to him and told him my name was May, like the month of May. May had been declared the miracle month. I also told him the senior Linda had a best friend named May, and he chuckled. He said, "My name is Pastor Jim Utley, and I welcome each one of you." He listened to me as I shared with him that I was writing a miracle book. He gave me a high-five and declared that, "This is truly the miracle month of May." To my surprise, a few seconds later he was cued, by dimming lights, to come to the pulpit to open the service in prayer. He began to pray for the soldiers who were on the battlefield, protecting our country.

Then it became time for Pastor Munsey to preach a sermon entitled "Talitha Cumi," from the book of Mark, chapter 5, verse 41. He read, "Damsel, I say unto thee, arise." He pointed out that, in the book of Mark, not all the disciples were with Jesus the day Jesus went out to heal the people. There were only three disciples with him. This made me think of the two people who were to come to the Sunday service but had cancelled. When the pastor was coming to the close of his sermon, he spoke of the woman who laid in a pool of blood. She believed if Jesus passed by her that she could touch the hem of his garment and be made whole. Directly after this point, Pastor Munsey asked all those persons who desired prayer to come to the altar, on the count of three. Before the number three was announced, I was up and making my way to the altar. I didn't have to go far, because I was already just a few feet away. So I was in the front row of the three or four hundred people lined up for prayer. I was standing there with my eyes closed, and all of a sudden I felt the touch of Pastor Munsey. He began to speak into my life. While in that awesome moment, I felt a touch on my shoulder from behind. It was Mama Davis. I had no idea she was attending this Sunday service. We had talked the night before, and she informed me that she was going back to her church for Sunday morning service.

She whispered in my ear that God had drawn her to Pastor Munsey's church because I was there. She felt she had to be there also. Comfort is an understatement as to how I really felt. I had Pastor Munsey in front of me, Mama Davis behind me and God all around me. When Pastor Steve Munsey saw Mama Davis, he placed his hands on hers and drew us in close together in a special hug. He said, "You two look like you go together." My entire body cried out in elation. He then smiled at me and said, "Oh, you are so anointed, you are full of the precious Holy Ghost." He allowed me to lean on his shoulder, where I surrendered to all that I had been feeling. He put his arms around me and let the spirit of God have its way. Finally, I had the opportunity to be restored by another preacher who saw my soul and the light of the Lord radiating upon me. It seemed like every vessel in my body was in rapture. These were the special words I had come to hear. Mama Davis was astonished that we received such a special touch from the Lord at Family Christian Center.

The next Sunday I attended a church where I had become fond of so many parishioners. I didn't arrive at my usual time. I considered myself late until I approached the parking lot and Minister Doris saw me and yelled out, "Hey, sister!" I turned to greet her and we both were very glad to see one another and agreed we never recalled being that late. I said to my sister in Christ that I believed God to be an on-time God. We both agreed we had been graced with God's traveling mercy. We gave thanks to God and embraced each other with a hug and well wishes for a blessed day. We expected that God was going to bless each of us real good for pressing our way to church.

When I entered the sanctuary, the door-keeper assisted me to a seat. She took me to the fifth row towards the front where one of the mother's of the church was sitting. She had placed her jacket on the end seat, and the usher asked her if anyone was sitting there. The lady politely moved her jacket and welcomed me. The preacher was ending a prophetic word before the congregation. The choir began to sing, "Pray, I am Going to Keep on Praying." The lead singer began to sing, "I'll pray for you, you pray for me, and watch God change things in your life." This song touched me right in the center of my stomach and filled my spirit with joy. My emotions became noticeable as I began to sing along, from my seat, the words that God would change things even in my family. I could only think about my son Vaughn, getting evicted with three children. My son had called me the night before pouring out to me all of his fears and asking me to pray harder for him and my grandchildren. He sadly mentioned that his felony rap sheet followed him wherever he would go with his kids. I hadn't slept all night. I prayed and hoped to touch the hem of Jesus.

As the preacher prepared to come to the preacher's stand I began to hear the choir softly sing "Watch God Change Things," and then the preacher joined in singing soulfully for the Lord. You could see the tears rolling down his face. I was drifting away from my seat, just singing and weeping. I felt blessed within to realize that real men do cry. I heard a whisper from my soul telling me to lean on Brother Kevin. The spirit of the Lord in him was always strong and encouraging. He was standing a seat ahead of me. As I sang the melody, he recognized the tone of my voice and began turning his head around as I walked toward him. He turned and when he saw my tears he asked me what was wrong. He reached for me to give me a hug, and I poured out my son's problems. I told him how I could barely make it to church. Brother Kevin put his arms around me and was very compassionate about my concerns. Until that day, I had sat directly behind him each time I attended the services. I would confide in him on every move that God blessed me with to set my sons free. We eventually became e-mail prayer partners and friends.

Well as the choir kept on singing, Brother Kevin and I were in the aisle. He was ministering to me, and I heard the preacher say, "Link up with somebody and pray for a miracle in their life. You don't know what it might have taken for them to get to church today." Brother Kevin pulled me close to him. God had blessed him with the words to sustain a praying mother's peace.

After the praise and worship song, we all took our seats, and the preacher began teaching, demonstrating, and preaching a powerful message. He referred to Exodus, chapter 19, New King James Version. While I was sitting and listening, Brother Kevin handed me a check for one thousand dollars for Vaughn and his children and left with the words "Help your family, sister." I instantly fell back in my seat with the words "Thank you" pouring from my lips.

I held the check out at the mother, seated right next to me. She held me by the hand and said, "You have been truly blessed today."

I couldn't wait to get outside the church after service and phone my dad and Vaughn. I wanted to let each of them know about the blessing that God put on Brother Kevin's heart. I explained to my son that he didn't have to worry as much because God had sent, through this young man, his gift of encouragement. This support came from a man who had never met my son or his children. He truly was a righteous man. He was someone who cared. I blessed God for another angel at this time of my family's life.

A few days later, late at night, Vaughn was in Summit, picking up his daughter, Versharia. A fire broke out across the street. My son told me that he lost all thoughts of himself or how his children needed him to survive. He could only think about saving the people who were involved in that fire. There were three children trapped and burning to death. The mother, on the floor below, was faced with fire burning uncontrollably. It forced her to jump out the window to save herself from the blazing flames. Vaughn was driven, spiritually, to save three burning children. He attempted to rush through the fire into the burning building. Another Good Samaritan entered the room and the windows exploded. Vaughn yelled, "No, no!" He and the other man were blown into another part of the apartment. They survived by the mercy and grace of God. Vaughn had been in the flames longer, but incurred no burns or scratches. He only had muscle pain and some asthma from inhaling so much smoke from the fire. Knowing his heart condition, I trusted God had his hands on that heart that he designed for Vaughn. He knew how much Vaughn could bear. I can't thank God enough for his shield of protection. I pray each and every day for the young woman who lost all of her children. Since then, my son has been having flashbacks of the three children burning to death. Vaughn was on the early morning news, on every station. I called Brother Kevin to tell him to turn the TV on, but there was no answer. He in turn five minutes later called me and said, "I believe I just saw Vaughn on TV." I told him yes, that was Vaughn. We both were in awe. Brother Kevin had blessed Vaughn and his three children. My son tried to save a woman and her three children from the burning fire. I truly believe Vaughn has the favor of God upon his life.

The Miracle Ending

Reader, please take with you this powerful thought: we are saved by the Lord's sovereign grace. I've learned this lesson by being gravely ill, undeniably humbled, and dangerously broken. With all my imperfections, I continue to praise and pray to the Lord. At this point, He has my complete attention. Don't we go to our father when we need help? The Lord has been my only constant companion, because for many years, my father didn't claim me and my mother gave me to her friend a few weeks after my birth. Yet she did not terminate me. I bless the Lord for her. The Lord created the most loving and spiritual home environment for me to grow up in. It is now part of my life's journey. I have witnessed his magnificent power, miracles and plans for my life's journey on earth.

Where else could I go for support, or on whom would I depend to guide me in my many times of need? It would have to be the one who created me. The one with whom I have a personal relationship, the only one who has complete control over my life, now and forever.

There is no other way for any of us to be saved and set free other than by His grace and mercy. I've been walking into His arms all my life and I have been running for the last nine years. Now, I write. I can honestly say I am coasting my way to the heavenly cross. It is the most amazing revelation I've experienced so far in my earthly life. I was once told by a prophet to hold on and don't give up. It is the best advice I can give to you. *Hold on and don't give up*! I'm a living witness that God's every word is true. Thank you for reading my life's testimony.

Angels in My Life

I thank God for all of my brothers and sisters who have been dispatched into my life as angels. It is the marvelous light of our Lord and Savior that shows us the way into each other's paths. You angels were sent for many different reasons. Even when someone says no to you is Gods way of redirecting you to something greater that he has for you. Each of you appeared at different times, according to my needs. The Lord promised that he would supply all of our needs.

My sons and I were lost sheep. I celebrate each of you who were assigned to our rescue. Thank you for listening to your inner voice to lend an ear, a helping hand, or a shoulder for me to cry on. Thank you for your many words of encouragement.

God hears all of our humble cries, and he promises to comfort us and wipe away all of our tears. It is said that into each and every one of our lives a little rain must fall. I thank each of you angels, personally, for choosing to do all that you could do for me and my family. We have had many personal and spiritual storms. It's so easy to turn away from other people's problems. I celebrate all of you angels who believe "If I can help somebody, then my living will not be in vain." God just needed a willing vessel. The storms in my life have been good for me. I have learned that all things in God's time, and we can't hurry God. God is always on time, never late. No one is left unheard.

About the Author

Mathell Givens is a first-time writer who hails from the Chicago area. Her book has been in the making for several years. She is the single mother of three sons, and has fourteen grandchildren and three great-grandchildren. Ms. Givens has never been afraid to accept the challenges that life offers. She is a God-fearing woman who respects her fellow man. She loves to sing and enjoys all types of music. She is fun-loving and believes that all people have the capacity to love and be loved. Ms. Givens is a woman of faith and feels that she has been highly favored in God's eyes. She is a believer that anything is possible with God as your pilot. Ms. Givens has dedicated her life to God and to helping people from all walks of life. It is her hope that this book inspires all who read it.